Web Services Essentials

Ethan Cerami

Beijing · Cambridge · Farnham · Köln · Sebastopol · Tokyo

Web Services Essentials
by Ethan Cerami

Copyright © 2002 O'Reilly Media, Inc. All rights reserved.
Printed in the United States of America.

Published by O'Reilly Media, Inc., 1005 Gravenstein Highway North, Sebastopol, CA 95472.

O'Reilly Media, Inc. books may be purchased for educational, business, or sales promotional use. On-line editions are also available for most titles (*safari.oreilly.com*). For more information, contact our corporate/institutional sales department: (800) 998-9938 or *corporate@oreilly.com*.

Editor:	Simon St.Laurent
Production Editor:	Claire Cloutier
Cover Designer:	Ellie Volckhausen
Interior Designer:	David Futato

Printing History:

February 2002:	First Edition.

ISBN: 978-0-596-00224-4
[LSI]   [2011-07-29]

To Amy:
I have you and that is all
I ever wanted anyway

Table of Contents

Part III. SOAP

Part IV. WSDL

Part V.   UDDI

Preface

Web services offer a new and evolving paradigm for building distributed web applications. This book focuses on the *essentials* of web services and covers four main technologies: XML-RPC, SOAP, WSDL, and UDDI. The book offers a high-level overview of each technology. It also describes the relevant API and discusses implementation options for each technology. The book includes a broad range of working examples so that you can immediately see web services in action.

Audience

This book is written for developers who are new to web services. It aims to to provide you with a "big-picture" perspective to enable you to understand the scope and extent of web services, while also providing you with enough nuts and bolts and sample code to start writing your own services.

When choosing between a proprietary system and an open source implementation, we tend to favor open source implementations. When choosing among programming languages, we tend to favor Java. To make the most of the book, you should therefore have solid Java programming experience. If you need to brush up on Java, consider these books:

- *Learning Java*, by Patrick Niemeyer and Jonathan Knudsen (O'Reilly & Associates, Inc.)
- *Java in a Nutshell*, Fourth Edition, by David Flanagan (O'Reilly)

A basic understanding of eXtensible Markup Language (XML) is also important. For a solid grounding in XML, consider these books:

- *Learning XML*, by Erik T. Ray (O'Reilly)
- *XML in a Nutshell: A Desktop Quick Reference*, by Elliotte Rusty Harold and W. Scott Means (O'Reilly)

Organization

The book is divided into five parts. Part I provides a general introduction to web services. Part II through Part V focus on core web service technologies, including XML-RPC, SOAP, WSDL, and UDDI. The book concludes with a glossary of common web service terms.

Part I, Introduction to Web Services

Chapter 1, *Introduction*, provides an overview of web services, the web service architecture, and the web service protocol stack. It also provides a snapshot of current standardization efforts of the World Wide Web Consortium (W3C).

Part II, XML-RPC

Chapter 2, *XML-RPC Essentials*, provides a comprehensive introduction to XML-RPC. This includes a technical overview of XML-RPC, including a detailed explanation of XML-RPC data types, requests, and responses. This chapter also includes sample XML-RPC code, written in Java and Perl.

Part III, SOAP

Chapter 3, *SOAP Essentials*, provides a comprehensive introduction to SOAP. This includes overviews of the SOAP specification, using SOAP via HTTP, and the W3C standardization effort surrounding SOAP.

Chapter 4, *Apache SOAP Quick Start*, provides a quick-start guide to using Apache SOAP, an open source Java implementation of the SOAP specification. This chapter includes detailed instructions on installing and deploying SOAP services and on writing basic service and client code.

Chapter 5, *Programming Apache SOAP*, provides an in-depth guide to programming Apache SOAP. This includes an overview of working with arrays, JavaBeans™, and literal XML documents. This chapter also includes a discussion on handling SOAP faults and maintaining session state.

Part IV, WSDL

Chapter 6, *WSDL Essentials*, provides a comprehensive introduction to WSDL. This includes an overview of the specification itself, numerous WSDL examples, and an introduction to WSDL-invocation tools.

Part V, UDDI

Chapter 7, *UDDI Essentials*, provides a comprehensive overview of UDDI. This includes an overview of the UDDI data model and tutorials for searching existing data and publishing new data.

Chapter 8, *UDDI Inquiry API: Quick Reference*, provides a quick reference to the UDDI Inquiry API.

Chapter 9, *UDDI 4J*, introduces UDDI4J, an open source Java implementation of UDDI. Example code illustrates how to search and publish UDDI data. A complete description of the UDDI4J API is also included.

Conventions Used in This Book

The following font conventions are used in this book:

Italic is used for:

- Pathnames, filenames, function names, and program names
- Internet addresses, such as domain names and URLs
- New terms where they are defined

Constant width is used for:

- Command lines and options that should be typed verbatim
- Names and keywords in programs, including method names, variable names, class names, value names, and XML-RPC headers
- XML element tags

Constant width bold is used for emphasis in program code lines.

Constant width italic is used for replaceable arguments in program code.

Comments and Questions

The information in this book has been tested and verified, but you may find that features or libraries have changed, or you may even find mistakes. You can send any errors you find, as well as suggestions for future editions, to:

O'Reilly & Associates, Inc.
1005 Gravenstein Highway North
Sebastopol, CA 95472
1-800-998-9938 (in the U.S. or Canada)
1-707-829-0515 (international/local)
1-707-829-0104 (fax)

You can also send us messages electronically. To be put on the mailing list or to request a catalog, send email to:

info@oreilly.com

To ask technical questions or comment on the book, send email to:

bookquestions@oreilly.com

We have a web site for the book, where we'll list examples, errata, and any plans for future editions. You can access this page at:

http://www.oreilly.com/catalog/webservess/

For more information abut this book and others, see the O'Reilly web site:

http://www.oreilly.com

Acknowledgments

Writing an O'Reilly book has always been a dream of mine. I certainly did not get here by myself. Therefore, I want to thank all those who helped turned this dream into reality.

First, I want to thank Simon St.Laurent, my editor at O'Reilly. Simon ushered this book from its very earliest stages until the very last round of copyediting. He was the first person to bring web services to my attention and provided constant and patient guidance at every step of the way. He also contributed Chapter 2, *XML-RPC Essentials*. I also want to thank all the technical reviewers who provided excellent feedback on early drafts of the book. Reviewers included Leigh Dodds, Timothy J. Ewald, Martin Gudgin, Simon Horrell, and Tim O'Reilly. Graham Glass, CEO of The Mind Electric, Inc., answered all of my many questions regarding the GLUE platform and WSDL in general. Tony Hong, cofounder of XMethods, Inc., also helped out with questions on SOAP interoperability and provided permission to reprint the WSDL file for the XMethods eBay Price Watcher Service. Claire Cloutier served as the production editor for the book and did an excellent job keeping the book well-organized and on schedule.

Second, I want to thank Gary Lazarus, my boss at Winstar Communications. Gary was gracious enough to provide me with a flexible schedule to complete this book. For this, I am forever grateful.

Third, I want to thank all my friends and family. You know who you are. As always, you have sustained and nourished me, and helped me keep a balanced life. Thank you.

Fourth, I want to thank my father-in-law, Ed Orsenigo. Your courage and determination are an inspiration to us all.

Lastly, I want to thank my wife, Amy. In the midst of writing this book, Amy and I actually found time to get married! September 1, 2001 was the happiest day of my life. Thanks, Amy, for supporting me, encouraging me, and bringing joy to everyone around you.

PART I

Introduction to Web Services

CHAPTER 1

Introduction

Today, the principal use of the World Wide Web is for interactive access to documents and applications. In almost all cases, such access is by human users, typically working through Web browsers, audio players, or other interactive front-end systems. The Web can grow significantly in power and scope if it is extended to support communication between applications, from one program to another.

—From the W3C XML Protocol Working Group Charter

Welcome to the world of web services. This chapter will ground you in the basics of web service terminology and architecture. It does so by answering the most common questions, including:

- What exactly is a web service?
- What is the web service protocol stack?
- What is XML messaging? Service description? Service discovery?
- What are XML-RPC, SOAP, WSDL, and UDDI? How do these technologies complement each other and work together?
- What security issues are unique to web services?
- What standards currently exist?

Introduction to Web Services

A web service is any service that is available over the Internet, uses a standardized XML messaging system, and is not tied to any one operating system or programming language. (See Figure 1-1.)

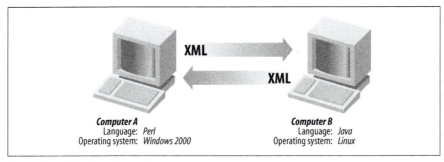

Figure 1-1. A basic web service

There are several alternatives for XML messaging. For example, you could use XML Remote Procedure Calls (XML-RPC) or SOAP, both of which are described later in this chapter. Alternatively, you could just use HTTP GET/POST and pass arbitrary XML documents. Any of these options can work. (See Figure 1-2.)

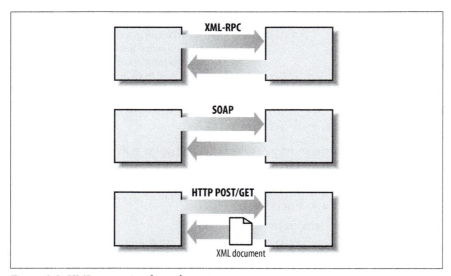

Figure 1-2. XML messaging for web services

Although they are not required, a web service may also have two additional (and desirable) properties:

A web service should be self-describing. If you publish a new web service, you should also publish a public interface to the service. At a minimum, your service should include human-readable documentation so that other developers can more easily integrate your service. If you have created a SOAP service, you should also ideally include a public interface written in a common XML grammar. The XML grammar can be used to identify all public methods, method arguments, and return values.

A web service should be discoverable. If you create a web service, there should be a relatively simple mechanism for you to publish this fact. Likewise, there should be some simple mechanism whereby interested parties can find the service and locate its public interface. The exact mechanism could be via a completely decentralized system or a more logically centralized registry system.

To summarize, a complete web service is, therefore, any service that:

- Is available over the Internet or private (intranet) networks
- Uses a standardized XML messaging system
- Is not tied to any one operating system or programming language
- Is self-describing via a common XML grammar
- Is discoverable via a simple find mechanism

The Web Today: The Human-Centric Web

To make web services more concrete, consider basic e-commerce functionality. For example, Widgets, Inc. sells parts through its web site, enabling customers to submit purchase orders and check on order status.

To check on the order status, a customer logs into the company web site via a web browser and receives the results as an HTML page. (See Figure 1-3.)

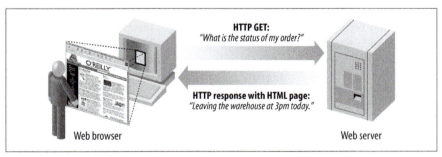

Figure 1-3. The human-centric Web

This basic model illustrates a *human-centric Web*, where humans are the primary actors initiating most web requests. It also represents the primary model on which most of the Web operates today.

Web Services: The Application-Centric Web

With web services, we move from a human-centric Web to an *application-centric Web*. This does not mean that humans are entirely out the picture! It just means that conversations can take place directly between applications as easily as between web browsers and servers.

For example, we can turn the order status application into a web service. Applications and agents can then connect to the service and utilize its functionality directly. For example, an inventory application can query Widgets, Inc. on the status of all orders. The inventory system can then process the data, manipulate it, and integrate it into its overall supply chain management software. (See Figure 1-4.)

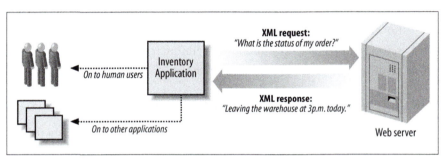

Figure 1-4. The application-centric Web

There are numerous areas where an application-centric Web could prove extremely helpful. Examples include credit card verification, package tracking, portfolio tracking, shopping bots, currency conversion, and language translation. Other options include centralized repositories for personal information, such as Microsoft's proposed .NET MyServices project. .NET MyServices aims to centralize calendar, email, and credit card information and to provide web services for sharing that data.

Web Services and the Semantic Web

Tim Berners-Lee, the original inventor of the Web, has recently argued for a "Semantic Web." The Semantic Web vision is application-centric, and shares many of the same ideas as web services. In fact, at the first W3C conference on web services, Berners-Lee stated that web services are an actualization of the Semantic Web vision. For an overview of the Semantic Web, see Berners-Lee's article in *Scientific American*: *http://www.sciam.com/2001/0501issue/0501berners-lee.html*.

The Web Services Vision: The Automated Web

An application-centric Web is not a new notion. For years, developers have created CGI programs and Java servlets designed primarily for use by other applications. For example, companies have developed credit card services, search systems, and news retrieval systems.

The crucial difference is that most of these systems consisted of ad hoc solutions. With web services, we have the promise of some standardization, which should hopefully lower the barrier to application integration.

> The web service architecture provides an interesting alternative for drastically decoupling presentation from content. For example, a site could consist of nothing but container pages that pass parameters to the real logic via SOAP or XML-RPC. This makes it easy to change presentation and also lets humans and computers "share" a single web service.

In the long term, web services also offer the promise of the *automated Web*. If services are easily discoverable, self-describing, and stick to common standards, it is possible to automate application integration. Some in the industry have referred to this as "just-in-time" application integration.

For example, consider the case of MegaElectric (ME). ME wants to buy parts from Widgets, Inc. and also wants to seamlessly integrate order status into a unified inventory system. At some point in the future, ME will be able to buy software that automates this entire process. Here's how it might work (refer to Figure 1-5):

1. The inventory application wakes up and connects to a centralized directory of web services: "Does Widgets, Inc. provide an order status service?" The directory returns information on Widgets, Inc.'s service and includes a pointer to the service description.

2. The inventory application connects to Widgets, Inc. and retrieves the service description.

3. The service description file includes complete details about how to connect to the specified service. The inventory application can therefore automatically invoke the order status service.

Is it possible to automate this process using existing web services technology? Not quite: only parts of the process can currently be automated. For example, as we will see in Chapter 9, it is possible to create Java programs that query service registries. Understanding the results and choosing which service to actually use, however, still requires some human intervention. It is

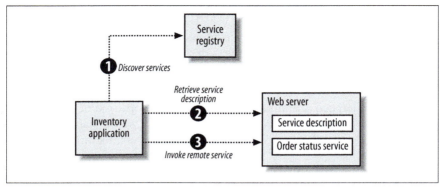

Figure 1-5. The automated Web

also possible to automatically invoke a service, based on a service description. For example, as we will see in Chapter 6, many automatic invocation tools already exist and work extremely well.

Even if all these steps could be automated, there is currently no mechanism for automating business relationships. For example, current service descriptions do not cover guarantees on pricing, delivery schedules, or legal ramifications if deliveries are not made. Given a service description, you also cannot assume that the service is bug-free or that the service is available 100 percent of the time.

These types of issues are not easily solved and are not easily automated. Completely automated web services and "just-in-time" application integration may therefore never be realized. Nonetheless, current web service technology does take us one step closer, and does enable us to automate portions of the process.

The Industry Landscape

There are currently many competing frameworks and proposals for web services. The three main contenders are Microsoft's .NET, IBM Web Services, and Sun Open Net Environment (ONE). While each of these frameworks has its own particular niche and spin, they all share the basic web service definition and vision put forth here. Furthermore, all of the frameworks share a common set of technologies, mainly SOAP, WSDL, and UDDI.

Rather than focusing on one particular implementation or framework, this book focuses on common definitions and technologies. Hopefully, this will better equip you to cut through the marketing hype and understand and evaluate the current contenders.

Web Service Architecture

There are two ways to view the web service architecture. The first is to examine the individual roles of each web service actor; the second is to examine the emerging web service protocol stack.

Web Service Roles

There are three major roles within the web service architecture:

Service provider
  This is the provider of the web service. The service provider implements the service and makes it available on the Internet.

Service requestor
  This is any consumer of the web service. The requestor utilizes an existing web service by opening a network connection and sending an XML request.

Service registry
  This is a logically centralized directory of services. The registry provides a central place where developers can publish new services or find existing ones. It therefore serves as a centralized clearinghouse for companies and their services.

Figure 1-6 shows the major web service roles and how they interact with each other.

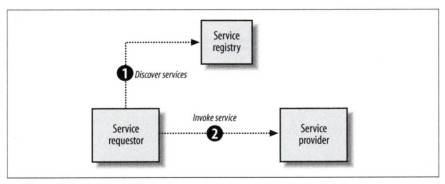

Figure 1-6. Web service roles

Web Service Protocol Stack

A second option for viewing the web service architecture is to examine the emerging web service protocol stack. The stack is still evolving, but currently has four main layers. Following is a brief description of each layer.

Service transport

This layer is responsible for transporting messages between applications. Currently, this layer includes hypertext transfer protocol (HTTP), Simple Mail Transfer Protocol (SMTP), file transfer protocol (FTP), and newer protocols, such as Blocks Extensible Exchange Protocol (BEEP).

XML messaging

This layer is responsible for encoding messages in a common XML format so that messages can be understood at either end. Currently, this layer includes XML-RPC and SOAP.

Service description

This layer is responsible for describing the public interface to a specific web service. Currently, service description is handled via the Web Service Description Language (WSDL).

Service discovery

This layer is responsible for centralizing services into a common registry, and providing easy publish/find functionality. Currently, service discovery is handled via Universal Description, Discovery, and Integration (UDDI).

As web services evolve, additional layers may be added, and additional technologies may be added to each layer. Figure 1-7 summarizes the current web service protocol stack. Each layer is described in detail later in this book.

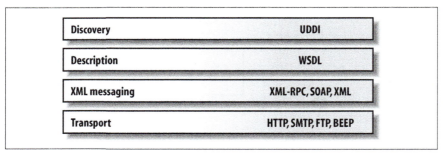

Figure 1-7. Web service protocol stack

Architectural Snapshot: The IBM Web Services Browser

To gain a high-level understanding of how the protocol stack actually works, try out the IBM Web Services Browser. The browser enables you to search for existing services, view their service descriptions, and automatically invoke those services. This lets you see each layer within the protocol stack without actually writing any code.

To get started, open a browser and go to *http://demo.alphaworks.ibm.com/browser/*. You should see the screen depicted in Figure 1-8.

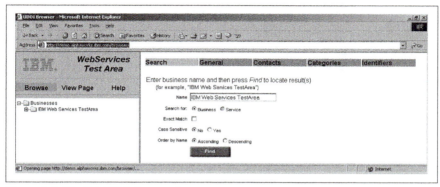

Figure 1-8. The IBM Web Services browser

In the righthand pane, you can search a centralized registry for existing web services. (The registry actually uses UDDI, but don't get too caught up in the details just yet.) Within the Search box, type "IBM Web Services" and click Search. IBM will search the centralized directory for you and display all matching results in the left pane. Select the last folder, entitled IBM Web Services TestArea, and you will see a list of available web services. (See Figure 1-9.)

Figure 1-9. Results of web service search

Click on GetWeatherService, and the right pane will display specific details about the service. (See Figure 1-10.) The data includes *binding points*, which indicate URLs for actually connecting to the service, and service description files that explain how to interface with the service. (These are WSDL files, but again, don't get too caught up in the details just yet.)

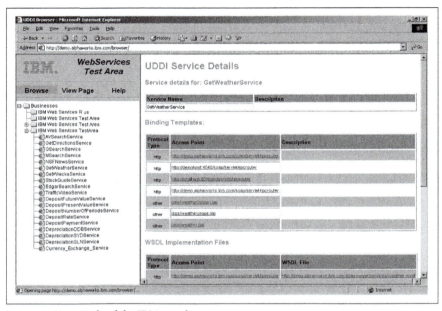

Figure 1-10. Details of the IBM weather service

Click the View Page link in the left pane. The right pane will now show a simple user interface for the weather service. Select a city and state, and IBM will automatically invoke the service and display the current weather conditions. (See Figure 1-11.)

If you pick another service, the service is added to the bottom of the right pane. For example, Figure 1-12 shows the stock quote service and the weather service bundled together.

The IBM browser does a good job of illustrating web services in action and highlighting the main layers within the protocol stack. It also does a good job of illustrating the potential of "just-in-time" application integration. Each service basically acts as an individual building block, and you can continue stacking more and more services to the same page. Best of all, you can do so without writing a single line of code!

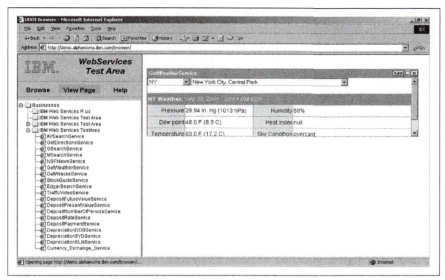

Figure 1-11. Invoking the IBM weather service

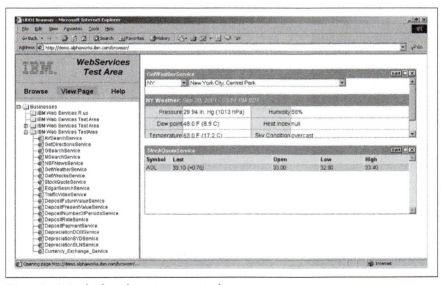

Figure 1-12. Multiple web services on a single page

XML Messaging

XML has exploded onto the computing scene in recent years. It has gained rapid acceptance because it enables diverse computer systems to share data more easily, regardless of operating system or programming language. There are dozens of XML tools, including parsers and editors that are available for nearly every operating system and every programming language, including Java, Perl, Python, C#, C, C++, and Ruby. When developers decided to build a web service messaging system, XML was therefore a natural choice. There are two main contenders for XML messaging: XML-RPC and SOAP. The following sections provide descriptions of both protocols.

XML-RPC

XML-RPC is a simple protocol that uses XML messages to perform RPCs. Requests are encoded in XML and sent via HTTP POST. XML responses are embedded in the body of the HTTP response. Because XML-RPC is platform-independent, it allows diverse applications to communicate. For example, a Java client can speak XML-RPC to a Perl server.

To gain a high-level understanding of XML-RPC, consider a simple weather service. The service expects a zip code and returns the current temperature for the area. Here is a sample XML-RPC request to the weather service (HTTP headers omitted):

```
<?xml version="1.0" encoding="ISO-8859-1"?>
<methodCall>
    <methodName>weather.getWeather</methodName>
    <params>
        <param><value>10016</value></param>
    </params>
</methodCall>
```

The request consists of a simple methodCall element that specifies the method name and any method parameters.

Here is a sample XML-RPC response from the weather service:

```
<?xml version="1.0" encoding="ISO-8859-1"?>
<methodResponse>
    <params>
        <param>
            <value><int>65</int></value>
        </param>
    </params>
</methodResponse>
```

The response consists of a single methodResponse element that specifies the return value. In this case, the return value is specified as an integer.

XML-RPC is the easiest way to get started with web services. In many ways, it is simpler than SOAP and easier to adopt. However, unlike SOAP, XML-RPC has no corresponding service description grammar. This prevents automatic invocation of XML-RPC services—a key ingredient for enabling just-in-time application integration. More details of XML-RPC are covered in Chapter 2.

SOAP

SOAP is an XML-based protocol for exchanging information between computers. Although SOAP can be used in a variety of messaging systems, and can be delivered via a variety of transport protocols, the main focus of SOAP is RPCs transported via HTTP. Like XML-RPC, SOAP is platform-independent and therefore enables diverse applications to communicate.

To gain a high-level understanding of SOAP, let's revisit our simple weather service. Here is a sample SOAP request (HTTP headers omitted):

```
<?xml version='1.0' encoding='UTF-8'?>
<SOAP-ENV:Envelope
    xmlns:SOAP-ENV="http://www.w3.org/2001/09/soap-envelope/"
    xmlns:xsi="http://www.w3.org/2001/XMLSchema-instance"
    xmlns:xsd="http://www.w3.org/2001/XMLSchema">
    <SOAP-ENV:Body>
        <ns1:getWeather
            xmlns:ns1="urn:examples:weatherservice"
            SOAP-ENV:encodingStyle="http://www.w3.org/2001/09/soap-encoding/">
            <zipcode xsi:type="xsd:string">10016</zipcode>
        </ns1:getWeather>
    </SOAP-ENV:Body>
</SOAP-ENV:Envelope>
```

As you can see, the SOAP request is slightly more complicated than the XML-RPC request. It makes use of both XML namespaces and XML Schemas. As in XML-RPC, however, the body of the SOAP request specifies both a method name and a list of parameters.

Here is a sample SOAP response from the weather service:

```
<?xml version='1.0' encoding='UTF-8'?>
<SOAP-ENV:Envelope
    xmlns:SOAP-ENV="http://www.w3.org/2001/09/soap-envelope/"
    xmlns:xsi="http://www.w3.org/2001/XMLSchema-instance"
    xmlns:xsd="http://www.w3.org/2001/XMLSchema">
    <SOAP-ENV:Body>
        <ns1:getWeatherResponse
            xmlns:ns1="urn:examples:weatherservice"
            SOAP-ENV:encodingStyle="http://www.w3.org/2001/09/soap-encoding/">
            <return xsi:type="xsd:int">65</return>
        </ns1:getWeatherResponse>
    </SOAP-ENV:Body>
</SOAP-ENV:Envelope>
```

The response indicates a single integer return value. Full details of SOAP are discussed in Chapter 3.

Service Description: WSDL

WSDL currently represents the service description layer within the web service protocol stack. In a nutshell, WSDL is an XML grammar for specifying a public interface for a web service. This public interface can include information on all publicly available functions, data type information for all XML messages, binding information about the specific transport protocol to be used, and address information for locating the specified service. WSDL is not necessarily tied to a specific XML messaging system, but it does include built-in extensions for describing SOAP services.

Example 1-1 provides a sample WSDL file. This file describes the public interface for the weather service we examined previously. Obviously, there are many details to consider when looking at the example. For now, just focus on two points. First, the message elements specify the individual XML messages that are transferred between computers. In this case, we have a getWeatherRequest and a getWeatherResponse. Second, the service element specifies that the service is available via SOAP at *http://localhost:8080/soap/ servlet/rpcrouter*.

Example 1-1. WeatherService.wsdl

```
<?xml version="1.0" encoding="UTF-8"?>
<definitions name="WeatherService"
    targetNamespace="http://www.ecerami.com/wsdl/WeatherService.wsdl"
    xmlns="http://schemas.xmlsoap.org/wsdl/"
    xmlns:soap="http://schemas.xmlsoap.org/wsdl/soap/"
    xmlns:tns="http://www.ecerami.com/wsdl/WeatherService.wsdl"
    xmlns:xsd="http://www.w3.org/2001/XMLSchema">

    <message name="getWeatherRequest">
       <part name="zipcode" type="xsd:string"/>
    </message>
    <message name="getWeatherResponse">
       <part name="temperature" type="xsd:int"/>
    </message>

    <portType name="Weather_PortType">
       <operation name="getWeather">
          <input message="tns:getWeatherRequest"/>
          <output message="tns:getWeatherResponse"/>
       </operation>
    </portType>

    <binding name="Weather_Binding" type="tns:Weather_PortType">
       <soap:binding style="rpc"
          transport="http://schemas.xmlsoap.org/soap/http"/>
```

Example 1-1. WeatherService.wsdl (continued)

```
        <operation name="getWeather">
          <soap:operation soapAction=""/>
          <input>
             <soap:body
                encodingStyle="http://schemas.xmlsoap.org/soap/encoding/"
                namespace="urn:examples:weatherservice"
                use="encoded"/>
          </input>
          <output>
             <soap:body
                encodingStyle="http://schemas.xmlsoap.org/soap/encoding/"
                namespace="urn:examples:weatherservice"
                use="encoded"/>
          </output>
       </operation>
    </binding>

    <service name="Weather_Service">
       <documentation>WSDL File for Weather Service</documentation>
       <port binding="tns:Weather_Binding" name="Weather_Port">
          <soap:address
             location="http://localhost:8080/soap/servlet/rpcrouter"/>
       </port>
    </service>
</definitions>
```

Using WSDL, a client can locate a web service and invoke any of the publicly available functions. With WSDL-aware tools, this process can be entirely automated, enabling applications to easily integrate new services with little or no manual code. For example, IBM has recently released the IBM Web Services Invocation Framework (WSIF). Using WSIF, you can specify the *WeatherService.wsdl* file and automatically invoke the service described. For example, the following command line:

```
java clients.DynamicInvoker http://localhost:8080/wsdl/WeatherService.wsdl
    getWeather 10016
```

generates the following output:

```
Reading WSDL document from 'http://localhost:8080/wsdl/WeatherService.wsdl'
Preparing WSIF dynamic invocation
Executing operation getWeather
Result:
temperature=65

Done!
```

WSDL and WSDL invocation tools are covered in Chapter 6.

Service Discovery: UDDI

UDDI currently represents the discovery layer within the web service protocol stack. UDDI was originally created by Microsoft, IBM, and Ariba, and represents a technical specification for publishing and finding businesses and web services.

At its core, UDDI consists of two parts. First, UDDI is a technical specification for building a distributed directory of businesses and web services. Data is stored within a specific XML format. The UDDI specification includes API details for searching existing data and publishing new data. Second, the UDDI Business Registry is a fully operational implementation of the UDDI specification. Launched in May 2001 by Microsoft and IBM, the UDDI registry now enables anyone to search existing UDDI data. It also enables any company to register itself and its services.

The data captured within UDDI is divided into three main categories:

White pages
> This category includes general information about a specific company; for example, business name, business description, and address.

Yellow pages
> This category includes general classification data for either the company or the service offered. For example, this data may include industry, product, or geographic codes based on standard taxonomies.

Green pages
> This category includes technical information about a web service (a pointer to an external specification and an address for invoking the web service).

Figure 1-13 shows a sample screenshot of the Microsoft UDDI site. From this site, you can easily publish your own services or search for existing ones.

Full details on UDDI are available in Chapter 7.

Service Transport

The bottom of the web service protocol stack is service transport. This layer is responsible for actually transporting XML messages between two computers.

Figure 1-13. The Microsoft UDDI site: searching for XMethods, Inc.

HTTP

Currently, HTTP is the most popular option for service transport. HTTP is simple, stable, and widely deployed. Furthermore, most firewalls allow HTTP traffic. This allows XML-RPC or SOAP messages to masquerade as HTTP messages. This is good if you want to easily integrate remote applications, but it does raise a number of security concerns. (See the "Security Considerations" section later in this chapter.)

While HTTP does get the job done, a number of critics have argued that HTTP is not ideal for web services. In particular, HTTP was originally designed for remote document retrieval, and is now being reworked to support RPCs. RPCs demand greater efficiency and reliability than document retrieval does.

 There are some developers who argue that HTTP is enough of a foundation for messaging and that the layers above HTTP are as much a problem as a solution. For some of this perspective, called Representational State Transfer, or REST, see *http://internet.conveyor.com/RESTwiki/moin.cgi.*

BEEP

One promising alternative to HTTP is the Blocks Extensible Exchange Protocol (BEEP). BEEP is a new IETF framework of best practices for building new protocols. In particular, BEEP is layered directly on TCP and includes a number of built-in features, including an initial handshake protocol, authentication, security, and error handling. Using BEEP, one can create new protocols for a variety of applications, including instant messaging, file transfer, content syndication, and network management.

SOAP is not tied to any specific transport protocol. In fact, you can use SOAP via HTTP, SMTP, or FTP. One promising idea is therefore to use SOAP over BEEP. Doing so provides several performance advantages over HTTP. Specifically, BEEP does require an initial handshake, but after the handshake, the protocol requires only 30 bytes of overhead for each message, making it much more efficient than HTTP.* Furthermore, BEEP supports multiple channels of data over the same connection, providing extra efficiency over HTTP.

A recent proposal for using SOAP over BEEP is available at *http://beepcore. org/beepcore/docs/beep-soap.jsp.*

 Another promising alternative to HTTP is Reliable HTTP (HTTP-R). HTTP-R is being developed by IBM, which plans to submit its proposal to the Internet Engineering Task Force (IETF). HTTP-R enhances HTTP to ensure message reliability. For example, HTTP-R ensures that a message gets delivered only once or gets reported as undeliverable. This is particularly critical for e-commerce services, such as electronic ordering systems and inventory management. A primer on HTTP-R is available from IBM at *http://www-106. ibm.com/developerworks/webservices/library/ws-phtt/.*

Security Considerations

Security is critical to web services. However, neither the XML-RPC nor SOAP specifications make any explicit security or authentication requirements. Furthermore, the web services community has proposed numerous security frameworks and protocols, but has yet to reach consensus on a comprehensive security package.

---

* The overhead for each HTTP message is dependent on numerous factors, including the requested URL, the type of client used, and the type of server information returned within the HTTP response. Overhead for typical browser and SOAP requests can therefore vary from approximately 100 to 300 bytes for each message.

Very broadly, there are three specific security issues: confidentiality, authentication, and network security.

Confidentiality

If a client sends an XML request to a server, can we ensure that the communication remains confidential?

Fortunately, both XML-RPC and SOAP run primarily on top of HTTP, and XML communications can therefore be encrypted via the Secure Sockets Layer (SSL). SSL is a proven technology, is widely deployed, and is therefore a very viable option for encrypting messages.

However, a key element of web services is that a single web service may consist of a chain of applications. For example, one large service might tie together the services of three other applications. In this case, SSL is not adequate; the messages need to be encrypted at each node along the service path, and each node represents a potential weak link in the chain. Currently, there is no agreed-upon solution to this issue, but one promising solution is the W3C XML Encryption Standard. This standard provides a framework for encrypting and decrypting entire XML documents or just portions of an XML document, and it is likely to receive widespread industry support. Information on the XML Encryption Standard is available at *http://www.w3.org/Encryption/*.

Authentication

If a client connects to a web service, how do we identify the user? And is the user authorized to use the service?

One solution is to leverage HTTP authentication. HTTP includes built-in support for Basic and Digest authentication, and services can therefore be protected in much the same manner as HTML documents are currently protected. Most security experts, however, agree that HTTP authentication is a relatively weak option.

As with encryption, there is no clear consensus on a strong authentication scheme, but there are several frameworks under consideration. The first is SOAP Security Extensions: Digital Signature (SOAP-DSIG). DSIG leverages public key cryptography to digitally sign SOAP messages. This enables the client or server to validate the identity of the other party. DSIG has been submitted to the W3C and is available at *http://www.w3.org/TR/SOAP-dsig/*.

Second, the Organization for the Advancement of Structured Information Standards (OASIS) is working on the Security Assertion Markup Language (SAML). SAML is designed to facilitate the exchange of authentication and authorization information between business partners. Information is available online at *http://www.oasis-open.org/committees/security/*.

In a related effort, several companies have put forth the XML Key Management Services (XKMS). XKMS defines a series of services for distributing and managing public keys and certificates. The protocol itself is built on SOAP and WSDL, and it is therefore an excellent example of a web service. The specification is available online at *http://www.w3.org/TR/xkms/*.

Network Security

In June 2000, Bruce Schneier, a noted computer expert, flatly stated that "SOAP is going to open up a whole new avenue for security vulnerabilities."[*] Schneier's basic argument is that HTTP was made for document retrieval. Extending HTTP via SOAP enables remote clients to invoke commands and procedures, something that firewalls are explicitly designed to prevent.

You could argue that CGI applications and servlets present the same security vulnerabilities. After all, these programs also enable remote applications to invoke commands and procedures. As SOAP becomes more widely deployed, however, Schneier's argument becomes more compelling. There is currently no easy answer to this problem, and it has been the subject of much debate. For now, if you are truly intent on filtering out SOAP or XML-RPC messages, one possibility is to filter out all HTTP POST requests that set their content type to text/xml (a requirement of both specifications). Another alternative is to filter for the SOAPAction HTTP header attribute (see Chapter 3 for details). Firewall vendors are also currently developing tools explicitly designed to filter web service traffic.

All Together Now

Once you understand each layer in the web service protocol stack, the next important step is to understand how all the pieces fit together. There are two ways of approaching the issue, either from the service requestor perspective or the service provider perspective. In this section, we examine both perspectives and look at a typical development plan for each.

---

[*] Crypto-Gram Newsletter, June 15, 2000 (*http://www.counterpane.com/crypto-gram-0006.html*).

Service Request Perspective

The service requestor is any consumer of web services. Here is a typical development plan for a service requestor:

1. First, you must identify and discover those services that are relevant to your application. This first step therefore usually involves searching the UDDI Business Directory for partners and services.

2. Once you have identified the service you want, the next step is to locate a service description. If this is a SOAP service, you are likely to find a WSDL document. If this is an XML-RPC service, you are likely to find some human-readable instructions for integration.

3. Third, you must create a client application. For example, you may create an XML-RPC or SOAP client in the language of your choice. If the service has a WSDL file, you also have the option of automatically creating client code via a WSDL invocation tool.

4. Finally, run your client application to actually invoke the web service.

A snapshot of the service requestor perspective is provided in Figure 1-14.

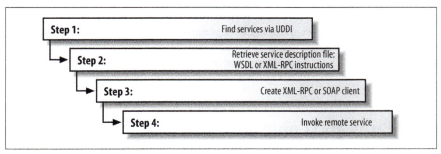

Figure 1-14. Developing web services: the service requestor perspective

Service Provider Perspective

The service provider is any provider of one or more web services. Here is a typical development plan for a service provider:

1. First, you must develop the core functionality of your service. This is usually the hardest part, as your application may connect to databases, Enterprise JavaBeans™ (EJBs), COM objects, or legacy applications.

2. Second, you must develop a service wrapper to your core functionality. This could be an XML-RPC or a SOAP service wrapper. This is usually a relatively simple step, as you are merely wrapping existing functionality into a larger framework.

3. Next, you should provide a service description. If you are creating a SOAP application, you should create a WSDL file. If you are creating an XML-RPC service, you should consider creating some human-readable instructions.

4. Fourth, you need to deploy the service. Depending on your needs, this could mean installing and running a standalone server or integrating with an existing web server.

5. Fifth, you need to publish the existence and specifications of your new service. This usually means publishing data to a global UDDI directory or perhaps a private UDDI directory specific to your company.

A snapshot of the service provider perspective is provided in Figure 1-15.

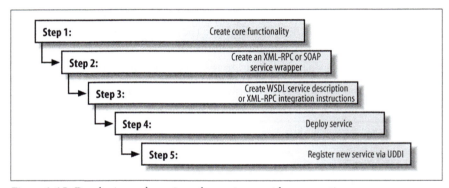

Figure 1-15. Developing web services: the service provider perspective

Standards and Coherence

Web services are still in their infancy, but they are poised to make great inroads in the world of distributed application development. The most crucial elements to the long-term success of web services, however, will be standardization and the coherency of those standards. Currently, none of the web service technologies described in this book has any official standing with the W3C or the IETF. SOAP and WSDL have both been submitted to the W3C, but have no official recommendation status. XML-RPC has not been submitted to any standards body. UDDI is currently under the purview of an industry consortium and will probably go through several more iterations before being handed over to a standards body.

In September 2000, the W3C created an XML Protocol Group. This group represented the W3C's first official foray into the world of web services. Its first task was to create an official recommendation for SOAP, and the group is currently finalizing a SOAP 1.2 specification. In January 2002, the W3C incorporated the XML Protocol Group into a more general Web Services Activity. The new Activity adds Working Groups for Web Services Architecutre and Web Services Description.

 Information about the W3C Web Services Activity is available at *http://www.w3.org/2002/ws/*.

Most people new to web services are initially overwhelmed by the long list of proposed standards and the complex interactions between each. Standardizing each layer in the web service protocol stack will be a major challenge. Making sure all the layers fit together and make coherent sense to developers will be an even greater challenge.

PART II

XML-RPC

CHAPTER 2

XML-RPC Essentials

XML-RPC provides an XML- and HTTP-based mechanism for making method or function calls across a network. XML-RPC offers a very simple, but frequently useful, set of tools for connecting disparate systems and for publishing machine-readable information. This chapter provides a complete overview of XML-RPC, covering the following topics:

- An introduction to the main concepts and history of XML-RPC
- An exploration of XML-RPC usage scenarios, examining its use in glue code and information publishing
- A technical overview of XML-RPC, including a detailed explanation of XML-RPC data types, requests, and responses
- An example demonstrating the use of XML-RPC to connect programs written in Java and Perl

XML-RPC Overview

XML-RPC permits programs to make function or procedure calls across a network. XML-RPC uses the HTTP protocol to pass information from a client computer to a server computer, describing the nature of requests and responses with a small XML vocabulary. Clients specify a procedure name and parameters in the XML request, and the server returns either a fault or a response in the XML response. XML-RPC parameters are a simple list of types and content—structs and arrays are the most complex types available. XML-RPC has no notion of objects and no mechanism for including information that uses other XML vocabularies. Despite those limitations, it has proven capable of a wide variety of tasks.

XML-RPC emerged in early 1998; it was published by UserLand Software and initially implemented in their Frontier product. It has remained largely stable since then.* The XML-RPC specification is available at *http://www.xmlrpc.com/spec*, and a list of implementations (55 at this writing, in a wide variety of languages) is available at *http://www.xmlrpc.com/directory/1568/implementations*.

Why XML-RPC?

In a programming universe seemingly obsessed with objects, XML-RPC may seem too limited for many applications. While XML-RPC certainly has limitations, its inherent simplicity gives it some significant advantages when developers need to integrate systems of very different types. XML-RPC's selection of data types is relatively small, but provides enough granularity that developers can express information in forms any programming language can use.

XML-RPC is used in two main areas, which overlap at times. Systems integrators and programmers building distributed systems often use XML-RPC as glue code, connecting disparate parts inside a private network. By using XML-RPC, developers can focus on the interfaces between systems, not the protocol used to connect those interfaces. Developers building public services can also use XML-RPC, defining an interface and implementing it in the language of their choice. Once that service is published to the Web, any XML-RPC–capable client can connect to that service, and developers can create their own applications that use that service.

Scenario 1: Glue Code with XML-RPC

As distributed systems have become more and more common (by design or by accident), developers have had to address integration problems more and more frequently. Systems that originally ran their own show have to work with other systems as organizations try to rationalize their information management and reduce duplication. This often means that Unix systems need to speak with Windows, which needs to speak with Linux, which needs to speak with mainframes. A lot of programmers have spent a lot of time building custom protocols and formats to let different systems speak to each other.

---

* For additional information on the early history of XML-RPC, explaining the roles of UserLand and Microsoft, see *http://davenet.userland.com/1999/01/29/microsoftXmlRpc*. The "snapshot of the spec we were working on with Microsoft" became XML-RPC, while the rest of the spec went on to become SOAP.

Instead of creating custom systems that need extensive testing, documentation, and debugging, developers can use XML-RPC to connect programs running on different systems and environments. Using this approach, developers can use existing APIs and add connections to those APIs as necessary. Some problems can be solved with a single procedure, while others require more complex interactions, but the overall approach is much like developing any other set of interfaces. In glue code situations, the distinction between client and server isn't especially significant—the terms only identify the program making the request and the program responding. The same program may have both client and server implementations, allowing it to use XML-RPC for both incoming and outgoing requests.

Scenario 2: Publishing Services with XML-RPC

XML-RPC can be used to publish information to the world, providing a computer-readable interface to information. The infrastructure for this use of XML-RPC is much like traditional web publishing to humans, with pretty much the same security and architecture issues, but it allows information recipients to be any kind of client that understands the XML-RPC interface. As in web publishing, XML-RPC publishing means that developers have control over the server, but not necessarily the client.

The O'Reilly Network's Meerkat headline syndicator, for example, presents both a human-readable interface (at *http://meerkat.oreillynet.com*) and an XML-RPC interface (documented at *http://www.oreillynet.com/pub/a/rss/ 2000/11/14/meerkat_xmlrpc.html*) to the world. Casual readers can use the forms-based interface to query the headlines, while developers who need to present the headline information in other forms can use XML-RPC. This makes it easy to separate content from presentation while still working in a Web-centric environment.

XML-RPC Technical Overview

XML-RPC consists of three relatively small parts:

XML-RPC data model
A set of types for use in passing parameters, return values, and faults (error messages)

XML-RPC request structures
An HTTP POST request containing method and parameter information

XML-RPC response structures
An HTTP response that contains return values or fault information

The data structures are used by both the request and response structures. The combination of the three parts defines a complete Remote Procedure Call.

 It's entirely possible to use XML-RPC without getting into the markup details presented later in this chapter. Even if you plan to stay above the details, however, you probably should read the following sections to understand the nature of the information you'll be passing across the network.

XML-RPC Data Model

The XML-RPC specification defines six basic data types and two compound data types that represent combinations of types. While this is a much more restricted set of types than many programming languages provide, it's enough to represent many kinds of information, and it seems to have hit the lowest common denominator for many kinds of program-to-program communications.

All of the basic types are represented by simple XML elements whose content provides the value. For example, to define a string whose value is "Hello World!", you'd write:

```
<string>Hello World!</string>
```

The basic types for XML-RPC are listed in Table 2-1.

Table 2-1. Basic data types in XML-RPC

Type	Value	Examples
int or i4	32-bit integers between -2,147,483,648 and 2,147,483,647.	`<int>27</int>` `<i4>27</i4>`
double	64-bit floating-point numbers	`<double>27.31415</double>` `<double>-1.1465</double>`
boolean	true (1) or false (0)	`<boolean>1</boolean>` `<boolean>0</boolean>`
string	ASCII text, though many implementations support Unicode	`<string>Hello</string>` `<string>bonkers! @</string>`

dateTime.iso8601	Dates in ISO8601 format: *CCYYMMDDTHH:MM:SS*	`<dateTime.iso8601>20021125T02:20:04`
		`</dateTime.iso8601>`
		`<dateTime.iso8601>20020104T17:27:30`
		`</dateTime.iso8601>`

base64	Binary information encoded as Base 64, as defined in RFC 2045	`<base64>SGVsbG8sIFdvcmxkIQ==` `</base64>`

For more information on how Base 64 encoding works, see section 6.8 of RFC 2045, "Multipurpose Internet Mail Extensions (MIME) Part One: Format of Internet Message Bodies", available at *http://www.ietf.org/rfc/rfc2045.txt*. Base 64 is not considered an efficient encoding format, but it does simplify the enclosure of binary information within XML documents. For best results, use it sparingly.

These basic types are always enclosed in value elements. Strings (and only strings) may be enclosed in a value element but omit the string element. These basic types may be combined into two more complex types, arrays and structs. Arrays represent sequential information, while structs represent name-value pairs, much like hashtables, associative arrays, or properties.

Arrays are indicated by the array element, which contains a data element holding the list of values. Like other data types, the array element must be enclosed in a value element. For example, the following array contains four strings:

```
<value>
  <array>
    <data>
      <value><string>This </string></value>
      <value><string>is </string></value>
      <value><string>an </string></value>
      <value><string>array.</string></value>
    </data>
  </array>
</value>
```

The following array contains four integers:

```
<value>
  <array>
    <data>
      <value><int>7</int></value>
      <value><int>1247</int></value>
      <value><int>-91</int></value>
      <value><int>42</int></value>
    </data>
  </array>
</value>
```

Arrays can also contain mixtures of different types, as shown here:

```
<value>
  <array>
    <data>
      <value><boolean>1</boolean></value>
      <value><string>Chaotic collection, eh?</string></value>
      <value><int>-91</int></value>
```

```
      <value><double>42.14159265</double></value>
    </data>
   </array>
</value>
```

Creating multidimensional arrays is simple—just add an array inside of an array:

```
<value>
 <array>
  <data>
    <value>
      <array>
        <data>
          <value><int>10</int></value>
          <value><int>20</int></value>
          <value><int>30</int></value>
        </data>
      </array>
    </value>
    <value>
      <array>
        <data>
          <value><int>15</int></value>
          <value><int>25</int></value>
          <value><int>35</int></value>
        </data>
      </array>
    </value>
  </data>
 </array>
</value>
```

It's a lot of markup, but for the most part, XML-RPC developers won't have to deal with this markup directly.

 XML-RPC won't do anything to guarantee that arrays have a consistent number or type of values. You'll need to make sure that you write code that consistently generates the right number and type of output values if consistency is necessary for your application.

Structs contain unordered content, identified by name. Names are strings, though you don't have to enclose them in string elements. Each struct element contains a list of member elements. Member elements each contain one name element and one value element. The order of members is not considered important. While the specification doesn't require names to be unique, you'll probably want to make sure they are unique for consistency. A simple struct might look like:

```
<value>
  <struct>
    <member>
      <name>givenName</name>
      <value><string>Joseph</string></value>
    </member>
    <member>
      <name>familyName</name>
      <value><string>DiNardo</string></value>
    </member>
    <member>
      <name>age</name>
      <value><int>27</int></value>
    </member>
  </struct>
</value>
```

Structs can also contain other structs, or even arrays. For example, this struct contains a string, a struct, and an array:

```
<value>
  <struct>
    <member>
      <name>name</name>
      <value><string>a</string></value>
    </member>
    <member>
      <name>attributes</name>
      <value><struct>
        <member>
          <name>href</name>
          <value><string>http://example.com</string></value>
        </member>
        <member>
          <name>target</name>
          <value><string>_top</string></value>
        </member>
      </struct></value>
    </member>
    <member>
      <name>contents</name>
      <value><array>
        <data>
          <value><string>This </string></value>
          <value><string>is </string></value>
          <value><string>an example.</string></value>
        </data>
      </array></value>
    </member>
  </struct>
</value>
```

Arrays can also contain structs. You can, in some cases, use these complex types to represent object structures, but at some point you may find it easier to use SOAP for that kind of complex transfer.

XML-RPC Request Structure

XML-RPC requests are a combination of XML content and HTTP headers. The XML content uses the data typing structure to pass parameters and contains additional information identifying which procedure is being called, while the HTTP headers provide a wrapper for passing the request over the Web.

Each request contains a single XML document, whose root element is a methodCall element. Each methodCall element contains a methodName element and a params element. The methodName element identifies the name of the procedure to be called, while the params element contains a list of parameters and their values. Each params element includes a list of param elements which in turn contain value elements.

For example, to pass a request to a method called circleArea, which takes a Double parameter (for the radius), the XML-RPC request would look like:

```
<?xml version="1.0"?>
<methodCall>
  <methodName>circleArea</methodName>
  <params>
    <param>
      <value><double>2.41</double></value>
    </param>
  </params>
</methodCall>
```

To pass a set of arrays to a sortArray procedure, the request might look like:

```
<?xml version="1.0"?>
<methodCall>
  <methodName>sortArray</methodName>
  <params>
    <param>
      <value>
        <array>
          <data>
            <value><int>10</int></value>
            <value><int>20</int></value>
            <value><int>30</int></value>
          </data>
        </array>
      </value>
```

```
        </param>
        <param>
          <value>
            <array>
              <data>
                <value><string>A</string></value>
                <value><string>C</string></value>
                <value><string>B</string></value>
              </data>
            </array>
          </value>
        </param>
      </params>
    </methodCall>
```

The HTTP headers for these requests will reflect the senders and the content. The basic template looks like:

```
POST /target HTTP/1.0
User-Agent: Identifier
Host: host.making.request
Content-Type: text/xml
Content-Length: length of request in bytes
```

The information in italics may change from client to client or from request to request. For example, if the circleArea method were available from an XML-RPC server listening at /xmlrpc, the request might look like:

```
POST /xmlrpc HTTP/1.0
User-Agent: myXMLRPCClient/1.0
Host: 192.168.124.2
Content-Type: text/xml
Content-Length: 169
```

Assembled, the entire request would look like:

```
POST /xmlrpc HTTP/1.0
User-Agent: myXMLRPCClient/1.0
Host: 192.168.124.2
Content-Type: text/xml
Content-Length: 169

<?xml version="1.0"?>
<methodCall>
    <methodName>circleArea</methodName>
    <params>
      <param>
        <value><double>2.41</double></value>
      </param>
    </params>
</methodCall>
```

It's an ordinary HTTP request, with a carefully constructed payload.

The User-Agent header will typically reflect the XML-RPC library used to assemble the request, not the particular program making the call. This is a bit of a change from the browser world, where "browser sniffing" using that header expects to identify the particular program—say, Opera 6.0 for Linux—making the request.

XML-RPC Response Structure

Responses are much like requests, with a few extra twists. If the response is successful—the procedure was found, executed correctly, and returned results—then the XML-RPC response will look much like a request, except that the methodCall element is replaced by a methodResponse element and there is no methodName element:

```
<?xml version="1.0"?>
<methodResponse>
  <params>
    <param>
      <value><double>18.24668429131</double></value>
    </param>
  </params>
</methodResponse>
```

An XML-RPC response can only contain one parameter, despite the use of the enclosing params element. That parameter, may, of course, be an array or a struct, so it is possible to return multiple values. Even if your method isn't designed to return a value (void methods in C, C++, or Java, for instance) you still have to return something. A "success value"—perhaps a boolean set to true (1)—is a typical approach to getting around this limitation.

If there was a problem in processing the XML-RPC request, the methodResponse element will contain a fault element instead of a params element. The fault element, like the params element, has only a single value. Instead of containing a response to the request, however, that value indicates that something went wrong. A fault response might look like:

```
<?xml version="1.0"?>
<methodResponse>
  <fault>
    <value><string>No such method!</string></value>
  </fault>
</methodResponse>
```

The response could also look like:

```
<?xml version="1.0"?>
<methodResponse>
  <fault>
    <value>
```

```
    <struct>
      <member>
        <name>code</name>
        <value><int>26</int></value>
      </member>
      <member>
        <name>message</name>
        <value><string>No such method!</string></value>
      </member>
    </struct>
  </value>
</fault>
</methodResponse>
```

XML-RPC doesn't standardize error codes at all. You'll need to check the documentation for particular packages to see how they handle faults.

Like requests, responses are packaged in HTTP and have HTTP headers. All XML-RPC responses use the 200 OK response code, even if a fault is contained in the message. Headers use a common structure similar to that of requests, and a typical set of headers might look like:

```
HTTP/1.1 200 OK
Date: Sat, 06 Oct 2001 23:20:04 GMT
Server: Apache.1.3.12 (Unix)
Connection: close
Content-Type: text/xml
Content-Length: 124
```

XML-RPC only requires HTTP 1.0 support, but HTTP 1.1 is compatible. The Server header indicates the kind of web server used to process requests for the XML-RPC implementation. The header may or may not reflect the XML-RPC server implementation that processed this particular request. The Content-Type must be set to text/xml; the Content-Length header specifies the length of the response in bytes. A complete response, with both headers and a response payload, would look like:

```
HTTP/1.1 200 OK
Date: Sat, 06 Oct 2001 23:20:04 GMT
Server: Apache.1.3.12 (Unix)
Connection: close
Content-Type: text/xml
Content-Length: 124

<?xml version="1.0"?>
<methodResponse>
  <params>
    <param>
      <value><double>18.24668429131</double></value>
    </param>
  </params>
</methodResponse>
```

After the response is delivered from the XML-RPC server to the XML-RPC client, the connection is closed. Follow-up requests need to be sent as separate XML-RPC connections.

Developing with XML-RPC

Using XML-RPC in your applications generally means adding an XML-RPC library and making some of your function calls through that library. Creating functions that will work smoothly with XML-RPC requires writing code that uses only the basic types XML-RPC supports. Otherwise, there is very little fundamental need to change your coding style. Adding XML-RPC support may require writing some wrapper code that connects your code with the library, but this generally isn't very difficult.

As XML-RPC becomes more and more widespread, some environments are building in XML-RPC. UserLand Frontier has done that for years, while the Perl and Python communities are discussing similar integration.

To demonstrate XML-RPC, we're going to create a server that uses Java to process XML-RPC messages, and Java and Perl clients to call procedures on that server. Although this demonstration is simple, it illustrates the connections needed to establish communications between programs using XML-RPC.

The Java side of the conversation uses the Apache XML Project's Apache XML-RPC, available at *http://xml.apache.org/xmlrpc/*. The Apache package includes a few key pieces that make integrating XML-RPC with Java easier:

- An automated registration process for adding methods to the XML-RPC server
- A built-in server that only speaks XML-RPC, reducing the need to create full-blown servlets
- A client package that makes calling remote methods fairly simple

This demonstration will use a procedure registered with the built-in server of the Apache package and a client for testing the procedure.

For much more information about the Apache XML-RPC package, including data type details and information about creating servlets for XML-RPC processing, see Chapter 3 of *Programming Web Services with XML-RPC* (O'Reilly), by Simon St.Laurent, Edd Dumbill, and Joe Johnston, available online at *http://www.oreilly.com/catalog/progxmlrpc/chapter/ch03.html*.

The procedure that we'll test returns the area of a circle and is defined in a class called AreaHandler, as shown in Example 2-1.

Example 2-1. A simple Java procedure

```java
package com.ecerami.xmlrpc;

public class AreaHandler {

    public double circleArea(double radius) {
        double value=(radius*radius*Math.PI);
        return value;
    }

}
```

The circleArea method of the AreaHandler class takes a double value representing the radius, and returns a double value representing the area of a circle that has that radius. There's nothing in the AreaHandler class that is specific to XML-RPC at all.

Making the circleArea method available via XML-RPC requires two steps. The method must be registered with the XML-RPC package, and some kind of server must make the package accessible via HTTP. The AreaServer class shown in Example 2-2 performs both these steps.

Example 2-2. Setting up a Java XML-RPC server

```java
package com.ecerami.xmlrpc;

import java.io.IOException;
import org.apache.xmlrpc.WebServer;
import org.apache.xmlrpc.XmlRpc;

public class AreaServer {

    public static void main(String[] args) {
        if (args.length < 1) {
            System.out.println("Usage: java AreaServer [port]");
            System.exit(-1);
        }

        try {
            startServer(args);
        } catch (IOException e) {
            System.out.println("Could not start server: " +
                e.getMessage());
        }
    }

    public static void startServer(String[] args) throws IOException {
        // Start the server, using built-in version
```

Example 2-2. Setting up a Java XML-RPC server (continued)

```
    System.out.println("Attempting to start XML-RPC Server...");
    WebServer server = new WebServer(Integer.parseInt(args[0]));

    server.start();

    System.out.println("Started successfully.");

    // Register our handler class as area
    server.addHandler("area", new AreaHandler());
    System.out.println("Registered AreaHandler class to area.");

    System.out.println("Now accepting requests. (Halt program to stop.)");

    }
}
```

The main method checks that there is an argument on the command line specifying on which port to run the server. The method then passes that information to startServer, which starts the built-in server. Once the server is started (it begins running when created), the program calls the addHandler method to register an instance of the AreaHandler class under the name area. The org.apache.xmlrpc.XmlRpc class deals with all of the method signature details, making it possible to start an XML-RPC service in about two lines of critical code. To fire up the server, just execute com.ecerami.xmlrpc. AreaServer from the command line, specifying a port.

```
C:\ora\xmlrpc\java>java com.ecerami.xmlrpc.AreaServer 8899
Attempting to start XML-RPC Server...
Started successfully.
Registered AreaHandler class to area.
Now accepting requests. (Halt program to stop.)
```

The AreaClient class shown in Example 2-3 tests the AreaServer, once started, from the command line. The AreaClient class also uses the XML-RPC library and only needs to use a few lines of code (in the areaCircle method) to make the actual call.

Example 2-3. A Java client to test the XML-RPC server

```
package com.ecerami.xmlrpc;

import java.io.IOException;
import java.util.Vector;
import org.apache.xmlrpc.XmlRpc;
import org.apache.xmlrpc.XmlRpcClient;
import org.apache.xmlrpc.XmlRpcException;

public class AreaClient {

    public static void main(String args[]) {
        if (args.length < 1) {
```

Example 2-3. A Java client to test the XML-RPC server (continued)

```
        System.out.println(
            "Usage: java AreaClient [radius]");
        System.exit(-1);
    }
    AreaClient client = new AreaClient( );
    double radius = Double.parseDouble(args[0]);

    try {
        double area = client.areaCircle(radius);
        // Report the results
        System.out.println("The area of the circle would be: " + area);

    } catch (IOException e) {
        System.out.println("IO Exception: " + e.getMessage( ));
    } catch (XmlRpcException e) {
        System.out.println("Exception within XML-RPC: " + e.getMessage( ));
    }
}

public double areaCircle (double radius)
  throws IOException, XmlRpcException {

        // Create the client, identifying the server
        XmlRpcClient client =
            new XmlRpcClient("http://localhost:8899/");

        // Create the request parameters using user input
        Vector params = new Vector( );
        params.addElement(new Double (radius));

        // Issue a request
        Object result = client.execute("area.circleArea", params);

        String resultStr = result.toString( );
        double area = Double.parseDouble(resultStr);
        return area;
    }

}
```

The main method parses the command line and reports results to the user, but the areaCircle method handles all of the interaction with the XML-RPC service. Unlike the server, which runs continuously, the client runs once in order to get a particular result. The same request may be reused or modified, but each request is a separate event. For this application, we just need to make one request, using the value from the command line as an argument. The client constructor takes a URL as an argument, identifying which server it should contact with requests.

Making requests also requires additional setup work that wasn't necessary in creating the server. While the server could rely on method signatures to figure out which parameters went to which methods, the client doesn't have any such information. The Apache implementation takes arguments in a Vector object, which requires using the Java wrapper classes (like the Double object for double primitives) around the arguments. Once that Vector has been constructed, it is fed to the execute method along with the name of the procedure being called. In this case, the name of the method is area. circleArea, reflecting that the AreaHandler class was registered on the server with the name area and that it contains a method called circleArea.

When the execute method is called, the client makes an XML-RPC request to the server specified in its constructor. The request calls the method identified by the first argument, area.circleArea in this case, and passes the contents of the second argument as parameters. This produces the following HTTP response.

```
POST / HTTP/1.1
Content-Length: 175
Content-Type: text/xml
User-Agent: Java1.3.0
Host: localhost:8899
Accept: text/html, image/gif, image/jpeg, *; q=.2, */*; q=.2
Connection: keep-alive

<?xml version="1.0" encoding="ISO-8859-1"?>
<methodCall><methodName>area.circleArea</methodName>
<params>
<param><value><double>3.0</double></value></param>
</params>
</methodCall>
```

The server responds with a methodResponse, which the execute function reports as an Object. Although the XML-RPC response will provide type information about that Object, and the underlying content will conform to that type, Object is as specific a type as the execute function can generally return while still conforming to Java's strong type-checking.

The result of all this work looks pretty simple:

```
C:\ora\xmlrpc\java>java com.ecerami.xmlrpc.AreaClient 3
The area of the circle would be: 28.274333882308138

C:\ora\xmlrpc\java>java com.ecerami.xmlrpc.AreaClient 4
The area of the circle would be: 50.26548245743669
```

Using XML-RPC to connect Java programs to Java programs isn't especially exciting, however. It certainly works—and it can be a great convenience when the only public access to a Java method is through XML-RPC—but much of XML-RPC's potential lies in connecting other environments. To demonstrate that this works with a broader array of environments, we'll create a Perl client that calls the same function.

The Perl client will use the Frontier::RPC module, an implementation of XML-RPC created by Ken MacLeod. (When MacLeod created this library, XML-RPC was primarily a part of UserLand Frontier.) The client component of the Frontier::RPC module is called Frontier::Client.

 Frontier::RPC and all of the modules it uses are available from CPAN at *http://www.cpan.org*.

The logic for the Perl version of the XML-RPC call is much like that of the Java version, except that Perl's flexibility allows us to skip packaging parameters into a vector. The program shown in Example 2-4 accepts a radius value from the command line, creates a new XML-RPC connection, and passes the radius value as a double to the area.circleArea method. Then the program prints the result.

Example 2-4. An XML-RPC client in Perl

```
use Frontier::Client;

$radius=@ARGV[0];

print "for radius: ", $radius, "\n";

my $client=Frontier::Client->new(url=>"http://127.0.0.1:8899");

print " The area of the circle would be: ", $client->call('area.circleArea',
    Frontier::RPC2::Double->new($radius)), "\n";
```

The trickiest part of the procedure call is the casting that needs to be done to ensure that the number is interpreted as a double. Without Frontier::RPC2::Double->new($radius), the Frontier::RPC module will interpret the radius as a string or an integer unless it has a decimal value. Frontier::RPC provides a set of modules that performs this work on Perl values in order to map Perl's loosely typed values to the explicit typing required by XML-RPC. When used on the command line, the Perl procedure call produces results much like those of the Java client:

```
C:\ora\xmlrpc\perl>perl circle.pl 3
for radius: 3
The area of the circle would be: 28.274333882308138

C:\ora\xmlrpc\perl>perl circle.pl 4
for radius: 4
The area of the circle would be: 50.26548245743669
```

For more information on both the Java and Perl implementations of XML-RPC, as well as implementations in Python, PHP, and Active Server Pages, see *Programming Web Services with XML-RPC* (O'Reilly).

Beyond Simple Calls

XML-RPC is a very simple concept with a limited set of capabilities. Those limitations are in many ways the most attractive feature of XML-RPC, as they substantially reduce the difficulty of implementing the protocol and testing its interoperability. While XML-RPC is simple, the creative application of simple tools can create sophisticated and powerful architectures. In cases where a wide variety of different systems need to communicate, XML-RPC may be the most appropriate lowest common denominator.

Some use cases only require basic functionality, like the library-style functionality described earlier. XML-RPC can support much richer development than these examples show, using combinations of arrays and structs to pass complex sets of information. While calculating the area of a circle may not be very exciting, working with matrices or processing sets of strings may be more immediately worthwhile. XML-RPC itself doesn't provide support for state management, but applications can use parameters to sustain conversations beyond a single request-response cycle, much as web developers use cookies to keep track of extended conversations.

Servers may be able to use XML-RPC to deliver information requested by clients, providing a window on a large collection of information. The O'Reilly Network's Meerkat uses XML-RPC this way, letting clients specify the information they need to receive through XML-RPC procedures. XML-RPC can also be very useful in cases where a client needs to deliver information to a server, both for logging-style operations and operations where the client needs to set properties on a server program. The richness of the interface is up to the developer, but the possibilities are definitely there.

PART III
SOAP

CHAPTER 3

SOAP Essentials

SOAP is an XML-based protocol for exchanging information between computers. Although SOAP can be used in a variety of messaging systems and can be delivered via a variety of transport protocols, the initial focus of SOAP is remote procedure calls transported via HTTP. SOAP therefore enables client applications to easily connect to remote services and invoke remote methods. For example (as we shall soon see), a client application can immediately add language translation to its feature set by locating the correct SOAP service and invoking the correct method.

Other frameworks, including CORBA, DCOM, and Java RMI, provide similar functionality to SOAP, but SOAP messages are written entirely in XML and are therefore uniquely platform- and language-independent. For example, a SOAP Java client running on Linux or a Perl client running on Solaris can connect to a Microsoft SOAP server running on Windows 2000.

SOAP therefore represents a cornerstone of the web service architecture, enabling diverse applications to easily exchange services and data.

Although still in its infancy, SOAP has received widespread industry support. Dozens of SOAP implementations now exist, including implementations for Java, COM, Perl, C#, and Python. At the same time, hundreds of SOAP services are blossoming across the Web.

This chapter aims to provide you with the essentials of SOAP. The following topics are covered:

- A quick overview of the SOAP protocol and a sample SOAP conversation
- Details about the SOAP XML Message specification
- An overview of the SOAP encoding rules, including rules for simple types, arrays, and structs

- Details about using SOAP via HTTP
- An overview of the W3C activities related to SOAP
- An overview of the four main SOAP implementations and a description of the main SOAP interoperability issues

SOAP 101

The SOAP specification defines three major parts:

SOAP envelope specification
> The SOAP XML Envelope defines specific rules for encapsulating data being transferred between computers. This includes application-specific data, such as the method name to invoke, method parameters, or return values. It can also include information about who should process the envelope contents and, in the event of failure, how to encode error messages.

Data encoding rules
> To exchange data, computers must agree on rules for encoding specific data types. For example, two computers that process stock quotes need an agreed-upon rule for encoding float data types; likewise, two computers that process multiple stock quotes need an agreed-upon rule for encoding arrays. SOAP therefore includes its own set of conventions for encoding data types. Most of these conventions are based on the W3C XML Schema specification.

RPC conventions
> SOAP can be used in a variety of messaging systems, including one-way and two-way messaging. For two-way messaging, SOAP defines a simple convention for representing remote procedure calls and responses. This enables a client application to specify a remote method name, include any number of parameters, and receive a response from the server.

To examine the specifics of the SOAP protocol, we begin by presenting a sample SOAP conversation. XMethods.net provides a simple weather service, listing current temperature by zip code. (See Figure 3-1.) The service method, getTemp, requires a zip code string and returns a single float value.

The SOAP Request

The client request must include the name of the method to invoke and any required parameters. Here is a sample client request sent to XMethods:

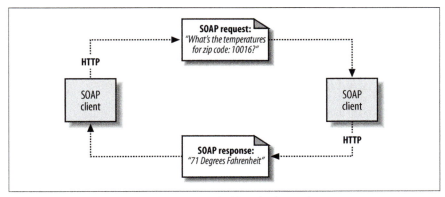

Figure 3-1. SOAP in action: connecting to the XMethods weather service

```
<?xml version='1.0' encoding='UTF-8'?>
<SOAP-ENV:Envelope
    xmlns:SOAP-ENV="http://schemas.xmlsoap.org/soap/envelope/"
    xmlns:xsi="http://www.w3.org/2001/XMLSchema-instance"
    xmlns:xsd="http://www.w3.org/2001/XMLSchema">
    <SOAP-ENV:Body>
        <ns1:getTemp
        xmlns:ns1="urn:xmethods-Temperature"
        SOAP-ENV:encodingStyle="http://schemas.xmlsoap.org/soap/encoding/">
            <zipcode xsi:type="xsd:string">10016</zipcode>
        </ns1:getTemp>
    </SOAP-ENV:Body>
</SOAP-ENV:Envelope>
```

There are a couple of important elements to note here. First, the request includes a single mandatory Envelope element, which in turn includes a mandatory Body element.

Second, a total of four XML namespaces are defined. Namespaces are used to disambiguate XML elements and attributes, and are often used to reference external schemas. In our sample SOAP request, we'll use namespaces to disambiguate identifiers associated with the SOAP Envelope (*http:// schemas.xmlsoap.org/soap/envelope/*), data encoding via XML Schemas (*http: //www.w3.org/2001/XMLSchema-instance* and *http://www.w3.org/2001/ XMLSchema*), and application identifiers specific to XMethods (*urn: xmethods-Temperature*). This enables application modularity, while also providing maximum flexibility for future changes to the specifications.

The Body element encapsulates the main "payload" of the SOAP message. The only element is getTemp, which is tied to the XMethods namespace and corresponds to the remote method name. Each parameter to the method appears as a subelement. In our case, we have a single zip code element, which is assigned to the XML Schema xsd:string data type and set to 10016. If additional parameters are required, each can have its own data type.

The SOAP Response

Here is the SOAP response from XMethods:

```
<?xml version='1.0' encoding='UTF-8'?>
<SOAP-ENV:Envelope
    xmlns:SOAP-ENV="http://schemas.xmlsoap.org/soap/envelope/"
    xmlns:xsi="http://www.w3.org/2001/XMLSchema-instance"
    xmlns:xsd="http://www.w3.org/2001/XMLSchema">
    <SOAP-ENV:Body>
        <ns1:getTempResponse
        xmlns:ns1="urn:xmethods-Temperature"
        SOAP-ENV:encodingStyle="http://schemas.xmlsoap.org/soap/encoding/">
            <return xsi:type="xsd:float">71.0</return>
        </ns1:getTempResponse>
    </SOAP-ENV:Body>
</SOAP-ENV:Envelope>
```

Just like the request, the response includes Envelope and Body elements, and the same four XML namespaces. This time, however, the Body element includes a single getTempResponse element, corresponding to our initial request. The response element includes a single return element, indicating an xsd:float data type. As of this writing, the temperature for zip code 10016 is 71 degrees Fahrenheit.

The SOAP Message

If you are eager to start coding your own SOAP applications, you may want to skip ahead to the "SOAP Implementations" section, later in this chapter. Otherwise, the following section provides additional details regarding the SOAP specification itself.

A one-way message, a request from a client, or a response from a server is officially referred to as a *SOAP message*. Every SOAP message has a mandatory Envelope element, an optional Header element, and a mandatory Body element. (See Figure 3-2.) Each of these elements has an associated set of rules, and understanding the rules will help you debug your own SOAP applications.

Envelope

Every SOAP message has a root Envelope element. In contrast to other specifications, such as HTTP and XML, SOAP does not define a traditional versioning model based on major and minor release numbers (e.g., HTTP 1.0

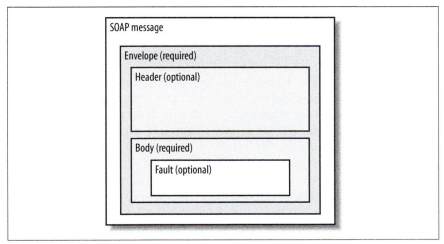

Figure 3-2. Main elements of the XML SOAP message

versus HTTP 1.1). Rather, SOAP uses XML namespaces to differentiate versions. The version must be referenced within the Envelope element. For example:

```
<SOAP-ENV:Envelope
    xmlns:SOAP-ENV="http://schemas.xmlsoap.org/soap/envelope/"
```

The SOAP 1.1 namespace URI is *http://schemas.xmlsoap.org/soap/envelope/*, whereas the SOAP 1.2 namespace URI is *http://www.w3.org/2001/09/soap-envelope*.[*] If the Envelope is in any other namespace, it is considered a versioning error.

Header

The optional Header element offers a flexible framework for specifying additional application-level requirements. For example, the Header element can be used to specify a digital signature for password-protected services; likewise, it can be used to specify an account number for pay-per-use SOAP services. Many current SOAP services do not utilize the Header element, but as SOAP services mature, the Header framework provides an open mechanism for authentication, transaction management, and payment authorization.

---

[*] The exact value of the SOAP 1.2 envelope namespace will likely change to reflect the final date of the SOAP 1.2 release. The value, *http://www.w3.org/2001/09/soap-envelope* reflects the specification from September, 2001.

The details of the Header element are intentionally open-ended, thereby providing maximum flexibility for application providers. The protocol does, however, specify two header attributes:

Actor attribute

The SOAP protocol defines a *message path* as a list of SOAP service nodes. Each of these intermediate nodes can perform some processing and then forward the message to the next node in the chain. By setting the Actor attribute, the client can specify the recipient of the SOAP header.

MustUnderstand attribute

Indicates whether a Header element is optional or mandatory. If set to true,[*] the recipient must understand and process the Header attribute according to its defined semantics, or return a fault. (See Table 3-2 for the MustUnderstand fault code.)

Here is an example Header:

```
<SOAP-ENV:Header>
    <ns1:PaymentAccount xmlns:ns1="urn:ecerami" SOAP-ENV:
        mustUnderstand="true">
        orsenigo473
    </ns1:PaymentAccount >
</SOAP-ENV:Header>
```

The Header specifies a payment account, which must be understood and processed by the SOAP server.

Body

The Body element is mandatory for all SOAP messages. As we have already seen, typical uses of the Body element include RPC requests and responses.

Fault

In the event of an error, the Body element will include a Fault element. The fault subelements are defined in Table 3-1 and include the faultCode, faultString, faultActor, and detail elements. Predefined SOAP fault codes are defined in Table 3-2. The following code is a sample Fault. The client has requested a method named ValidateCreditCard, but the service does not support such a method. This represents a client request error, and the server returns the following SOAP response:

---

[*] SOAP 1.1 uses integer values of 1/0 for the MustUnderstand attribute; SOAP 1.2 uses Boolean values of true/1/false/0.

```
<?xml version='1.0' encoding='UTF-8'?>
<SOAP-ENV:Envelope
    xmlns:SOAP-ENV="http://schemas.xmlsoap.org/soap/envelope/"
    xmlns:xsi="http://www.w3.org/1999/XMLSchema-instance"
    xmlns:xsd="http://www.w3.org/1999/XMLSchema">
    <SOAP-ENV:Body>
        <SOAP-ENV:Fault>
            <faultcode xsi:type="xsd:string">SOAP-ENV:Client</faultcode>
            <faultstring xsi:type="xsd:string">
                Failed to locate method (ValidateCreditCard) in class
                (examplesCreditCard) at /usr/local/ActivePerl-5.6/lib/
                site_perl/5.6.0/SOAP/Lite.pm line 1555.
            </faultstring>
        </SOAP-ENV:Fault>
    </SOAP-ENV:Body>
</SOAP-ENV:Envelope>
```

Table 3-1. SOAP fault subelements

Element name	Description
faultCode	A text code used to indicate a class of errors. See Table 3-2 for a listing of predefined fault codes.
faultString	A human-readable explanation of the error.
faultActor	A text string indicating who caused the fault. This is useful if the SOAP message travels through several nodes in the SOAP message path, and the client needs to know which node caused the error. A node that does not act as the ultimate destination must include a faultActor element.
detail	An element used to carry application-specific error messages. The detail element can contain child elements, called detail entries.

Table 3-2. SOAP fault codes

Name	Description
SOAP-ENV:VersionMismatch	Indicates that the SOAP Envelope element included an invalid namespace, signifying a version mismatch.
SOAP-ENV:MustUnderstand	Indicates that the recipient is unable to properly process a Header element with a mustUnderstand attribute set to true. This ensures that mustUnderstand elements are not silently ignored.
SOAP-ENV:Client	Indicates that the client request contained an error. For example, the client has specified a nonexistent method name, or has supplied the incorrect parameters to the method.
SOAP-ENV:Server	Indicates that the server is unable to process the client request. For example, a service providing product data may be unable to connect to the database.

SOAP Encoding

SOAP includes a built-in set of rules for encoding data types. This enables the SOAP message to indicate specific data types, such as integers, floats, doubles, or arrays. Most of the time, the encoding rules are implemented directly by the SOAP toolkit you choose, and are therefore hidden from you. It is nonetheless useful to understand the basics of SOAP encoding, particularly if you are intercepting SOAP messages and trying to debug an application. Note also that while the W3C specification encourages the use of SOAP encoding rules, these rules are not required; this enables you to choose a different encoding schema, should the need arise.

When exploring the SOAP encoding rules, it is important to note that the XML 1.0 specification does not include rules for encoding data types. The original SOAP specification therefore had to define its own data encoding rules. Subsequent to early drafts of the SOAP specification, the W3C released the XML Schema specification. The XML Schema Part 2: Datatypes specification provides a standard framework for encoding data types within XML documents. The SOAP specification therefore adopted the XML Schema conventions. However, even though the latest SOAP specification adopts all the built-in types defined by XML Schema, it still maintains its own convention for defining constructs not standardized by XML Schema, such as arrays and references. Arrays are discussed in detail in the "Compound Types" section, later in this chapter.

SOAP data types are divided into two broad categories: scalar types and compound types. Scalar types contain exactly one value, such as a last name, price, or product description. Compound types contain multiple values, such as a purchase order or a list of stock quotes. Compound types are further subdivided into arrays and structs. Arrays contain multiple values, each of which is specified by an ordinal position. Structs also contain multiple values, but each element is specified by an accessor name.

The encoding style for a SOAP message is set via the SOAP-ENV: encodingStyle attribute. To use SOAP 1.1 encoding, use the value http:// schemas.xmlsoap.org/soap/encoding/. To use SOAP 1.2 encoding, use the value http://www.w3.org/2001/09/soap-encoding.

Scalar Types

For scalar types, SOAP adopts all the built-in simple types specified by the XML Schema specification. This includes strings, floats, doubles, and integers. Table 3-3 lists the main simple types, excerpted from the XML Schema Part 0: Primer (*http://www.w3.org/TR/2000/WD-xmlschema-0-20000407/*).

Table 3-3. A list of the main XML Schema built-in simple types

Simple type	Example(s)
string	Web services
Boolean	true, false, 1, 0
float	-INF, -1E4, -0, 0, 12.78E-2, 12, INF, NaN
double	-INF, -1E4, -0, 0, 12.78E-2, 12, INF, NaN
decimal	-1.23, 0, 123.4, 1000.00
binary	100010
integer	-126789, -1, 0, 1, 126789
nonPositiveInteger	-126789, -1, 0
negativeInteger	-126789, -1
long	-1, 12678967543233
int	-1, 126789675
short	-1, 12678
byte	-1, 126
nonNegativeInteger	0, 1, 126789
unsignedLong	0, 12678967543233
unsignedInt	0, 1267896754
unsignedShort	0, 12678
unsignedByte	0, 126
positiveInteger	1, 126789
date	1999-05-31
time	13:20:00.000, 13:20:00.000-05:00

For example, here is a SOAP response with a double data type:

```
<?xml version='1.0' encoding='UTF-8'?>
<SOAP-ENV:Envelope
    xmlns:SOAP-ENV="http://www.w3.org/2001/09/soap-envelope"
    xmlns:xsi="http://www.w3.org/2001/XMLSchema-instance"
    xmlns:xsd="http://www.w3.org/2001/XMLSchema">
    <SOAP-ENV:Body>
        <ns1:getPriceResponse
            xmlns:ns1="urn:examples:priceservice"
            SOAP-ENV:encodingStyle="http://www.w3.org/2001/09/soap-encoding">
            <return xsi:type="xsd:double">54.99</return>
        </ns1:getPriceResponse>
    </SOAP-ENV:Body>
</SOAP-ENV:Envelope>
```

As you can see, the xsi:type attribute is set to xsd:double, indicating a return double value.

The SOAP specification provides several options for indicating the data type of a specific XML element. The first option is to specify an xsi:type attribute for each element. The second option is to store data type information within an external XML Schema or even within human-readable documentation. SOAP toolkits vary in their implementation of this requirement. The Apache SOAP toolkit, for example, automatically includes an xsi:type attribute with every element, whereas the Microsoft SOAP toolkit omits the xsi:type attribute and assumes an external XML Schema definition. The examples within this chapter are derived from Apache SOAP and therefore use the xsi:type attribute. See the "SOAP Interoperability" section, later in this chapter, for additional details.

Compound Types

SOAP arrays have a very specific set of rules, which require that you specify both the element type and array size. SOAP also supports multidimensional arrays, but not all SOAP implementations support multidimensional functionality. (Check your chosen SOAP toolkit for details.)

To create an array, you must specify it as an xsi:type of Array. The array must also include an arrayType attribute. This attribute is required to specify the data type for the contained elements and the dimension(s) of the array. For example, the following attribute specifies an array of 10 double values: arrayType="xsd:double[10]". In contrast, the following attribute specifies a two-dimensional array of strings: arrayType="xsd:string[5,5]".

Here is a sample SOAP response with an array of double values:

```
<?xml version='1.0' encoding='UTF-8'?>
<SOAP-ENV:Envelope
    xmlns:SOAP-ENV="http://www.w3.org/2001/09/soap-envelope"
    xmlns:xsi="http://www.w3.org/2001/XMLSchema-instance"
    xmlns:xsd="http://www.w3.org/2001/XMLSchema">
    <SOAP-ENV:Body>
        <ns1:getPriceListResponse
            xmlns:ns1="urn:examples:pricelistservice"
            SOAP-ENV:encodingStyle="http://www.w3.org/2001/09/soap-encoding">
            <return
                xmlns:ns2="http://www.w3.org/2001/09/soap-encoding"
                xsi:type="ns2:Array" ns2:arrayType="xsd:double[2]">
                <item xsi:type="xsd:double">54.99</item>
                <item xsi:type="xsd:double">19.99</item>
            </return>
        </ns1:getPriceListResponse>
    </SOAP-ENV:Body>
</SOAP-ENV:Envelope>
```

Note that the `arrayType` is set to `xsd:double[2]`. Each element in the array is specified as an `item` element.

In contrast to arrays, structs contain multiple values, but each element is specified with a unique accessor element. For example, consider an item within a product catalog. In this case, the struct might contain a product SKU, product name, description, and price. Here is how such a struct would be represented in a SOAP message:

```
<?xml version='1.0' encoding='UTF-8'?>
<SOAP-ENV:Envelope
    xmlns:SOAP-ENV="http://www.w3.org/2001/09/soap-envelope"
    xmlns:xsi="http://www.w3.org/2001/XMLSchema-instance"
    xmlns:xsd="http://www.w3.org/2001/XMLSchema">
    <SOAP-ENV:Body>
        <ns1:getProductResponse
            xmlns:ns1="urn:examples:productservice"
            SOAP-ENV:encodingStyle="http://www.w3.org/2001/09/soap-encoding">
            <return xmlns:ns2="urn:examples" xsi:type="ns2:product">
                <name xsi:type="xsd:string">Red Hat Linux</name>
                <price xsi:type="xsd:double">54.99</price>
                <description xsi:type="xsd:string">
                    Red Hat Linux Operating System
                </description>
                <SKU xsi:type="xsd:string">A358185</SKU>
            </return>
        </ns1:getProductResponse>
    </SOAP-ENV:Body>
</SOAP-ENV:Envelope>
```

Each element in a struct is specified with a unique accessor name. For example, the message above includes four accessor elements: `name`, `price`, `description`, and `SKU`. Each element can have its own data type; for example, `name` is specified as a `string`, whereas `price` is specified as a `double`.

 All of the sample SOAP messages (including arrays, structs, and literal XML documents) within this section were created with the Apache SOAP toolkit. See Chapter 5 for complete details.

Literal Encoding

As previously noted, you are not required to use the SOAP encoding style. In fact, occasionally you may want to ignore the SOAP encoding rules completely and embed an entire XML document (or just a portion of the document) directly into your SOAP message. Doing so is referred to as literal XML encoding, and it requires that you specify a literal XML encoding style.

Within Apache SOAP, the literal XML style is specified with the namespace *http://xml.apache.org/xml-soap/literalxml*.

For example, the following is a second option for encoding product information. Rather than encoding the product as a SOAP struct, the data is encoded as a literal XML document:

```xml
<?xml version='1.0' encoding='UTF-8'?>
<SOAP-ENV:Envelope
    xmlns:SOAP-ENV="http://www.w3.org/2001/09/soap-envelope"
    xmlns:xsi="http://www.w3.org/2001/XMLSchema-instance"
    xmlns:xsd="http://www.w3.org/2001/XMLSchema">
    <SOAP-ENV:Body>
        <ns1:getProductResponse
            xmlns:ns1="urn:examples:XMLproductservice"
            SOAP-ENV:encodingStyle=
                "http://xml.apache.org/xml-soap/literalxml">
            <return>
                <product sku="A358185">
                <name>Red Hat Linux</name>
                <description>Red Hat Linux Operating System</description>
                <price>54.99</price></product>
            </return>
        </ns1:getProductResponse>
    </SOAP-ENV:Body>
</SOAP-ENV:Envelope>
```

For a more extensive discussion of SOAP encoding rules, refer to *Programming Web Services with SOAP* by James Snell, Doug Tidwell, and Pavel Kulchenko (O'Reilly).

SOAP via HTTP

SOAP is not tied to any one transport protocol. In fact, SOAP can be transported via SMTP, FTP, IBM's MQSeries, or Microsoft Message Queuing (MSMQ). However, the SOAP specification includes details on HTTP only, and HTTP remains the most popular SOAP transport protocol.

Quite logically, SOAP requests are sent via an HTTP request and SOAP responses are returned within the content of the HTTP response. While SOAP requests can be sent via an HTTP GET, the specification includes details on HTTP POST only. (HTTP POST is preferred because most servers place a character limit on GET requests.) Additionally, both HTTP requests and responses are required to set their content type to text/xml.

As an additional requirement, clients must specify a SOAPAction header. The SOAPAction header is a server-specific URI used to indicate the intent of the request. This makes it possible to quickly determine the nature of the SOAP request, without actually examining the SOAP message payload. In practice, the header is frequently used by firewalls as a mechanism for blocking out SOAP requests or for quickly dispatching SOAP messages to specific SOAP servers.

The SOAP specification mandates that the client must provide a SOAPAction header, but the actual value of the SOAPAction header is dependent on the SOAP server implementation. For example, to access the AltaVista BabelFish Translation service, hosted by XMethods, you must specify the urn:xmethodsBabelFish#BabelFish as the SOAPAction header. Even if the server does not require a full SOAPAction header, the client must specify an empty string (""), or a null value. For example:

```
SOAPAction: ""
SOAPAction:
```

Here is a sample request sent via HTTP to the XMethods Babelfish Translation service:

```
POST /perl/soaplite.cgi HTTP/1.0
Host: services.xmethods.com
Content-Type: text/xml; charset=utf-8
Content-Length: 538
SOAPAction: "urn:xmethodsBabelFish#BabelFish"

<?xml version='1.0' encoding='UTF-8'?>
<SOAP-ENV:Envelope
    xmlns:SOAP-ENV="http://schemas.xmlsoap.org/soap/envelope/"
    xmlns:xsi="http://www.w3.org/1999/XMLSchema-instance"
    xmlns:xsd="http://www.w3.org/1999/XMLSchema">
    <SOAP-ENV:Body>
        <ns1:BabelFish
        xmlns:ns1="urn:xmethodsBabelFish"
        SOAP-ENV:encodingStyle="http://schemas.xmlsoap.org/soap/encoding/">
            <translationmode xsi:type="xsd:string">en_fr</translationmode>
            <sourcedata xsi:type="xsd:string">Hello, world!</sourcedata>
        </ns1:BabelFish>
    </SOAP-ENV:Body>
</SOAP-ENV:Envelope>
```

Note the content type and the SOAPAction header. Also note that the BabelFish method requires two String parameters. The translation mode en_fr will translate from English to French.

Here is the response from XMethods:

```
HTTP/1.1 200 OK
Date: Sat, 09 Jun 2001 15:01:55 GMT
Server: Apache/1.3.14 (Unix) tomcat/1.0 PHP/4.0.1pl2
SOAPServer: SOAP::Lite/Perl/0.50
Cache-Control: s-maxage=60, proxy-revalidate
Content-Length: 539
```

```
Content-Type: text/xml

<?xml version="1.0" encoding="UTF-8"?>
<SOAP-ENV:Envelope
    xmlns:SOAP-ENC="http://schemas.xmlsoap.org/soap/encoding/"
    SOAP-ENV:encodingStyle="http://schemas.xmlsoap.org/soap/encoding/"
    xmlns:xsi="http://www.w3.org/1999/XMLSchema-instance"
    xmlns:SOAP-ENV="http://schemas.xmlsoap.org/soap/envelope/"
    xmlns:xsd="http://www.w3.org/1999/XMLSchema">
    <SOAP-ENV:Body>
        <namesp1:BabelFishResponse xmlns:namesp1="urn:xmethodsBabelFish">
            <return xsi:type="xsd:string">Bonjour, monde!</return>
        </namesp1:BabelFishResponse>
    </SOAP-ENV:Body>
</SOAP-ENV:Envelope>
```

SOAP responses delivered via HTTP are required to follow the same HTTP status codes. For example, a status code of 200 OK indicates a successful response. A status code of 500 Internal Server Error indicates that there is a server error and that the SOAP response includes a Fault element.

Many people, including members of the W3C XML Protocol Working Group, have argued that the meaning and use of the SOAPAction header is extremely vague. As a result, SOAP 1.2 has changed the status of SOAPAction from required to optional. Future versions of the specification may maintain the header, but deprecate it, in order to ensure backward compatibility.

SOAP and the W3C

SOAP 1.1 was originally submitted to the W3C in May 2000. Official submitters included large companies, such as Microsoft, IBM, and Ariba, and smaller companies, such as UserLand Software and DevelopMentor.

In September 2000, the W3C created a new XML Protocol Working Group. The goal of the group is to hammer out an XML protocol for information exchange and recommend the protocol as an official W3C recommendation.

In July 2001, the XML Protocol Working Group released a "working draft" of SOAP 1.2. Within the W3C, this document is officially a work in progress, meaning that the document is likely to be updated many times before it is finalized. However, so far, SOAP 1.2 does not represent a radical departure from SOAP 1.1 and is primarily aimed at clarifying ambiguous issues within the SOAP 1.1 specification. Most developers should therefore find the transition from 1.1 to 1.2 relatively painless.

The W3C has broken the SOAP 1.2 specification into two parts. Part I describes the SOAP messaging framework and envelope specification. Part II describes the SOAP encoding rules, the SOAP-RPC convention, and HTTP binding details.

Once finalized, SOAP may work its way up to official W3C recommendation status. Until that time, however, it is important to note that SOAP has no official commitment from the W3C. Even SOAP 1.1 has a status of "Note", meaning that it is currently open to the W3C membership for discussion.

 SOAP originally stood for Simple Object Access Protocol. The W3C was uncomfortable with maintaining this definition, primarily because the specification does not actually mandate the use of objects. On the other hand, the W3C was also reluctant to define a new name, such as XML Protocol, or XML-P, primarily because the term SOAP was already well established among developers. Hence, in a bizarre twist of fate, the name SOAP stays, but the W3C now says it no longer stands for anything.

For the latest details on the XML Protocol Working Group, go to *http://www.w3.org/2000/xp/Group/*. The working group also hosts a public email discussion list, available at *xml-dist-app@w3.org*.

 SOAP Version 1.1 is available online at *http://www.w3.org/TR/SOAP/*. The working draft of SOAP Version 1.2 is available at *http://www.w3.org/TR/soap12/*. Note that the W3C also hosts a submission for "SOAP Messages with Attachments", which separates from the core SOAP specification. This specification enables SOAP messages to include binary attachments, such as images and sound files. For full details, see the W3C Note at *http://www.w3.org/TR/SOAP-attachments*.

SOAP Implementations

Dozens of SOAP implementations now freely exist on the Internet. In fact, as of this writing, SOAPWare.org has referenced a total of 65 implementations. Here are four of the most popular and widely cited implementations.

Apache SOAP (http://xml.apache.org/soap/)
Open source Java implementation of the SOAP protocol; based on the IBM SOAP4J implementation

Microsoft SOAP ToolKit 2.0 (http://msdn.microsoft.com/soap/default.asp)
COM implementation of the SOAP protocol for C#, C++, Visual Basic, or other COM-compliant languages

SOAP::Lite for Perl (http://www.soaplite.com/)
Perl implementation of the SOAP protocol, written by Paul Kulchenko, that includes support for WSDL and UDDI

GLUE from the Mind Electric (http://www.themindelectric.com)
Java implementation of the SOAP protocol that includes support for WSDL and UDDI

Complete information on Apache SOAP is provided in Chapter 4 and Chapter 5. SOAP::Lite and GLUE are discussed briefly in Chapter 6. For a more complete list, or to find a SOAP implementation for your language or platform of choice, check out *http://www.soapware.org/directory/4/implementations.*

SOAP Interoperability

SOAP was specifically designed to solve platform and language interoperability problems. It is therefore ironic that SOAP itself has its own interoperability problems, but alas, this is currently true. For example, as of this writing, there are known interoperability issues between Apache SOAP, SOAP::Lite for Perl, and the Microsoft SOAP ToolKit. Apache SOAP requires all parameters to be typed via the xsi:type attribute, whereas the Microsoft SOAP ToolKit does not require this; each implementation provides different levels of enforcement for the mustUnderstand attribute; and Microsoft SOAP supports multidimensional arrays, whereas Apache SOAP and SOAP::Lite for Perl support only one-dimensional arrays.

The interoperability problems stem from two main issues. First, and foremost, SOAP is still in its infancy. SOAP was submitted to the W3C in May 2000 and has yet to receive a formal recommendation from the W3C. Second, dozens of SOAP implementations currently exist, and it will take much effort to ensure that they all interoperate with each other.

Hopefully, all the interoperability issues will be worked out soon. The implementations themselves will mature and the SOAP specification will also mature as it makes its way through the W3C process. For additional information on SOAP interoperability, check out the Microsoft Interoperability Site (*http://www.mssoapinterop.org*) or the XMethods Interoperability Lab (*http://www.xmethods.net/ilab/*). Each of these sites provides a suite of interoperability tests and includes updated results for most of the major SOAP implementations.

CHAPTER 4

Apache SOAP Quick Start

Apache SOAP is an open source Java implementation of the SOAP specification. The original Apache code is based on IBM's SOAP4J, which IBM donated to the Apache open source community. Like all Apache projects, Apache SOAP is free for both noncommercial and commercial purposes. The source code is readily available, and an active group of programmers is busy adding new features for future releases.

This chapter provides a quick start introduction to using Apache SOAP. The goal is to present the most important essentials so that you can start coding and get to work. Four specific topics will be covered:

- Installation instructions for using Apache SOAP with the open source Jakarta Tomcat server

- A "Hello, SOAP!" client/service application for demonstrating basic SOAP RPC coding

- An overview of deploying and managing SOAP services via the web-based administration tool and the command-line `ServiceManagerClient` tool

- Tips for viewing live SOAP conversations using the `TcpTunnelGui` tool

Installing Apache SOAP

If you are only creating SOAP clients, all you need to do is download the correct suite of files and include the relevant JAR files within your CLASS-PATH (details to follow). If, however, you are creating SOAP services, you need the right files plus a Java servlet engine. For example, you can install Apache SOAP to BEA WebLogic Application Server, IBM WebSphere, or Allaire JRun. This section includes specific instructions for installing to the open source Apache Jakarta Tomcat 3.2 server. Tomcat is free, easy to set up, and gets you running in just a few minutes.

You need a Java servlet engine to set up SOAP services because the Apache SOAP service, called rpcrouter, is really just a Java servlet that has been configured to receive SOAP requests.

Downloading the Required Java Files

To install Apache SOAP to Jakarta Tomcat, you need to download five distribution files. First, download the Tomcat and Apache SOAP distributions:

- Apache Jakarta Tomcat: *http://jakarta.apache.org/tomcat/*
- Apache SOAP: *http://xml.apache.org/soap/*

Then, download the Xerces Java Parser, Java Mail, and JavaBeans Activation Framework distributions:

- Xerces Java Parser (Version 1.1.2 or higher): *http://xml.apache.org/xerces-j/index.html*
- Java Mail: *http://java.sun.com/products/javamail/*
- JavaBeans Activation Framework: *http://java.sun.com/products/javabeans/glasgow/jaf.html*

Setting Up the Tomcat CLASSPATH

Next, you need to set the CLASSPATH for Jakarta Tomcat. Specifically, you must include the following JAR files and directories:

- *soap.jar*
- *xerces.jar*
- *mail.jar*
- *activation.jar*
- Directory for your SOAP application class files

To set the Tomcat CLASSPATH, edit the server startup file (on Windows, this file is *tomcat.bat*; on Unix, it is *tomcat.sh*). For example, I added the following lines to the section entitled "Set Up the Runtime Classpath" in my *tomcat.bat* file:

```
echo Adding xerces.jar to beginning of CLASSPATH
set CP=c:\web_services\lib\xerces.jar;%CP%
echo Adding soap.jar to CLASSPATH
set CP=%CP%;C:\web_services\lib\soap.jar
echo Adding mail.jar and activation.jar to CLASSPATH
set CP=%CP%;c:\web_services\lib\mail.jar;c:\web_services\lib\activation.jar
echo Adding SOAP Examples Directory
set CP=%CP%;c:\web_services\examples\classes
```

Note that the Tomcat distribution includes its own XML parser, but the built-in parser is not namespace-aware and therefore will not work with Apache SOAP. Hence, you need to force Tomcat to use Xerces (1.1.2 or higher) by prepending *xerces.jar* to the very beginning of your CLASS-PATH. For example:

```
set CP=c:\web_services\lib\xerces.jar;%CP%
```

Configuring Tomcat

As the final step, you must register the Apache SOAP service with Tomcat. To do so, just add the following lines to the Tomcat configuration file (*conf/server.xml*):

```
<Context path="/soap" docBase="C:\web_services\soap-2_2\webapps\soap"
         debug="1" reloadable="true">
</Context>
```

Make sure to set the correct docBase to reflect your local installation.

Starting Tomcat

You are now ready to start the Tomcat server. On Windows, run the *startup.bat* file. On Unix, run *startup.sh*. If you are running Windows, you should see the startup window in Figure 4-1. By default, Tomcat will start on port 8080, and you should see the text "Starting HttpConnectionHandler on 8080" within the startup window.

Figure 4-1. Starting Tomcat

Running the SOAP Administrator

With Tomcat running, you can now access the SOAP Administrator. Open a browser window, and go to *http://localhost:8080/soap*. If you see the welcome screen in Figure 4-2, everything is installed correctly, and you can start deploying your own SOAP services.

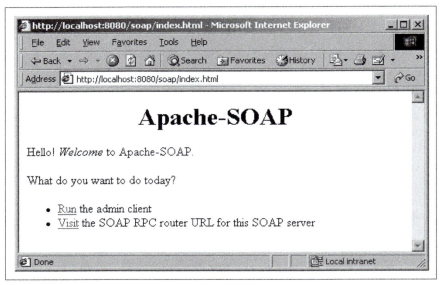

Figure 4-2. Apache SOAP welcome screen

Hello, SOAP!

With Apache SOAP now installed, we're ready to tackle our first SOAP application, "Hello, SOAP!" The "Hello, SOAP!" service provides a single sayHello( ) method, which accepts a first-name parameter and returns a personalized greeting. We'll begin by exploring the general architecture outlined in Figure 4-3. This diagram includes all the elements responsible for processing data and traces the steps of a sample "Hello, SOAP!" conversation.

1. The Apache SOAP client generates a SOAP request and sends the request via an HTTP POST. The client request specifies the *helloservice* service and the sayHello method. The request also includes a single parameter called *firstName*.

2. The Jakarta Tomcat server receives the incoming request and forwards it to the Apache rpcrouter servlet.

3. The rpcrouter looks up the requested *helloservice*, instantiates a HelloService object, and invokes the sayHello( ) method.

4. The HelloService object extracts the firstName parameter (e.g., "Amy") and returns a greeting (e.g., "Hello, Amy!").

5. The rpcrouter captures the greeting, packages the result into a SOAP response, and returns the response to the client.

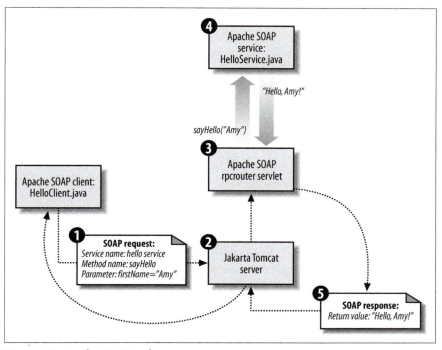

Figure 4-3. Apache SOAP architecture

Service Code

We will examine the service-side code first. (See Example 4-1.) The most striking aspect of the service code is that this is just a regular Java class. There is no need to import any Apache SOAP–specific libraries or to implement any SOAP-specific interfaces. Rather, you just need to implement the methods supported by your service. In Example 4-1, we provide an implementation of the sayHello( ) method. This method takes a single String parameter, firstName, and returns a greeting. That's all there is to it!

Example 4-1. HelloService.java

```
package com.ecerami.soap;

/**
 * "Hello, SOAP!" SOAP Service
 * Provides a personalized greeting to any client application
 */
```

Example 4-1. HelloService.java (continued)

```
public class HelloService {

  /**
   *  Says Hello to Client
   */
  public String sayHello (String firstName) {
    return new String ("Hello, "+firstName+"!");
  }
}
```

Client Code

In contrast to the service code, writing client code does require interfacing with the Apache SOAP API. Regardless of the complexity, however, client code generally follows the same five steps:

1. Create an RPC Call object. The Call object encapsulates all the details for invoking a remote SOAP service. For example, it includes the SOAP service name and the method name to invoke.

2. Build a list of parameters to pass to the remote service. Apache SOAP includes built-in support for passing a large number of data types, including primitive data types, strings, vectors, and arrays. As we will see in Chapter 5, Apache SOAP also supports the passing of JavaBeans and literal XML documents.

3. Invoke the remote method. Behind the scenes, the client packages the relevant data into a SOAP request, sends it to the SOAP server, and receives and parses the SOAP response.

4. Check for any errors within the SOAP response.

5. Extract the return value from the SOAP response.

The complete client code for the "Hello, SOAP!" application is shown in Example 4-2.

Example 4-2. HelloClient.java

```
package com.ecerami.soap;

/**
 * "Hello, SOAP!" SOAP Client
 * usage:  java HelloClient first_name
 */
import java.net.*;
import java.util.Vector;
import org.apache.soap.SOAPException;
import org.apache.soap.Fault;
import org.apache.soap.Constants;
import org.apache.soap.rpc.Call;
```

Example 4-2. HelloClient.java (continued)

```java
import org.apache.soap.rpc.Parameter;
import org.apache.soap.rpc.Response;

public class HelloClient {

  /**
   * Static Main method
   */
  public static void main (String[] args) {
    String firstName = args[0];
    System.out.println ("Hello SOAP Client");
    HelloClient helloClient = new HelloClient();
    try {
      String greeting = helloClient.getGreeting(firstName);
      System.out.print (greeting);
    } catch (SOAPException e) {
      String faultCode = e.getFaultCode();
      String faultMsg = e.getMessage();
      System.err.println ("SOAPException Thrown (details below):");
      System.err.println ("FaultCode:  "+faultCode);
      System.err.println ("FaultMessage:  "+faultMsg);
    } catch (MalformedURLException e) {
      System.err.println (e);
    }
  }

  /**
   * getGreeting Method
   */
  public String getGreeting (String firstName)
    throws SOAPException, MalformedURLException {

    // Create SOAP RPC Call Object
    Call call = new Call ();

    // Set Encoding Style to standard SOAP encoding
    call.setEncodingStyleURI(Constants.NS_URI_SOAP_ENC);

    // Set Object URI and Method Name
    call.setTargetObjectURI ("urn:examples:helloservice");
    call.setMethodName ("sayHello");

    // Set Method Parameters
    Parameter param = new Parameter("firstName", String.class,
      firstName, Constants.NS_URI_SOAP_ENC);

    Vector paramList = new Vector ();
    paramList.addElement (param);
    call.setParams (paramList);

    // Set the URL for the Web Service
    URL url = new URL ("http://localhost:8080/soap/servlet/rpcrouter");
```

Example 4-2. HelloClient.java (continued)

```java
// Invoke the Service
Response resp = call.invoke (url, "");

// Check for Faults
if (!resp.generatedFault()) {
  // Extract Return value
  Parameter result = resp.getReturnValue ();
  String greeting = (String) result.getValue();
  return greeting;
}
else {
  // Extract Fault Code and String
  Fault f = resp.getFault();
  String faultCode = f.getFaultCode();
  String faultString = f.getFaultString();
  System.err.println("Fault Occurred (details follow):");
  System.err.println("Fault Code:  "+faultCode);
  System.err.println("Fault String:  "+faultString);
  return new String ("Fault Occurred.  No greeting for you!");
  }
 }
}
```

This code expects a single command-line argument, indicating a first name. For example, the command line:

```
java com.ecerami.soap.HelloClient Amy
```

will generate the following output:

```
Hello SOAP Client
Hello, Amy!
```

The bulk of the SOAP-specific code occurs in the getGreeting( ) method. So we'll begin our code dissection there.

The RPC Call object

To generate a SOAP request, you must first instantiate an org.apache.soap.rpc.Call object:

```
Call call = new Call ( );
```

The Call object encapsulates all the details of your SOAP request. For example, we need to set the SOAP encoding style. For the default SOAP encoding style, use Constants.NS_URI_SOAP_ENC:

```
call.setEncodingStyleURI(Constants.NS_URI_SOAP_ENC);
```

Other encoding styles will be discussed in Chapter 5. The Call object also encapsulates the URI of the desired SOAP service and the method name to invoke:

```
call.setTargetObjectURI ("urn:examples:helloservice");
call.setMethodName ("sayHello");
```

API: org.apache.soap.rpc.Call

void setEncodingStyleURI(String encodingStyleURI)
> Sets the encoding style URI for the parameters passed inside the SOAP Envelope. Takes the following parameter:

encodingStyleURI
>> The encoding style URI. Use Constants.NS_URI_SOAP_ENC for the default encoding style: *http://schemas.xmlsoap.org/soap/encoding/*. Use Constants.NS_URI_LITERAL_XML for passing literal XML documents.

void setTargetObjectURI(String targetObjectURI)
> Sets the target object URI. Takes the following parameter:

targetObjectURI
>> The URI of the remote service. This is usually the URN of the service to be invoked; for example, *urn:examples:helloservice*.

void setMethodName(String methodName)
> Sets the remote method name. Takes the following parameter:

methodName
>> The name of the remote method; for example, sayHello.

void setParams(Vector params)
> Sets the vector of parameters that will be passed from client to server. Takes the following parameter:

params
>> The vector of parameters. The vector must consist of org.apache.soap.rpc.Parameter objects.

Response invoke(URL url, String SOAPActionURI) throws SOAPException
> Invokes the remote method. Behind the scenes, the method will connect to the specified server, send the SOAP request, and retrieve and parse the SOAP response. In the event of fatal errors, including failed network connections or violations of the SOAP protocol, the method will throw a SOAPException. Takes the following parameter:

url
>> The absolute URL of the SOAP server.

SOAPActionURI
> Optional SOAPAction HTTP header. SOAPAction is generally used to indicate the URI for the SOAP service. An empty string ("") indicates that the SOAP target is specified in the HTTP request URI.

Setting parameters

To pass data to a remote method, you must create one or more parameters. For each parameter, you must instantiate an org.apache.soap.rpc.Parameter object. The Parameter constructor expects four arguments:

- Parameter name.
- Class type; for example, String.class, Integer.class, or Double.class.
- Parameter value.
- Encoding style. If set to null, the parameter will use the encoding style of the Class object.

API:org.apache.soap.rpc.Parameter

Parameter (String name, Class type, Object value, String encodingStyleURI)
    Constructs a new Parameter object. Takes the following parameters:

    name
        The parameter name.

    type
        The Java class type; for example, String.class, Double.class, or String[].class.

    value
        The parameter value.

    encodingStyleURI
        The encoding-style URI for the parameter. If set to null, the parameter will default to the style specified for the Call object.

public java.lang.Object getValue( )
    Retrieves the value of the Parameter object.

For example, we add a single String parameter:

```
Parameter param = new Parameter("firstName", String.class,
    firstName, Constants.NS_URI_SOAP_ENC);
```

Passing primitive data types (e.g., ints, doubles, or floats) follows an identical process. The only difference is that you must specify the object wrapper, such as Integer, Double, or Float. For example, the following code creates a Double parameter:

```
discountParam = new Parameter ("discount", Double.class,
    discount, Constants.NS_URI_SOAP_ENC);
```

Each parameter is added to a Vector object, and this entire Vector object is then passed to the Call object via the setParams( ) method:

```
Vector paramList = new Vector ();
paramList.addElement (param);
call.setParams (paramList);
```

When you create parameters, each parameter has a name/value pair, but the order of the parameters is critical. Upon receiving your method call, the rpcrouter will unpack each parameter in the exact order in which it was received and attempt to find a matching method signature. For example, a SOAP request with two parameters, String firstName and int age, will attempt to find methodName (String, int). If the client reverses the parameter order, a "no signature match" error will occur.

Invoking a remote service

Once the Call object is set, we are ready to execute the remote service via the invoke( ) method. The invoke( ) method takes two parameters:

The URL of the SOAP server
> For the Apache distribution, this is the absolute URL to the rpcrouter servlet; for example, *http://localhost:8080/soap/servlet/rpcrouter*.

The SOAPAction header
> According to the SOAP specification, the SOAPAction header is a required HTTP header for client applications sending SOAP requests via HTTP. SOAPAction is generally used to indicate the URI for the SOAP service. Nonetheless, an empty string ("") indicates that the SOAP target is specified in the HTTP request URI. The Apache SOAP server implementation requires that you specify a SOAPAction header, but it will ignore the actual value. You can therefore safely use an empty string or a null value.

Our client code specifies the localhost Apache server and an empty string SOAPAction header:

```
URL url = new URL ("http://localhost:8080/soap/servlet/rpcrouter");
Response resp = call.invoke (url, "");
```

If all goes well, the invoke( ) method will return an org.apache.soap.rpc. Response object. The Response object encapsulates all data regarding the server SOAP response, including any return parameters or fault conditions.

Checking for errors

Distributed computing that is enabled by SOAP is inherently vulnerable to multiple points of failure. For example:

- The SOAP server may be down or unable to keep up with a high volume of transactions.
- The SOAP server may be unable to complete the requested service.

- The SOAP client may be unable to open a network connection.
- The SOAP client may be incompatible with the SOAP server.

There are two groups of SOAP errors: SOAPExceptions and SOAP faults. SOAPExceptions refer to fatal errors in network connectivity or violations of the SOAP protocol. For example, if a SOAP server returns a SOAP response, but neglects to include the required Body element, the client will detect the protocol violation and immediately throw a SOAPException. In contrast, SOAP faults refer to errors at the application layer. For example, if a client requests a nonexistent service or method, the SOAP server will generate a fault and will propagate the fault back to the client. If a remote service method is unable to complete execution, it too can trigger a fault.

SOAPExceptions are thrown by the Call.invoke() method, whereas SOAP faults are embedded in the Response object and need to be explicitly extracted.

API: org.apache.soap.SOAPException

String getFaultCode()
> Returns the SOAP fault code, identifying the primary origin of the error. A return value of SOAP-ENV:Client indicates that the client caused the error. A return value of SOAP-ENV:Server indicates that the server caused the error.

String getMessage()
> Returns a human-readable explanation of the error.

API: org.apache.soap.Fault

String getFaultCode()
> Returns the SOAP fault code, identifying the primary origin of the error. A return value of SOAP-ENV:Client indicates that the client caused the error. A return value of SOAP-ENV:Server indicates that the server caused the error.

String getFaultString()
> Returns a human-readable explanation of the error.

HelloClient.java includes code for capturing both SOAPExceptions and SOAP faults. For example, the main() method captures the SOAPException and displays the cause of the error:

```
catch (SOAPException e) {
    String faultCode = e.getFaultCode( );
    String faultMsg = e.getMessage( );
    System.err.println ("SOAPException Thrown (details below):");
    System.err.println ("FaultCode:  "+faultCode);
    System.err.println ("FaultMessage:  "+faultMsg);
}
```

The fault code indicates the origin of the error. A return value of SOAP-ENV:
Client indicates that the client caused the error. A return value of SOAP-ENV:
Server indicates that the server caused the error.

HelloClient.java also checks for SOAP faults by checking the Response.
generatedFault( ) method. If this method returns true, the code extracts the
Fault object and queries it for details:

```
Fault f = resp.getFault( );
String faultCode = f.getFaultCode( );
String faultString = f.getFaultString( );
System.err.println("Fault Occurred (details follow):");
System.err.println("Fault Code:  "+faultCode);
System.err.println("Fault String:  "+faultString);
```

Extracting the return value

For the final step, we extract the return value. To do so, call the Response.
getReturnValue( ) method. Then call Parameter.getValue( ) and cast to the
expected class:

```
if (!resp.generatedFault( )) {
    // Extract Return value
    Parameter result = resp.getReturnValue( );
    String greeting = (String) result.getValue( );
    return greeting;
}
```

API: org.apache.soap.rpc.Response

boolean generatedFault( )
> Indicates whether a fault was generated. If this method returns true, use
> getFault( ) to retrieve the embedded fault.

Fault getFault( )
> Retrieves the embedded Fault object.

Parameter getReturnValue( )
> Retrieves the return parameter.

Deploying SOAP Services

There are two ways to deploy new SOAP services. The first option is to use the web-based administrator. The second is to use the command-line tool.

Web-Based Administrator

To use the web-based administrator, open a new browser, go to *http://localhost:8080/soap*, and click the Run the Admin Client link. This screen (see Figure 4-4) provides three basic tools:

List
    To obtain a complete list of all deployed services
Deploy
    To deploy a new SOAP service
UnDeploy
    To undeploy an existing SOAP service

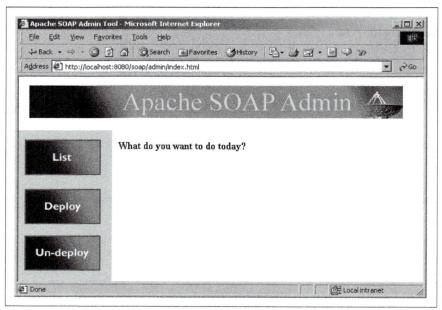

Figure 4-4. Apache SOAP administration client

To deploy the `HelloService` class, click the Deploy button.

The Deploy a Service page contains half a dozen fields for deploying your web service. (See Figure 4-5.) Let's focus on the most important fields:

Uniform Resource Names (URNs)

A Uniform Resource Name (URN) is a Uniform Resource Identifier (URI) that is both persistent and location-independent. The official URN syntax as detailed in IETF RFC 2141 is:

```
<URN> ::= "urn:" <NID> ":" <NSS>
```

where `<NID>` is the namespace identifier and `<NSS>` is the namespace-specific string. For example, `urn:isbn:0596000588` refers to the O'Reilly book, *XML in a Nutshell*.

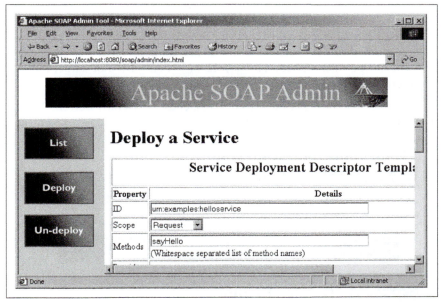

Figure 4-5. Apache SOAP: Deploy a Service page

ID

> This field sets the name of your SOAP service. It is recommended that you use the URN syntax when naming your SOAP service (see the earlier sidebar for details regarding URNs). For our first example, set the ID to `urn:examples:helloservice`.

Scope

> Each time a SOAP service is invoked, a specific server object handles the request. Scope defines the lifetime of this instantiated object. Request indicates that the object will exist during the lifetime of one SOAP

request/response cycle. Session indicates that the object will exist during the entire session between client and server, and will therefore be maintained across multiple request/response conversations. Application indicates that only one object is instantiated and will process all incoming requests. For our first example, set the scope to Request.

Methods

This field includes a complete list of all methods supported by your service. Methods are separated by whitespace characters. The HelloService class only supports one method: sayHello.

Java provider

The Java provider is the completely qualified name of the Java service class that will handle incoming SOAP requests. For "Hello, World!", set the Java provider to com.ecerami.soap.HelloService. Note that this class must be available via the Tomcat CLASSPATH. The Static field indicates whether the specified methods are static. If set to Yes, the object will not be instantiated. The sayHello( ) method is not static, and we therefore keep the Static field set to the default of No.

Once you have completed these four fields, click the Deploy button. To verify that your service has indeed been deployed, click the List button, and you should see your service displayed. (See Figure 4-6.)

Figure 4-6. Apache SOAP: Service Listing page

ServiceManagerClient Command-Line Tool

To deploy a new SOAP service, you can also use the Apache command-line tool, ServiceManagerClient. The command-line tool has the following usage:

```
Usage: java org.apache.soap.server.ServiceManagerClient
[-auth username:password] url operation arguments
```

The following operations are supported:

list
: Provides a complete list of existing SOAP services

deploy deployment-descriptor-file.xml
: Deploys the SOAP service specified in the deployment descriptor file

query servicename
: Displays the deployment descriptor of the specified service

undeploy service-name
: Undeploys the specified service

To deploy a new SOAP service, you must specify a deployment descriptor file. The deployment descriptor file contains all the information for your deployed service, including the service URN, list of service methods, scope, and Java provider. For example, here is the deployment descriptor for the "Hello, SOAP!" service:

```
<isd:service
    xmlns:isd="http://xml.apache.org/xml-soap/deployment"
    id="urn:examples:helloservice" checkMustUnderstands="false">
    <isd:provider type="java" scope="Request" methods="sayHello">
        <isd:java class="com.ecerami.soap.HelloService" static="false"/>
    </isd:provider>
</isd:service>
```

Note that there is a one-to-one correspondence between the elements and attributes specified in the deployment descriptor and the HTML form fields of the web administration tool:

Service element
: Specifies the URN for the SOAP service

Provider element
: Specifies the service provider type, scope, methods, and Java class

To deploy the "Hello, SOAP!" service via the command-line tool, use the following command:

```
java org.apache.soap.server.ServiceManagerClient http://localhost:8080/soap/
    servlet/rpcrouter deploy helloservice.xml
```

To verify that the service was indeed registered, use the list operation:

```
java org.apache.soap.server.ServiceManagerClient http://localhost:8080/soap/
    servlet/rpcrouter list
```

You should see the following output:

```
Deployed Services:
urn:examples:helloservice
```

To retrieve the deployment descriptor of an existing service, use the query operation. For example, the following command:

```
java org.apache.soap.server.ServiceManagerClient http://localhost:8080/soap/
    servlet/rpcrouter query urn:examples:helloservice
```

will display the helloservice deployment descriptor.

The TcpTunnelGui Tool

It is often quite useful to view the actual SOAP conversation between client and server. This can aid in understanding the intricacies of the SOAP protocol and in debugging live applications. To help you along, the Apache SOAP distribution includes a handy TcpTunnelGui tool. The tool requires three command-line parameters:

listenport
> The TcpTunnelGui tool will intercept and display all messages going to the listenport.

tunnelhost
> The tunnel hostname. For local installations, set this to localhost.

tunnelport
> The TcpTunnelGui tool will intercept all messages and forward them to the tunnelport. For Jakarta Tomcat, set this to 8080.

For example, the following command line will intercept all messages going to port 8070 and forward them to the localhost, port 8080:

```
java org.apache.soap.util.net.TcpTunnelGui 8070 localhost 8080
```

To view your actual SOAP conversation, you must modify the client code to use port 8070. For example:

```
URL url = new URL ("http://localhost:8070/soap/servlet/rpcrouter");
Response resp = call.invoke (url, "");
```

A sample screenshot of the "Hello, SOAP!" conversation is provided in Figure 4-7. Messages from the client are displayed in the left column; messages from the server are displayed in the right column.

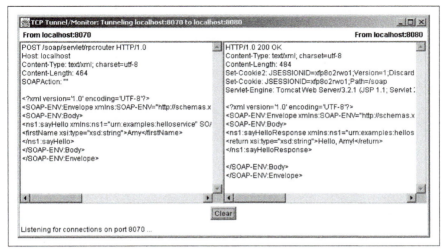

Figure 4-7. The TcpTunnelGui tool in action

Here is the full text of a sample request message:

```
POST /soap/servlet/rpcrouter HTTP/1.0
Host: localhost
Content-Type: text/xml; charset=utf-8
Content-Length: 464
SOAPAction: ""

<?xml version='1.0' encoding='UTF-8'?>
<SOAP-ENV:Envelope
    xmlns:SOAP-ENV="http://schemas.xmlsoap.org/soap/envelope/"
    xmlns:xsi="http://www.w3.org/1999/XMLSchema-instance"
    xmlns:xsd="http://www.w3.org/1999/XMLSchema">
    <SOAP-ENV:Body>
        <ns1:sayHello
            xmlns:ns1="urn:examples:helloservice"
            SOAP-ENV:encodingStyle="http://schemas.xmlsoap.org/soap/encoding/">
            <firstName xsi:type="xsd:string">Amy</firstName>
        </ns1:sayHello>
    </SOAP-ENV:Body>
</SOAP-ENV:Envelope>
```

Here is the full text of a sample response message:

```
HTTP/1.0 200 OK
Content-Type: text/xml; charset=utf-8
Content-Length: 484
Set-Cookie2: JSESSIONID=810j57jod1;Version=1;Discard;Path="/soap"
Set-Cookie: JSESSIONID=810j57jod1;Path=/soap
Servlet-Engine: Tomcat Web Server/3.2.1
(JSP 1.1; Servlet 2.2; Java 1.3.0; Windows 2000 5.0 x86;
    java.vendor=Sun Microsystems Inc.)
```

```
<?xml version='1.0' encoding='UTF-8'?>
<SOAP-ENV:Envelope
    xmlns:SOAP-ENV="http://schemas.xmlsoap.org/soap/envelope/"
    xmlns:xsi="http://www.w3.org/1999/XMLSchema-instance"
    xmlns:xsd="http://www.w3.org/1999/XMLSchema">
    <SOAP-ENV:Body>
        <ns1:sayHelloResponse
            xmlns:ns1="urn:examples:helloservice"
            SOAP-ENV:encodingStyle="http://schemas.xmlsoap.org/soap/encoding/">
            <return xsi:type="xsd:string">Hello, Amy!</return>
        </ns1:sayHelloResponse>
    </SOAP-ENV:Body>
</SOAP-ENV:Envelope>
```

Web Resources

Here are some web resources that provide more information about Apache SOAP.

- Apache SOAP web site: *http://xml.apache.org/soap/*.
- Mailing-list archives: Apache SOAP maintains a "soap-user" mailing list. Complete archives are available at *http://marc.theaimsgroup.com/ ?l=soap-user*.

CHAPTER 5

Programming Apache SOAP

With a basic understanding of Apache SOAP, we are now ready for more in-depth coverage of select topics. These topics include:

- Passing arrays between client and server
- Passing JavaBeans between client and server
- Registering new type mappings
- Working with literal XML documents
- Handling SOAP faults and exceptions
- Maintaining session state

This chapter is built around a series of five example SOAP applications that will help explain these topics. The first four applications illustrate services provided by a fictional e-commerce company that sells software over the Web. The final application provides a simple counting service that illustrates the creation of stateful SOAP services. Each application includes full client code, service code, and a description of relevant APIs.

 Apache SOAP can use SMTP for the transport of SOAP messages. Nonetheless, all examples within this chapter assume the (more popular) use of HTTP.

Working with Arrays

The "Hello, SOAP!" application from Chapter 4 illustrated the passing of strings and primitive data types. The next step up the SOAP ladder is working with arrays. Fortunately, Apache SOAP provides built-in support for arrays, making this task relatively painless.

To illustrate the basic concepts, we will create a simple e-commerce product catalog. Clients can connect to the catalog service and send a list of stockkeeping units (SKUs). The catalog service looks up each SKU and returns a list of current prices. Behind the scenes, the client passes an array of strings to the server, and the server returns an array of doubles.

Service Code

We will examine the service code first. (See Example 5-1.) The PriceListService constructor creates a product hashtable of two current products. To keep the code simple, the prices are hardcoded. The getPriceList( ) method expects an array of string SKUs and generates a corresponding array of doubles. We assume that the client always requests current, valid SKUs.

Example 5-1. PriceListService.java

```java
package com.ecerami.soap;

import java.util.Hashtable;

/**
 * A Sample SOAP Service
 * Provides a Price List for specified list of SKUs
 */
public class PriceListService {
  protected Hashtable products;    // Product "Database"

  /**
   * Zero Argument Constructor
   * Load product database with two sample products
   */
  public PriceListService ( ) {
    products = new Hashtable( );
    //   Red Hat Linux
    products.put("A358185", new Double (54.99));
    //   McAfee PGP Personal Privacy
    products.put("A358565", new Double (19.99));
  }

  /**
   *  Provides Price List for specified SKUs.
   *  We assume that the client always specifies valid, current SKUs
   */
  public double[] getPriceList (String sku[]) {
    double prices[] = new double [sku.length];
    for (int i=0; i<sku.length; i++) {
      Double price = (Double) products.get(sku[i]);
      prices[i] = price.doubleValue( );
    }
    return prices;
  }
}
```

Client Code

The client code is shown in Example 5-2, later in this section. When invoking the client application, you can specify as many SKUs as you like on the command line. For example, the following command line:

```
java com.ecerami.soap.PriceListClient A358185 A358565
```

will generate the following output:

```
Price List Checker:  SOAP Client
SKU:   A358185 --> 54.99
SKU:   A358565 --> 19.99
```

In examining the client code, first note the `TargetObjectURI` and method name:

```
call.setTargetObjectURI ("urn:examples:pricelistservice");
call.setMethodName ("getPriceList");
```

Here, we are assuming that the `pricelistservice` has already been deployed via the web administrator tool. Alternatively, you could use the command-line tool and the following deployment descriptor:

```
<isd:service
    xmlns:isd="http://xml.apache.org/xml-soap/deployment"
    id="urn:examples:pricelistservice" checkMustUnderstands="false">
    <isd:provider type="java" scope="Request" methods="getPriceList">
        <isd:java class="com.ecerami.soap.PriceListService" static="false"/>
    </isd:provider>
</isd:service>
```

To pass an array from client to server, you must create a new `Parameter` object. The important distinction is that you must specify an array class, such as `String[].class` or `Double[].class`, to the `Parameter` constructor. For example, our new client creates an array parameter of string SKUs:

```
Parameter param = new Parameter("sku", String[].class,
    skus, Constants.NS_URI_SOAP_ENC);
```

The array parameter is then added to a `Vector` of parameters, and the `Vector` is passed to the `Call` object, just as in our "Hello, SOAP!" application.

To extract an array from the `Response` object, you just need to cast to the appropriate array type. For example, the `PriceListClient` code expects an array of doubles:

```
Parameter result = resp.getReturnValue ();
double priceList[] = (double []) result.getValue();
```

In conclusion, there is really nothing special about passing arrays. Note, however, that the current version of Apache SOAP only supports one-dimensional arrays. Additional dimensions may be supported in the near future. Check the Apache SOAP web site for current release notes.

Example 5-2. PriceListClient.java

```
package com.ecerami.soap;

/**
 * A Sample SOAP Client
 * Retrieves Price List for Specified SKUs
 * usage:   java PriceClient sku#1 sku#2 sku#N
 */
import java.net.*;
import java.util.Vector;
import org.apache.soap.*;
import org.apache.soap.rpc.*;

public class PriceListClient {

  /**
   * Static Main method
   */
  public static void main (String[] args) {
    System.out.println ("Price List Checker:  SOAP Client");
    String skus[] = new String [args.length];
    for (int i=0; i<args.length; i++)
      skus[i] = new String (args[i]);
    PriceListClient priceListClient = new PriceListClient();
    try {
      double price[] = priceListClient.getPriceList(skus);
      for (int i=0; i<price.length; i++) {
        System.out.print ("SKU:  "+skus[i]);
        System.out.println (" --> "+price[i]);
      }
    } catch (SOAPException e) {
      System.err.println (e);
    } catch (MalformedURLException e) {
      System.err.println (e);
    }
  }

  /**
   * getPriceList Method
   */
  public double[] getPriceList (String skus[])
    throws SOAPException, MalformedURLException {
    Parameter skuParam;

    // Create SOAP RPC Call Object
    Call call = new Call ();

    // Set Encoding Style to standard SOAP encoding
    call.setEncodingStyleURI(Constants.NS_URI_SOAP_ENC);
```

Example 5-2. PriceListClient.java (continued)

```java
// Set Object URI and Method Name
call.setTargetObjectURI ("urn:examples:pricelistservice");
call.setMethodName ("getPriceList");

//  Set Method Parameters
Vector paramList = new Vector ();
Parameter param = new Parameter("sku", String[].class,
    skus, Constants.NS_URI_SOAP_ENC);
paramList.addElement (param);
call.setParams (paramList);

//  Set the URL for the Web Service
URL url = new URL ("http://localhost:8080/soap/servlet/rpcrouter");

// Invoke the Service
Response resp = call.invoke (url, null);

// Check for Success
if (!resp.generatedFault( )) {
  // Extract Return value
  Parameter result = resp.getReturnValue ();
  double priceList[] = (double []) result.getValue( );
  return priceList;
}
//  Check for Faults
else {
  //  Extract Fault Code and String
  Fault f = resp.getFault( );
  String faultCode = f.getFaultCode( );
  String faultString = f.getFaultString( );
  System.err.println("Fault Occurred (details follow):");
  System.err.println("Fault Code:  "+faultCode);
  System.err.println("Fault String:  "+faultString);
  return null;
  }
 }
}
```

For reference, here is the full text of a sample SOAP request (HTTP headers are not included). Note the array encoding:

```xml
<?xml version='1.0' encoding='UTF-8'?>
<SOAP-ENV:Envelope
    xmlns:SOAP-ENV="http://www.w3.org/2001/09/soap-envelope"
    xmlns:xsi="http://www.w3.org/2001/XMLSchema-instance"
    xmlns:xsd="http://www.w3.org/2001/XMLSchema">
<SOAP-ENV:Body>
<ns1:getPriceList
```

```
          xmlns:ns1="urn:examples:pricelistservice"
          SOAP-ENV:encodingStyle="http://www.w3.org/2001/09/soap-encoding">
     <sku
          xmlns:ns2="http://www.w3.org/2001/09/soap-encoding"
          xsi:type="ns2:Array" ns2:arrayType="xsd:string[2]">
          <item xsi:type="xsd:string">A358185</item>
          <item xsi:type="xsd:string">A358565</item>
     </sku>
     </ns1:getPriceList>
     </SOAP-ENV:Body>
     </SOAP-ENV:Envelope>
```

Here is a complete SOAP response:

```
     <?xml version='1.0' encoding='UTF-8'?>
     <SOAP-ENV:Envelope
          xmlns:SOAP-ENV="http://www.w3.org/2001/09/soap-envelope"
          xmlns:xsi="http://www.w3.org/2001/XMLSchema-instance"
          xmlns:xsd="http://www.w3.org/2001/XMLSchema">
          <SOAP-ENV:Body>
             <ns1:getPriceListResponse
                xmlns:ns1="urn:examples:pricelistservice"
                SOAP-ENV:encodingStyle="http://www.w3.org/2001/09/soap-encoding">
                <return
                    xmlns:ns2="http://www.w3.org/2001/09/soap-encoding"
                    xsi:type="ns2:Array" ns2:arrayType="xsd:double[2]">
                    <item xsi:type="xsd:double">54.99</item>
                    <item xsi:type="xsd:double">19.99</item>
                </return>
             </ns1:getPriceListResponse>
          </SOAP-ENV:Body>
     </SOAP-ENV:Envelope>
```

Working with JavaBeans

Working with strings, primitive data types, and arrays will only get you so far. Fortunately, Apache SOAP also includes support for JavaBeans and literal XML documents. According to the official JavaSoft documentation, a JavaBean is a reusable software component that can be visually manipulated within any building tool. More generally, however, a JavaBean is any Java class that follows the JavaBean naming convention. This convention requires that all accessible properties be made available via get/set methods. For example, a Color property must have a corresponding pair of getColor( )/setColor( ) methods. The only exceptions to this rule are boolean properties that require an is/set naming convention. The JavaBean convention also requires that you provide a zero-argument constructor.

By using Java reflection, a visual tool can determine the available Bean properties and make these properties available via easy-to-use text boxes or radio buttons. Along the same lines, Apache SOAP's built-in `BeanSerializer` class can, by using reflection, transform any JavaBean into an XML element or receive an XML element and automatically build a corresponding JavaBean. This requires that both the client and service code have access to the class file for the JavaBean. The SOAP call does not actually download the code for the JavaBean, only the state of the JavaBean. Understanding how this works requires a more detailed understanding of Java-to-XML transformation and the SOAP service deployment options.

The ProductBean

To illustrate the most important JavaBean concepts, our second SOAP example enables the retrieval of the complete state of a JavaBean. We now want more than just the product price. Rather, we want to retrieve the product name, description, and price, and we want all this data encapsulated into one JavaBean. For example, given the following command line:

```
java com.ecerami.soap.ProductClient A358565
```

the program will generate the following output:

```
Product Checker:  SOAP Client
SKU:  A358565
Name:  McAfee PGP
Description:  McAfee PGP Personal Privacy
Price:  19.99
```

The first step is to create a product JavaBean, called `ProductBean`. (See Example 5-3.) The `ProductBean` has four properties: name, description, price, and SKU. Each property has a get/set method, and we also provide a zero-argument constructor, making this a valid JavaBean.

Example 5-3. ProductBean.java

```java
package com.ecerami.soap;

/**
 * A Product Bean
 * Encapsulates data regarding one product
 */
public class ProductBean {
    private String name;          // Product Name
    private String description;   // Product Description
    private double price;         // Product Price
    private String sku;           // Product SKU
```

Example 5-3. ProductBean.java (continued)

```java
/**
 * Zero-argument Constructor
 */
public ProductBean () { }

/**
 * Constructor with full arguments
 */
public ProductBean (String name, String description, double price,
  String sku) {
  this.name = name;
  this.description = description;
  this.price = price;
  this.sku = sku;
}

// Setters
public void setName (String name) {
  this.name = name;
}

public void setDescription (String description) {
    this.description = description;
}

public void setPrice (double price) {
  this.price = price;
}

public void setSKU (String sku) {
  this.sku = sku;
}

// Getters
public String getName () { return name; }
public String getDescription () { return description; }
public double getPrice () { return price; }
public String getSKU () { return sku; }
}
```

Service Code

The next step is to write the service code. (See Example 5-4.) The
ProductService constructor creates two sample ProductBeans and loads these
into the product hashtable. The getProduct( ) method searches for a specific SKU string and returns the corresponding ProductBean. Again, we
assume that the user always specifies a valid, current SKU.

Example 5-4. ProductService.java

```
package com.ecerami.soap;

import java.util.Hashtable;

/**
 * A Sample SOAP Service
 * Provides Product Information for requested Stockkeeping Unit (SKU)
 */
public class ProductService {
  protected Hashtable products;    // Product "Database"

  /**
   * Constructor
   * Load product database with two sample products
   */
  public ProductService ( ) {
    products = new Hashtable( );
    ProductBean product1 = new ProductBean
      ("Red Hat Linux", "Red Hat Linux Operating System",
      54.99, "A358185");
    ProductBean product2 = new ProductBean
      ("McAfee PGP", "McAfee PGP Personal Privacy",
      19.99, "A358565");
    products.put(product1.getSKU( ), product1);
    products.put(product2.getSKU( ), product2);
  }

  /**
   *  Provides Product Info for requested SKU.
   *  We assume that the client always specifies a valid, current SKU
   */
  public ProductBean getProduct (String sku) {
    ProductBean product = (ProductBean) products.get(sku);
    return product;
  }
}
```

You can deploy the ProductService in the same manner as in the previous examples. Nonetheless, you will need to fill in a few additional fields of information for the type-mapping registry. The Apache SOAP type-mapping registry provides a way to map XML Schema data types to Java classes and vice versa. By default, the registry is prepopulated with basic data types, including primitive data types, strings, vectors, dates, and arrays. If you are passing a new data type, you need to explicitly register the new type and indicate which Java classes will be responsible for serializing and deserializing your new type.

To register a new mapping, scroll down to the bottom of the Deploy a Service page. (See Figure 5-1.)

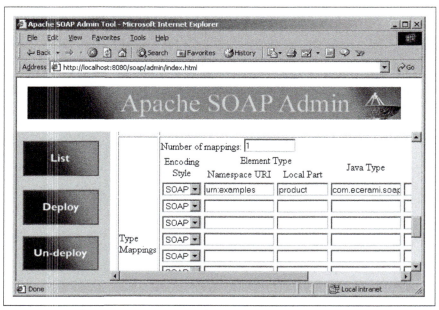

Figure 5-1. Deploying a SOAP service with a new type-mapping entry

Next to Number of mappings, enter the total number of new mappings. For each mapping, enter the correct data into the form fields. Alternatively, you can deploy the service via the command-line tool. To set type mappings within a deployment descriptor file, use the isd:mappings element. The isd: mappings element requires a single isd:map element, which includes a number of attributes. The attributes correspond exactly to the web administration tool. These attributes are described in the following table.

Web administration field	isd:map attribute	Description
Encoding style	encodingStyle	This is the encoding style for your new data type. For example: encodingStyle="http://schemas. xmlsoap.org/soap/encoding/" For JavaBeans, use the default SOAP encoding style.
Element type: namespace URI	xmlns:x	If you are strictly following the URN syntax, this is the URN namespace identifier. For example, if you are using urn:examples: productservice, this field should be set to urn:examples.

Web administration field	isd:map attribute	Description
Element type: local part	qname	This is the name of your new data type. The name should be descriptive enough to convey the encapsulated data. For our example, set this field to product.
Java type	javaType	This is the fully qualified name of your new Java class. In our example, this is the ProductBean: com.ecerami.soap. ProductBean.
Java-to- XML serializer	java2XMLClassName	This is the fully qualified name of the Java class responsible for converting your Java class into XML. As noted previously, Apache SOAP includes a built-in BeanSerializer capable of serializing any arbitrary JavaBean. The fully qualified name is org.apache.soap. encoding.soapenc.BeanSerializer.
XML-to-Java deserializer	xml2JavaClassName	This is the fully qualified name of the Java class responsible for taking an XML element and reconstructing your Java object. The Apache BeanSerializer is also capable of deserial- izing. Hence, for JavaBeans, these last two fields are usually set to the same value.

If you choose to deploy a SOAP service via the command-line tool, here is the complete deployment descriptor file:

```
<isd:service
  xmlns:isd="http://xml.apache.org/xml-soap/deployment"
  id="urn:examples:productservice" checkMustUnderstands="false">
  <isd:provider type="java" scope="Request" methods="getProduct">
    <isd:java class="com.ecerami.soap.ProductService" static="false"/>
  </isd:provider>
  <isd:mappings defaultRegistryClass="">
    <isd:map
      encodingStyle="http://schemas.xmlsoap.org/soap/encoding/"
      xmlns:x="urn:examples"
      qname="x:product"
      javaType="com.ecerami.soap.ProductBean"
      xml2JavaClassName="org.apache.soap.encoding.soapenc.BeanSerializer"
      java2XMLClassName=
        "org.apache.soap.encoding.soapenc.BeanSerializer"/>
  </isd:mappings>
</isd:service>
```

If you choose to deploy your service via the web administration tool, verify that your new mappings have been registered. Click List services, then click on the productservice link. At the bottom of the service details page, you should see the new type mapping. (See Figure 5-2.)

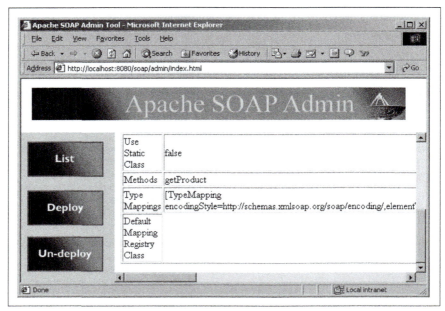

Figure 5-2. The new registered type mapping

Client Code

In the same way that we registered a new type mapping for the server code, we must now register a new type mapping within our client code. Unfortunately, this adds to the complexity of the client code, but remember that registering a new mapping is the same for server or client code. The only difference is that for server code, you can easily add new mappings via the simple web deployment tool, whereas the client code requires a more intimate knowledge of the SOAP API.

The complete client code is available in Example 5-5, shown later in this section. After setting the TargetObjectURI and method name, we set out to register a new type mapping.

First, we instantiate a new BeanSerializer object:

```
BeanSerializer bSerializer = new BeanSerializer( );
```

This is the same class we used when deploying the server code. It is responsible for Java-to-XML serialization and XML-to-Java deserialization.

Second, we need to create a new SOAP mapping registry:

```
SOAPMappingRegistry registry = new SOAPMappingRegistry( );
```

This creates a default registry object, which is already prepopulated with the mappings for strings, primitive data types, and arrays.

Third, we must create a Qualified Namespace object. This object must match the namespace URI and local part fields specified for the service deployment. In the case of our product parameter, the fields do indeed match up:

```
QName qname = new QName ("urn:examples", "product");
```

Fourth, we must register our new mapping for the ProductBean by calling the mapTypes() method:

```
registry.mapTypes (Constants.NS_URI_SOAP_ENC, qname,
    com.ecerami.soap.ProductBean.class, bSerializer,
    bSerializer);
```

The arguments to the mapTypes() method correspond exactly to the fields on the Deploy a Service page. These fields include the encoding type, qualified name, Java-to-XML serializer, and XML-to-Java deserializer.

The fifth and final step in registering a new type is to associate our new SOAP mapping registry with the current Call object:

```
call.setSOAPMappingRegistry(registry);
```

Once registered, any XML elements corresponding to urn:examples:product will be automatically reconstructed into the corresponding ProductBean. By casting properly, the ProductBean can then be retrieved from the Response object:

```
Parameter result = resp.getReturnValue ();
ProductBean product = (ProductBean) result.getValue();
```

Example 5-5. ProductClient.java

```
package com.ecerami.soap;

/**
 * A Sample SOAP Client
 * Retrieves Product Info for Specified Stockkeeping Unit (SKU)
 * usage:  java ProductClient sku#
 */
import java.net.*;
import java.util.Vector;
import org.apache.soap.*;
import org.apache.soap.rpc.*;
import org.apache.soap.encoding.soapenc.BeanSerializer;
import org.apache.soap.encoding.SOAPMappingRegistry;
import org.apache.soap.util.xml.QName;

public class ProductClient {

  /**
```

Example 5-5. ProductClient.java (continued)

```
 * Static Main method
 */
public static void main (String[] args) {
  String sku = args[0];
  System.out.println ("Product Checker:  SOAP Client");
  ProductClient productClient = new ProductClient();
  try {
    ProductBean product = productClient.getProduct (sku);
    System.out.println ("SKU:  "+product.getSKU());
    System.out.println ("Name:  "+product.getName());
    System.out.println ("Description:  "+product.getDescription());
    System.out.println ("Price:  "+product.getPrice());
  } catch (SOAPException e) {
    System.err.println (e);
  } catch (MalformedURLException e) {
    System.err.println (e);
  }
}

/**
 * getProduct Method
 */
public ProductBean getProduct (String sku)
  throws SOAPException, MalformedURLException {
  Parameter skuParam;

  //  Create SOAP RPC Call Object
  Call call = new Call ();

  // Set Encoding Style to standard SOAP encoding
  call.setEncodingStyleURI(Constants.NS_URI_SOAP_ENC);

  // Set Object URI and Method Name
  call.setTargetObjectURI ("urn:examples:productservice");
  call.setMethodName ("getProduct");

  //  Add JavaXML Mapping for Product Bean
  //  First, Create a Bean Serializer
  BeanSerializer bSerializer = new BeanSerializer();

  //  Second, Get the current SOAPMappingRegistry
  //  This object is pre-registered with basic mappings
  SOAPMappingRegistry registry = new SOAPMappingRegistry();

  //  Third, Create a new Qualified Namespace for Product Bean
  QName qname = new QName ("urn:examples", "product");

  //  Fourth, Register new mapping for ProductBean
  registry.mapTypes (Constants.NS_URI_SOAP_ENC, qname,
    com.ecerami.soap.ProductBean.class, bSerializer,
    bSerializer);
```

Example 5-5. ProductClient.java (continued)

```java
    // Fifth, Set MappingRegistry for the Call object
    call.setSOAPMappingRegistry(registry);

    // Set Method Parameters
    Vector paramList = new Vector ();
    skuParam = new Parameter("sku", String.class,
      sku, Constants.NS_URI_SOAP_ENC);
    paramList.addElement (skuParam);
    call.setParams (paramList);

    // Set the URL for the Web Service
    URL url = new URL ("http://localhost:8080/soap/servlet/rpcrouter");

    // Invoke the Service
    Response resp = call.invoke (url, null);

    // Check for Success
    if (!resp.generatedFault()) {
      // Extract Return value
      Parameter result = resp.getReturnValue ();
      ProductBean product = (ProductBean) result.getValue();
      return product;
    }
    // Check for Faults
    else {
      // Extract Fault Code and String
      Fault f = resp.getFault();
      String faultCode = f.getFaultCode();
      String faultString = f.getFaultString();
      System.err.println("Fault Occurred (details follow):");
      System.err.println("Fault Code:   "+faultCode);
      System.err.println("Fault String: "+faultString);
      return null;
    }
  }
}
```

For reference, here is the full text of a sample SOAP request (HTTP headers are not included):

```xml
<?xml version='1.0' encoding='UTF-8'?>
<SOAP-ENV:Envelope
    xmlns:SOAP-ENV="http://www.w3.org/2001/09/soap-envelope"
    xmlns:xsi="http://www.w3.org/2001/XMLSchema-instance"
    xmlns:xsd="http://www.w3.org/2001/XMLSchema">
    <SOAP-ENV:Body>
        <ns1:getProduct
            xmlns:ns1="urn:examples:productservice"
            SOAP-ENV:encodingStyle="http://www.w3.org/2001/09/soap-encoding">
```

```
          <sku xsi:type="xsd:string">A358185</sku>
        </ns1:getProduct>
    </SOAP-ENV:Body>
  </SOAP-ENV:Envelope>
```

Here is a sample SOAP response:

```
<?xml version='1.0' encoding='UTF-8'?>
<SOAP-ENV:Envelope
    xmlns:SOAP-ENV="http://www.w3.org/2001/09/soap-envelope"
    xmlns:xsi="http://www.w3.org/2001/XMLSchema-instance"
    xmlns:xsd="http://www.w3.org/2001/XMLSchema">
    <SOAP-ENV:Body>
        <ns1:getProductResponse
            xmlns:ns1="urn:examples:productservice"
            SOAP-ENV:encodingStyle="http://www.w3.org/2001/09/soap-encoding">
            <return xmlns:ns2="urn:examples" xsi:type="ns2:product">
                <name xsi:type="xsd:string">Red Hat Linux</name>
                <price xsi:type="xsd:double">54.99</price>
                <description xsi:type="xsd:string">
                    Red Hat Linux Operating System
                </description>
                <SKU xsi:type="xsd:string">A358185</SKU>
            </return>
        </ns1:getProductResponse>
    </SOAP-ENV:Body>
</SOAP-ENV:Envelope>
```

API: org.apache.soap.rpc.Call

```
void setSOAPMappingRegistry(SOAPMappingRegistry smr)
```
Sets the SOAP mapping registry. This is useful if you need to serialize/
deserialize your own Java classes. Takes the following parameter:

```
smr
```
The SOAP mapping registry.

Working with Literal XML Documents

In addition to JavaBeans, Apache SOAP also supports the passing of literal
XML documents. Our third example demonstrates the main concepts. The
client code will send a product query by sending a product element with a
SKU attribute. For example:

```
<product sku="A358185"/>
```

The server will respond with a complete product XML document. For example, the following command line:

```
java com.ecerami.soap.ProductXMLClient A358185
```

API: org.apache.soap.encoding.SOAPMappingRegistry

`SOAPMappingRegistry( )`

Constructs a new `SOAPMappingRegistry` object. The object will be pre-populated with mappings for basic data types, including primitive data types, strings, vectors, dates, and arrays.

`void mapTypes(String encodingStyleURI, QName elementType, Class javaType, Serializer s, Deserializer ds) ( )`

Registers a new type mapping. Takes the following parameters:

`encodingStyleURI`

The encoding style for your new data type. To use the default SOAP encoding style, use `Constants.NS_URI_SOAP_ENC`.

`name`

The qualified name for your new data type.

`javaType`

The Java class type; for example, `ProductBean.class`.

`s`

The Java class responsible for serializing your Java class into XML. Use `BeanSerializer` for JavaBeans.

`ds`

The Java class responsible for deserializing XML into Java. Use `BeanSerializer` for JavaBeans.

---

will generate this XML response:

```
<product sku="A358185">
    <name>Red Hat Linux</name>
    <description>Red Hat Linux Operating System</description>
    <price>54.99</price>
</product>
```

Working with literal XML documents requires some knowledge of the XML Document Object Model (DOM) API. Even if you are not familiar with the DOM API, however, you should be able to follow the general flow of the example code.

Service Code

The full service code is shown in Example 5-6. Note that the `ProductXMLService` class extends `ProductService` from the previous example and therefore utilizes the same product hashtable. Note also that the new getProduct( ) method accepts a DOM Element and returns a DOM Element. Within the method, we'll first extract the SKU attribute code:

```
String sku = request.getAttribute("sku");
```

We will then search the product hashtable. If a match is found, we can build an entire XML document via the DOM API. As a shortcut, we can use the Apache utility method to retrieve a DocumentBuilder object:

```
DocumentBuilder docBuilder = XMLParserUtils.getXMLDocBuilder( );
Document doc = docBuilder.newDocument( );
```

With the document in hand, we can then proceed to add the proper hierarchy of XML elements. For example, the following code creates a product name element with the corresponding text subelement:

```
Text productNameText = doc.createTextNode(product.getName( ));
Element nameNode = doc.createElement("name");
nameNode.appendChild(productNameText);
```

Example 5-6. ProductXMLService.java

```
package com.ecerami.soap;

import java.util.Hashtable;
import org.w3c.dom.*;
import javax.xml.parsers.DocumentBuilder;
import org.apache.soap.util.xml.XMLParserUtils;

/**
 * A Sample SOAP Service
 * Provides Product Name for requested Stockkeeping Unit (SKU)
 * Information is passed as Literal XML Documents.
 */
public class ProductXMLService extends ProductService{

    /**
     *  Provides Product Info for requested XML document.
     */
    public Element getProduct (Element request)
      throws ProductNotFoundException {
      //  Extract sku attribute
      String sku = request.getAttribute("sku");
      ProductBean product = (ProductBean) products.get(sku);

      // Create XML Document to store Product data
      DocumentBuilder docBuilder = XMLParserUtils.getXMLDocBuilder( );
      Document doc = docBuilder.newDocument( );

      // Create Product Name Element
      Text productNameText = doc.createTextNode(product.getName( ));
      Element nameNode = doc.createElement("name");
      nameNode.appendChild(productNameText);
```

Example 5-6. ProductXMLService.java (continued)

```
   // Create Product Description Element
   Text productDescriptionText =
     doc.createTextNode(product.getDescription());
   Element descriptionNode = doc.createElement("description");
   descriptionNode.appendChild(productDescriptionText);

   // Create Product Name Element
   Text productPriceText = doc.createTextNode(
     Double.toString(product.getPrice()));
   Element priceNode = doc.createElement("price");
   priceNode.appendChild(productPriceText);

   // Create Root Product Element
   Element productNode = doc.createElement("product");
   productNode.setAttribute("sku", sku);
   productNode.appendChild(nameNode);
   productNode.appendChild(descriptionNode);
   productNode.appendChild(priceNode);
   return productNode;
 }
}
```

Client Code

The full client code is shown in Example 5-7. Fortunately, most of the code is similar to that in the previous three examples. As in the service code, we'll also utilize the DOM API to build a new XML document.

First, we'll set the encoding style to XML literal:

```
   call.setEncodingStyleURI(Constants.NS_URI_LITERAL_XML);
```

This enables the passing of whole XML documents within the SOAP request.

Second, we'll create a new XML document. We'll use the same technique that we used to write the server code, with the goal of creating a single product element (e.g., <product sku="A358185"/>). With the element in hand, we will then create a new Parameter object:

```
   skuParam = new Parameter("productNode", org.w3c.dom.Element.class,
       productNode, Constants.NS_URI_LITERAL_XML);
```

Note that we will again set the encoding style to XML literal.

As usual, the final step is to cast the return value correctly. In this case, we'll cast to the DOM Element class:

```
   Parameter result = resp.getReturnValue ();
   Element xmlResult = (Element) result.getValue();
```

We can then print out the Element string using Apache's handy DOM2Writer:

```
DOM2Writer domWriter = new DOM2Writer( );
System.out.println ("Server Response:  ");
System.out.println (domWriter.nodeToString(product));
```

Example 5-7. ProductXMLClient.java

```
package com.ecerami.soap;

/**
 * A Sample SOAP Client
 * Retrieves Product Info for Specified Stockkeeping Unit (SKU)
 * Data is returned as an XML Literal Document
 * usage:   java ProductXMLClient sku#
 */
import java.net.*;
import java.util.Vector;
import org.w3c.dom.*;
import org.apache.soap.*;
import org.apache.soap.rpc.*;
import javax.xml.parsers.DocumentBuilder;
import org.apache.soap.util.xml.XMLParserUtils;
import org.apache.soap.util.xml.DOM2Writer;

public class ProductXMLClient {

  /**
   * Static Main method
   */
  public static void main (String[] args) {
    String sku = args[0];
    System.out.println ("XML Product Checker:  SOAP Client");
    ProductXMLClient productXMLClient = new ProductXMLClient( );
    try {
      Element product = productXMLClient.getProduct (sku);
      DOM2Writer domWriter = new DOM2Writer( );
      System.out.println ("Server Response:  ");
      System.out.println (domWriter.nodeToString(product));
    } catch (SOAPException e) {
      System.err.println (e);
    } catch (MalformedURLException e) {
      System.err.println (e);
    }
  }

  /**
   * getProduct Method
   */
  public Element getProduct (String sku)
    throws SOAPException, MalformedURLException {
    Parameter skuParam;

    // Create SOAP RPC Call Object
    Call call = new Call ();
```

Example 5-7. ProductXMLClient.java (continued)

```java
// Set Encoding Style to XML Literal
call.setEncodingStyleURI(Constants.NS_URI_LITERAL_XML);

// Set Object URI and Method Name
call.setTargetObjectURI ("urn:examples:XMLproductservice");
call.setMethodName ("getProduct");

//  Set Method Parameters
Vector paramList = new Vector ();

//  Create XML Document to store SKU
DocumentBuilder docBuilder = XMLParserUtils.getXMLDocBuilder();
Document doc = docBuilder.newDocument();

// Create product element with sku attribute
Element productNode = doc.createElement("product");
productNode.setAttribute("sku", sku);

skuParam = new Parameter("productNode", org.w3c.dom.Element.class,
  productNode, Constants.NS_URI_LITERAL_XML);
paramList.addElement (skuParam);
call.setParams (paramList);

//  Set the URL for the Web Service
URL url = new URL ("http://localhost:8080/soap/servlet/rpcrouter");

// Invoke the Service
Response resp = call.invoke (url, null);

// Check for Success
if (!resp.generatedFault()) {
  // Extract Return value
  Parameter result = resp.getReturnValue ();
  Element xmlResult = (Element) result.getValue();
  return xmlResult;
}
//  Check for Faults
else {
  //  Extract Fault Code and String
  Fault f = resp.getFault();
  String faultCode = f.getFaultCode();
  String faultString = f.getFaultString();
  System.err.println("Fault Occurred (details follow):");
  System.err.println("Fault Code:  "+faultCode);
  System.err.println("Fault String:  "+faultString);
  return null;
  }
 }
}
```

For reference, here is a complete SOAP request:

```
<?xml version='1.0' encoding='UTF-8'?>
<SOAP-ENV:Envelope
    xmlns:SOAP-ENV="http://www.w3.org/2001/09/soap-envelope"
    xmlns:xsi="http://www.w3.org/2001/XMLSchema-instance"
    xmlns:xsd="http://www.w3.org/2001/XMLSchema">
    <SOAP-ENV:Body>
        <ns1:getProduct
            xmlns:ns1="urn:examples:XMLproductservice"
            SOAP-ENV:encodingStyle=
              "http://xml.apache.org/xml-soap/literalxml">
            <productNode>
                <product sku="A358185"/>
            </productNode>
        </ns1:getProduct>
    </SOAP-ENV:Body>
</SOAP-ENV:Envelope>
```

Here is a sample SOAP response:

```
<?xml version='1.0' encoding='UTF-8'?>
<SOAP-ENV:Envelope
    xmlns:SOAP-ENV="http://www.w3.org/2001/09/soap-envelope"
    xmlns:xsi="http://www.w3.org/2001/XMLSchema-instance"
    xmlns:xsd="http://www.w3.org/2001/XMLSchema">
    <SOAP-ENV:Body>
        <ns1:getProductResponse
            xmlns:ns1="urn:examples:XMLproductservice"
            SOAP-ENV:encodingStyle=
               "http://xml.apache.org/xml-soap/literalxml">
            <return>
                <product sku="A358185">
                <name>Red Hat Linux</name>
                <description>Red Hat Linux Operating System</description>
                <price>54.99</price></product>
            </return>
        </ns1:getProductResponse>
    </SOAP-ENV:Body>
</SOAP-ENV:Envelope>
```

Handling SOAP Faults

As explained in Chapter 4, SOAP faults indicate errors at the application level. For example, a request for a nonexistent service or method name will trigger a fault. Service objects can also trigger faults, providing a means of propagating errors back to the client. Propagating exceptions and errors back to the client is particularly critical for building robust applications. For example, in the catalog applications we have created so far, we have assumed that the user will always pass a valid, current SKU. What happens

---

when the user requests a SKU for a nonexistent product? To explore this question, and thereby illustrate several fault-handling options, let's examine an updated version of the ProductService example.

Service Code

The complete service code is presented in Example 5-8. The ProductService2 class extends the original ProductService class and uses the same product hashtable. The new getProductInfo() method receives a String SKU parameter and checks the product hashtable.

Example 5-8. ProductService2.java

```
package com.ecerami.soap;

import java.util.Hashtable;

/**
 * A Sample SOAP Service
 * Provides Product Information for requested Stockkeeping Unit (SKU)
 */
public class ProductService2 extends ProductService {

  /**
   *  Provides Product Info for requested SKU.
   *  If SKU is not found, method throws a ProductNotFoundException
   */
  public ProductBean getProductInfo (String sku)
    throws ProductNotFoundException {
    ProductBean product = (ProductBean) products.get(sku);
    if (product==null)
      throw new ProductNotFoundException ("SKU Not Found:  "+sku);
    return product;
  }
}
```

If a match is found, the method returns the correct ProductBean. Otherwise, the method throws a ProductNotFoundException. The ProductNotFoundException code is presented in Example 5-9.

Example 5-9. ProductNotFoundException.java

```
package com.ecerami.soap;

import org.apache.soap.Fault;

/**
 * ProductNotFoundException
 * Encapsulates any exceptions related to retrieving
 * product/price for Specified Stockkeeping Unit (SKU)
```

Example 5-9. ProductNotFoundException.java (continued)

```
*/
public class ProductNotFoundException extends Exception {
  private Fault fault;

  public ProductNotFoundException (String faultString) {
    super (faultString);
  }

  public ProductNotFoundException (String faultString, Fault fault) {
    super (faultString);
    this.fault = fault;
  }

  public Fault getFault () { return fault; }
}
```

Client Code

The revised client code is presented in Example 5-10. Most of the getProduct( ) method is the same as in the original ProductClient code, and therefore I have only included those pieces that illustrate the new fault-handling capability. First, if a fault is detected, the client code extracts the Fault object and embeds it into a ProductNotFoundException:

```
Fault fault = resp.getFault( );
String faultString = fault.getFaultString( );
throw new ProductNotFoundException (faultString, fault);
```

This enables us to examine the Fault object later. Second, the main( ) method includes a new printFaultDetails( ) method for printing out any fault details embedded in the Response object. Before we examine this method, however, we'll test the code by sending a nonexistent SKU. Let's try the SKU number Z358185. If you are using the TcpTunnelGui tool, you will see the following response from the SOAP server:

```
<?xml version='1.0' encoding='UTF-8'?>
<SOAP-ENV:Envelope
    xmlns:SOAP-ENV="http://schemas.xmlsoap.org/soap/envelope/"
    xmlns:xsi="http://www.w3.org/1999/XMLSchema-instance"
    xmlns:xsd="http://www.w3.org/1999/XMLSchema">
    <SOAP-ENV:Body>
        <SOAP-ENV:Fault>
            <faultcode>SOAP-ENV:Server</faultcode>
            <faultstring>
                Exception from service object: SKU Not Found:  Z358185
            </faultstring>
            <faultactor>/soap/servlet/rpcrouter</faultactor>
        </SOAP-ENV:Fault>
    </SOAP-ENV:Body>
</SOAP-ENV:Envelope>
```

As you can see, ProductNotFoundException is not propagated directly back to the client. Rather, the rpcrouter captures the exception, generates a SOAP Fault element, and inserts the embedded ProductNotFoundException message inside the faultstring subelement. On the client end, we capture the fault and throw our own ProductNotFoundException.

The SOAP specification also allows for the SOAP response to include fault details. Fault details can provide a finer-grained description of errors and thereby aid in debugging. To access the list of fault details, use the Fault getDetailEntries() method. This will return a vector of DOM Elements. You can then query each element for its name and value:

```
for (int i=0; i< detailEntries.size(); i++) {
    Element detail = (Element) detailEntries.elementAt(i);
    String name = detail.getNodeName();
    String value = DOMUtils.getChildCharacterData(detail);
    System.err.println (name);
    System.err.println (value);
}
```

No fault details are normally included in the SOAP response, and this method will not print anything. Nonetheless, Apache SOAP does provide two built-in fault listeners that provide very helpful fault details. The first, DOMFaultListener, will insert the entire stack trace for any exception thrown within the service object. The second, ExceptionFaultListener, will insert the name of the thrown exception. Unfortunately, you cannot set fault listeners via the web administration tool. You therefore must use the command-line tool and the isd:faultListener element. For example, the following addition to the deployment descriptor file will add the DomFaultListener:

```
<isd:faultListener>
    org.apache.soap.server.DOMFaultListener
</isd:faultListener>
```

With the DOMFaultListener in place, the server will now generate errors like this:

```
<?xml version='1.0' encoding='UTF-8'?>
<SOAP-ENV:Envelope xmlns:SOAP-ENV="http://schemas.xmlsoap.org/soap/envelope/"
xmlns:xsi="http://www.w3.org/1999/XMLSchema-instance" xmlns:xsd="http://www.
    w3.org/1999/XMLSchema">
<SOAP-ENV:Body>
<SOAP-ENV:Fault>
<faultcode>SOAP-ENV:Server</faultcode>
<faultstring>Exception from service object: SKU Not Found:  Z358185</
    faultstring>
<faultactor>/soap/servlet/rpcrouter</faultactor>
<detail>
<stackTrace>com.ecerami.soap.ProductNotFoundException: SKU Not Found:
    Z358185
```

```
        at com.ecerami.soap.ProductService2.getProductInfo(ProductService2.java:
            26)
        at java.lang.reflect.Method.invoke(Native Method)
        at org.apache.soap.server.RPCRouter.invoke(RPCRouter.java:146)
        at org.apache.soap.providers.RPCJavaProvider.invoke(RPCJavaProvider.
            java:129)
        at org.apache.soap.server.http.RPCRouterServlet.doPost(RPCRouterServlet.
            java:286)
        at javax.servlet.http.HttpServlet.service(HttpServlet.java:760)
        at javax.servlet.http.HttpServlet.service(HttpServlet.java:853)
        at org.apache.tomcat.core.ServletWrapper.doService(ServletWrapper.java:
            404)
        at org.apache.tomcat.core.Handler.service(Handler.java:286)
        at org.apache.tomcat.core.ServletWrapper.service(ServletWrapper.java:
            372)
        at org.apache.tomcat.core.ContextManager.internalService(ContextManager.
            java:797)
        at org.apache.tomcat.core.ContextManager.service(ContextManager.java:
            743)
        at org.apache.tomcat.service.http.HttpConnectionHandler.
            processConnection(HttpConnectionHandler.java:210)
        at org.apache.tomcat.service.TcpWorkerThread.runIt(PoolTcpEndpoint.java:
            416)
        at org.apache.tomcat.util.ThreadPool$ControlRunnable.run(ThreadPool.
            java:498)
        at java.lang.Thread.run(Thread.java:484)
    </stackTrace>
    </detail>
  </SOAP-ENV:Fault>
  </SOAP-ENV:Body>
  </SOAP-ENV:Envelope>
```

As you can see, the detail element is now included, and it contains a single
stackTrace element. The printFaultDetails() method, using the code
shown in Example 5-10, will now detect a detail entry and print out the
entire stack trace.

Example 5-10. ProductClient2.java

```
package com.ecerami.soap;

/**
 * A Sample SOAP Client
 * Retrieves Product Info for Specified Stockkeeping Unit (SKU)
 * usage:  java ProductClient sku#
*/
import java.net.*;
import java.util.Vector;
import org.apache.soap.*;
import org.apache.soap.rpc.*;
import org.apache.soap.encoding.soapenc.BeanSerializer;
import org.apache.soap.encoding.SOAPMappingRegistry;
```

Example 5-10. ProductClient2.java (continued)

```java
import org.apache.soap.util.xml.QName;
import org.w3c.dom.Element;
import org.apache.soap.util.xml.DOMUtils;

public class ProductClient2 {

  /**
   * Static Main method
   */
  public static void main (String[] args) {
    String sku = args[0];
    System.out.println ("Product Checker:  SOAP Client");
    ProductClient2 productClient2 = new ProductClient2( );
    try {
      ProductBean product = productClient2.getProduct (sku);
      System.out.println ("SKU:  "+product.getSKU( ));
      System.out.println ("Name:  "+product.getName( ));
      System.out.println ("Description:  "+product.getDescription( ));
      System.out.println ("Price:  "+product.getPrice( ));
    } catch (ProductNotFoundException e) {
      System.err.println (e);
      printFaultDetails (e.getFault( ));
    } catch (SOAPException e) {
      System.err.println (e);
    } catch (MalformedURLException e) {
      System.err.println (e);
    }
  }

  /**
   * Extract and Print Fault Details
   */
  public static void printFaultDetails (Fault fault) {
    // Extract Detail Entries
    Vector detailEntries = fault.getDetailEntries( );
    if (detailEntries != null) {
      // Print each Detail Entry
      for (int i=0; i< detailEntries.size( ); i++) {
        Element detail = (Element) detailEntries.elementAt(i);
        String name = detail.getNodeName( );
        String value = DOMUtils.getChildCharacterData(detail);
        System.err.println (name);
        System.err.println (value);
      }
    }
  }

  /**
   * getProduct Method
   */
  public ProductBean getProduct (String sku)
```

Example 5-10. ProductClient2.java (continued)

```
  throws SOAPException,MalformedURLException,ProductNotFoundException {
  Parameter skuParam;

  ... Same as ProductClient.java

  // Check for Success
  if (!resp.generatedFault()) {
    // Extract Return value
    Parameter result = resp.getReturnValue ();
    ProductBean product = (ProductBean) result.getValue();
    return product;
  }
  // Check for Faults
  else {
    //  Extract Fault Code and String
    Fault fault = resp.getFault();
    String faultString = fault.getFaultString();
    throw new ProductNotFoundException (faultString, fault);
  }
 }
}
```

Maintaining Session State

Our final topic is the maintenance of session state. As you may recall from Chapter 4, each deployed SOAP service has an associated Scope property. Each time a service is invoked, the rpcrouter servlet will invoke the remote service object. The Scope property defines the lifetime of this remote object.

Request
> Indicates that the object will exist during the lifetime of one SOAP request/response cycle

Session
> Indicates that the rpcrouter will instantiate one object per client, and will maintain these objects across multiple request/response conversations

Application
> Indicates that only one object is instantiated, and this one object will process all incoming requests

To make the Scope property more concrete, our final example illustrates a session-counting service. The server code keeps a current counter in memory and returns this value to the client. When Scope is set to Session, the rpcrouter will instantiate a new service object for each client. The server is therefore able to maintain individual session counts for each client. When Scope is set to Application, the rpcrouter will instantiate only one service object; the server therefore counts the total number of requests from all clients.

Service Code

The complete service code is shown in Example 5-11. The code maintains a single instance variable, called counter. For each client request, counter is incremented.

Example 5-11. CounterService.java

```
package com.ecerami.soap;

/**
 * A Sample SOAP Service
 * Illustrates Session v. Application Scope
 *
 * When this service is deployed with Scope="Session",
 * server will instantiate one instance of CounterService
 * per client.  CounterService will then maintain total
 * number of requests per session.
 *
 * When this service is deployed with Scope="Application",
 * server will instantiate just one instance of CounterService.
 * CounterService will then maintain total number of requests
 * across all sessions.
 *
 */
public class CounterService {
  private int counter;    //  Number of requests

  /**
   * Constructor
   */
  public CounterService () { counter = 0; }

  /**
   *  Return number of requests
   */
  public int getCounter () { return ++counter; }
}
```

Client Code

The complete client code is shown in Example 5-12. The goal of the client code is to call the remote getCounter( ) method and retrieve the current count value.

Example 5-12. CounterClient.java

```java
package com.ecerami.soap;

/**
 * A Sample SOAP Client
 * Retrieves Current Counter value from CounterService
 * Illustrates Session v. Application Scope
 */
import java.util.*;
import java.net.*;
import org.apache.soap.*;
import org.apache.soap.rpc.*;

public class CounterClient {
  private Call call;    // Reusable Call Object

  /**
   * Static Main method
   */
  public static void main (String[] args) {
    System.out.println ("Session/Application Counter:  SOAP Client");
    CounterClient counterClient = new CounterClient();
    counterClient.process();
  }

  /**
   * Constructor
   * Create reusable Call object
   */
  public CounterClient () {
    call = new Call();
  }

  /**
   * Start counting
   */
  public void process () {
    try {
      for (int i=0; i<5; i++) {
        int counter = getCounter ();
        System.out.println ("Counter:  "+counter);
      }
    } catch (CounterException e) {
      System.err.println (e);
    } catch (SOAPException e) {
      System.err.println (e);
    } catch (MalformedURLException e) {
      System.err.println (e);
    }
  }
}
```

Example 5-12. CounterClient.java (continued)

```java
/**
 * getCounter Method
 */
public int getCounter ()
  throws SOAPException, MalformedURLException,
      CounterException {

  // Set Encoding Style to standard SOAP encoding
  call.setEncodingStyleURI(Constants.NS_URI_SOAP_ENC);

  // Set Object URI and Method Name
  call.setTargetObjectURI ("urn:examples:counterservice");
  call.setMethodName ("getCounter");

  //  Set the URL for the Web Service
  URL url = new URL ("http://localhost:8080/soap/servlet/rpcrouter");

  // Invoke the Service
  Response resp = call.invoke (url, null);

  // Check for Success
  if (!resp.generatedFault()) {
    // Extract Return value
    Parameter result = resp.getReturnValue ();
    Integer counter = (Integer) result.getValue();
    return counter.intValue();
  }
  //  Check for Faults
  else {
      //  Extract Fault Code and String
      Fault f = resp.getFault();
      String faultCode = f.getFaultCode();
      String faultString = f.getFaultString();
      throw new CounterException (faultCode+": "+faultString);
  }
}

/**
 * CounterException
 * Encapsulates any exceptions related to retrieving
 * application/session counter.
 */
class CounterException extends Exception {
  private String msg;

  public CounterException (String msg) {
    super(msg);
  }
}
}
```

Behind the scenes, Apache SOAP uses cookies to differentiate client requests. For example, the first request to the CounterService generates the following HTTP response:

```
HTTP/1.0 200 OK
Content-Type: text/xml; charset=utf-8
Content-Length: 477
Set-Cookie2: JSESSIONID=tfr2ps35b1;Version=1;Discard;Path="/soap"
Set-Cookie: JSESSIONID=tfr2ps35b1;Path=/soap
Servlet-Engine: Tomcat Web Server/3.2.1 (JSP 1.1; Servlet 2.2; Java 1.3.0;
    Windows 2000 5.0 x86; java.vendor=Sun Microsystems Inc.)
<?xml version='1.0' encoding='UTF-8'?>
<SOAP-ENV:Envelope
    xmlns:SOAP-ENV="http://schemas.xmlsoap.org/soap/envelope/"
    xmlns:xsi="http://www.w3.org/1999/XMLSchema-instance"
    xmlns:xsd="http://www.w3.org/1999/XMLSchema">
    <SOAP-ENV:Body>
        <ns1:getCounterResponse
            xmlns:ns1="urn:examples:counterservice"
            SOAP-ENV:encodingStyle=
                "http://schemas.xmlsoap.org/soap/encoding/">
            <return xsi:type="xsd:int">1</return>
        </ns1:getCounterResponse>
    </SOAP-ENV:Body>
</SOAP-ENV:Envelope>
```

The fifth and sixth lines of the HTTP response set a Jakarta Tomcat session cookie, called JSESSIONID. Clients can use this cookie to maintain session state across multiple calls to the server.

By default, the SOAP Call object recognizes cookies and will automatically send them back to the server. The only requirement is that you reuse the same Call object across all requests within the same session. For example, our client code creates a reusable Call object within the constructor:

```
public CounterClient () {
    call = new Call();
}
```

To maintain session, the code just reuses the same Call object. The Call object automatically returns any session cookies, and the server is able to maintain a separate counter for each client.

CHAPTER 6

WSDL Essentials

WSDL is a specification defining how to describe web services in a common XML grammar. WSDL describes four critical pieces of data:

- Interface information describing all publicly available functions
- Data type information for all message requests and message responses
- Binding information about the transport protocol to be used
- Address information for locating the specified service

In a nutshell, WSDL represents a contract between the service requestor and the service provider, in much the same way that a Java interface represents a contract between client code and the actual Java object. The crucial difference is that WSDL is platform- and language-independent and is used primarily (although not exclusively) to describe SOAP services.

Using WSDL, a client can locate a web service and invoke any of its publicly available functions. With WSDL-aware tools, you can also automate this process, enabling applications to easily integrate new services with little or no manual code. WSDL therefore represents a cornerstone of the web service architecture, because it provides a common language for describing services and a platform for automatically integrating those services.

This chapter covers all aspects of WSDL, including the following topics:

- An overview of the WSDL specification, complete with detailed explanations of the major WSDL elements
- Two basic WSDL examples to get you started
- A brief survey of WSDL invocation tools, including the IBM Web Services Invocation Framework (WSIF), SOAP::Lite, and The Mind Electric's GLUE platform

- A discussion of how to automatically generate WSDL files from existing SOAP services
- An overview of using XML Schema types within WSDL, including the use of arrays and complex types

The WSDL Specification

WSDL is an XML grammar for describing web services. The specification itself is divided into six major elements:

definitions
> The definitions element must be the root element of all WSDL documents. It defines the name of the web service, declares multiple namespaces used throughout the remainder of the document, and contains all the service elements described here.

types
> The types element describes all the data types used between the client and server. WSDL is not tied exclusively to a specific typing system, but it uses the W3C XML Schema specification as its default choice. If the service uses only XML Schema built-in simple types, such as strings and integers, the types element is not required. A full discussion of the types element and XML Schema is deferred to the end of the chapter.

message
> The message element describes a one-way message, whether it is a single message request or a single message response. It defines the name of the message and contains zero or more message part elements, which can refer to message parameters or message return values.

portType
> The portType element combines multiple message elements to form a complete one-way or round-trip operation. For example, a portType can combine one request and one response message into a single request/ response operation, most commonly used in SOAP services. Note that a portType can (and frequently does) define multiple operations.

binding
> The binding element describes the concrete specifics of how the service will be implemented on the wire. WSDL includes built-in extensions for defining SOAP services, and SOAP-specific information therefore goes here.

service
> The service element defines the address for invoking the specified service. Most commonly, this includes a URL for invoking the SOAP service.

To help you keep the meaning of each element clear, Figure 6-1 offers a concise representation of the WSDL specification. As you continue reading the remainder of the chapter, you may wish to refer back to this diagram.

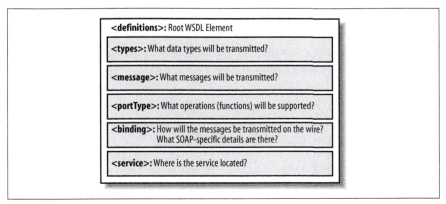

Figure 6-1. The WSDL specification in a nutshell

In addition to the six major elements, the WSDL specification also defines the following utility elements:

documentation

> The documentation element is used to provide human-readable documentation and can be included inside any other WSDL element.

import

> The import element is used to import other WSDL documents or XML Schemas. This enables more modular WSDL documents. For example, two WSDL documents can import the same basic elements and yet include their own service elements to make the same service available at two physical addresses. Note, however, that not all WSDL tools support the import functionality as of yet.

> WSDL is not an official recommendation of the W3C and, as such, has no official status within the W3C. WSDL Version 1.1 was submitted to the W3C in March 2001. Original submitters included IBM, Microsoft, Ariba, and a half dozen other companies. Most probably, WSDL will be placed under the consideration of the new W3C Web Services Activity's Web Services Description Working Group, which will decide if the specification advances to an official recommendation status. The WSDL Version 1.1 specification is available online at *http://www.w3.org/TR/wsdl*.

Basic WSDL Example: HelloService.wsdl

To make the previously described WSDL concepts as concrete as possible, let's examine our first sample WSDL file.

Example 6-1 provides a sample *HelloService.wsdl* document. The document describes the HelloService from Chapter 4.

As you may recall, the service provides a single publicly available function, called *sayHello*. The function expects a single string parameter, and returns a single string greeting. For example, if you pass the parameter world, the service returns the greeting, "Hello, world!"

Example 6-1. HelloService.wsdl

```
<?xml version="1.0" encoding="UTF-8"?>
<definitions name="HelloService"
   targetNamespace="http://www.ecerami.com/wsdl/HelloService.wsdl"
   xmlns="http://schemas.xmlsoap.org/wsdl/"
   xmlns:soap="http://schemas.xmlsoap.org/wsdl/soap/"
   xmlns:tns="http://www.ecerami.com/wsdl/HelloService.wsdl"
   xmlns:xsd="http://www.w3.org/2001/XMLSchema">

   <message name="SayHelloRequest">
      <part name="firstName" type="xsd:string"/>
   </message>
   <message name="SayHelloResponse">
      <part name="greeting" type="xsd:string"/>
   </message>

   <portType name="Hello_PortType">
      <operation name="sayHello">
         <input message="tns:SayHelloRequest"/>
         <output message="tns:SayHelloResponse"/>
      </operation>
   </portType>

   <binding name="Hello_Binding" type="tns:Hello_PortType">
      <soap:binding style="rpc"
         transport="http://schemas.xmlsoap.org/soap/http"/>
      <operation name="sayHello">
         <soap:operation soapAction="sayHello"/>
         <input>
            <soap:body
               encodingStyle="http://schemas.xmlsoap.org/soap/encoding/"
               namespace="urn:examples:helloservice"
               use="encoded"/>
         </input>
         <output>
```

Example 6-1. HelloService.wsdl (continued)

```
        <soap:body
            encodingStyle="http://schemas.xmlsoap.org/soap/encoding/"
            namespace="urn:examples:helloservice"
            use="encoded"/>
      </output>
    </operation>
  </binding>

  <service name="Hello_Service">
    <documentation>WSDL File for HelloService</documentation>
    <port binding="tns:Hello_Binding" name="Hello_Port">
      <soap:address
          location="http://localhost:8080/soap/servlet/rpcrouter"/>
    </port>
  </service>
</definitions>
```

The WSDL elements are discussed in the next section of this chapter. As you examine each element in detail, you may want to refer to Figure 6-2, which summarizes the most important aspects of Example 6-1.

Figure 6-2. A bird's-eye view of HelloService.wsdl

definitions

The definitions element specifies that this document is the *HelloService*. It also specifies numerous namespaces that will be used throughout the remainder of the document:

```
<definitions name="HelloService"
    targetNamespace="http://www.ecerami.com/wsdl/HelloService.wsdl"
    xmlns="http://schemas.xmlsoap.org/wsdl/"
    xmlns:soap="http://schemas.xmlsoap.org/wsdl/soap/"
    xmlns:tns="http://www.ecerami.com/wsdl/HelloService.wsdl"
    xmlns:xsd="http://www.w3.org/2001/XMLSchema">
```

The use of namespaces is important for differentiating elements, and it enables the document to reference multiple external specifications, including the WSDL specification, the SOAP specification, and the XML Schema specification.

The definitions element also specifies a targetNamespace attribute. The targetNamespace is a convention of XML Schema that enables the WSDL document to refer to itself. In Example 6-1, we specified a targetNamespace of *http://www.ecerami.com/wsdl/HelloService.wsdl*. Note, however, that the namespace specification does not require that the document actually exist at this location; the important point is that you specify a value that is unique, different from all other namespaces that are defined.

Finally, the definitions element specifies a default namespace: *xmlns=http:// schemas.xmlsoap.org/wsdl/*. All elements without a namespace prefix, such as message or portType, are therefore assumed to be part of the default WSDL namespace.

message

Two message elements are defined. The first represents a request message, *SayHelloRequest,* and the second represents a response message, *SayHelloResponse*:

```
<message name="SayHelloRequest">
  <part name="firstName" type="xsd:string"/>
</message>
<message name="SayHelloResponse">
  <part name="greeting" type="xsd:string"/>
</message>
```

Each of these messages contains a single part element. For the request, the part specifies the function parameters; in this case, we specify a single firstName parameter. For the response, the part specifies the function return values; in this case, we specify a single greeting return value.

The part element's type attribute specifies an XML Schema data type. The value of the type attribute must be specified as an XML Schema QName— this means that the *value* of the attribute must be namespace-qualified. For example, the firstName type attribute is set to xsd:string; the xsd prefix references the namespace for XML Schema, defined earlier within the definitions element.

If the function expects multiple arguments or returns multiple values, you can specify multiple part elements.

portType

The portType element defines a single operation, called *sayHello*. The operation itself consists of a single input message (*SayHelloRequest*) and a single output message (*SayHelloResponse*):

```
<portType name="Hello_PortType">
    <operation name="sayHello">
        <input message="tns:SayHelloRequest"/>
        <output message="tns:SayHelloResponse"/>
    </operation>
</portType>
```

Much like the type attribute defined earlier, the message attribute must be specified as an XML Schema QName. This means that the value of the attribute must be namespace-qualified. For example, the input element specifies a message attribute of tns:SayHelloRequest; the tns prefix references the targetNamespace defined earlier within the definitions element.

WSDL supports four basic patterns of operation:

One-way
> The service receives a message. The operation therefore has a single input element.

Request-response
> The service receives a message and sends a response. The operation therefore has one input element, followed by one output element (illustrated previously in Example 6-1). To encapsulate errors, an optional fault element can also be specified.

Solicit-response
> The service sends a message and receives a response. The operation therefore has one output element, followed by one input element. To encapsulate errors, an optional fault element can also be specified.

Notification
> The service sends a message. The operation therefore has a single output element.

These patterns of operation are also shown in Figure 6-3. The request-response pattern is most commonly used in SOAP services.

binding

The binding element provides specific details on how a portType operation will actually be transmitted over the wire. Bindings can be made available via multiple transports, including HTTP GET, HTTP POST, or SOAP. In fact, you can specify multiple bindings for a single portType.

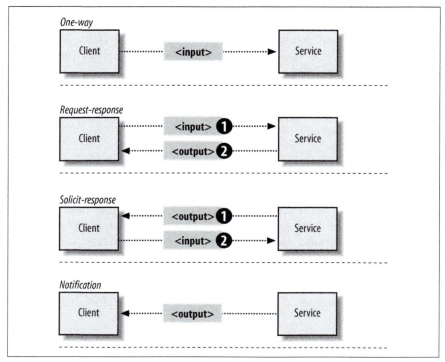

Figure 6-3. Operation patterns supported by WSDL 1.1

The binding element itself specifies name and type attributes:

```
<binding name="Hello_Binding" type="tns:Hello_PortType">
```

The type attribute references the portType defined earlier in the document. In our case, the binding element therefore references tns:Hello_PortType, defined earlier in the document. The binding element is therefore saying, "I will provide specific details on how the *sayHello* operation will be transported over the Internet."

SOAP binding

WSDL 1.1 includes built-in extensions for SOAP 1.1. This enables you to specify SOAP-specific details, including SOAP headers, SOAP encoding styles, and the SOAPAction HTTP header. The SOAP extension elements include:

soap:binding

This element indicates that the binding will be made available via SOAP. The style attribute indicates the overall style of the SOAP message format. A style value of rpc specifies an RPC format. This means that the body of the SOAP request will include a wrapper XML element indicating the function name. Function parameters are then embedded inside the wrapper element. Likewise, the body of the SOAP response will include a wrapper XML element that mirrors the function request. Return values are then embedded inside the response wrapper element.

A style value of document specifies an XML document call format. This means that the request and response messages will consist simply of XML documents. The document style is flatter than the rpc style and does not require the use of wrapper elements. (See the upcoming note for additional details.)

The transport attribute indicates the transport of the SOAP messages. The value http://schemas.xmlsoap.org/soap/http indicates the SOAP HTTP transport, whereas http://schemas.xmlsoap.org/soap/smtp indicates the SOAP SMTP transport.

soap:operation

This element indicates the binding of a specific operation to a specific SOAP implementation. The soapAction attribute specifies that the SOAPAction HTTP header be used for identifying the service. (See Chapter 3 for details on the SOAPAction header.)

soap:body

This element enables you to specify the details of the input and output messages. In the case of HelloWorld, the body element specifies the SOAP encoding style and the namespace URN associated with the specified service.

> The choice between the rpc style and the document style is controversial. The topic has been hotly debated on the WSDL newsgroup (*http://groups.yahoo.com/group/wsdl*). The debate is further complicated because not all WSDL-aware tools even differentiate between the two styles. Because the rpc style is more in line with the SOAP examples from previous chapters, I have chosen to stick with the rpc style for all the examples within this chapter. Note, however, that most Microsoft .NET WSDL files use the document style.

service

The service element specifies the location of the service. Because this is a SOAP service, we use the soap:address element, and specify the local host address for the Apache SOAP rpcrouter servlet: http://localhost:8080/soap/servlet/rpcrouter.

Note that the service element includes a documentation element to provide human-readable documentation.

WSDL Invocation Tools, Part I

Given the WSDL file in Example 6-1, you could manually create a SOAP client to invoke the service. A better alternative is to *automatically* invoke the service via a WSDL invocation tool. (See Figure 6-4.)

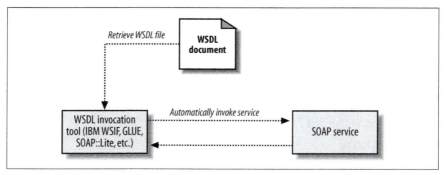

Figure 6-4. WSDL invocation tools

Many WSDL invocation tools already exist. This section provides a brief overview of three invocation tools.

GLUE

The Mind Electric provides a complete web service platform called GLUE (available at *http://www.themindelectric.com*). The platform itself provides extensive support for SOAP, WSDL, and UDDI. Some of its advanced functionality, including support for complex data types, will be explored later in this chapter.

For now, you can try out the GLUE invoke command-line tool. Here is the command-line usage:

```
usage: invoke URL method arg1 arg2 arg3...
```

For example, to invoke the HelloService, make sure that your Apache Tomcat server is running, and place the *HelloService.wsdl* file within a publicly available directory. Then, issue the following command:

```
invoke http://localhost:8080/wsdl/HelloService.wsdl sayHello World
```

Once invoked, GLUE will immediately download the specified WSDL file, invoke the *sayHello* method, and pass World as a parameter. GLUE will then automatically display the server response:

```
Output: result = Hello, World!
```

That's all there is to it!

GLUE also supports an excellent logging facility that enables you to easily view all SOAP messages. To activate the logging facility, set the electric. logging system property. The easiest option is to modify the *invoke.bat* file. The original file looks like this:

```
call java electric.glue.tools.Invoke %1 %2 %3 %4 %5 %6 %7 %8 %9
```

Modify the file to include the logging property via the –D option to the Java interpreter:

```
call java -Delectric.logging="SOAP" electric.glue.tools.Invoke %1 %2 %3 %4
    %5 %6 %7 %8 %9
```

When you invoke the HelloService, GLUE now generates the following output:

```
LOG.SOAP: request to http://207.237.201.187:8080/soap/servlet/rpcrouter
<?xml version='1.0' encoding='UTF-8'?>
<soap:Envelope
    xmlns:xsi='http://www.w3.org/2001/XMLSchema-instance'
    xmlns:xsd='http://www.w3.org/2001/XMLSchema'
    xmlns:soap='http://schemas.xmlsoap.org/soap/
    envelope/' xmlns:soapenc='http://schemas.xmlsoap.org/soap/encoding/'
    soap:encodingStyle='http://schemas.xmlsoap.org/soap/encoding/'>
    <soap:Body>
        <n:sayHello xmlns:n='urn:examples:helloservice'>
            <firstName xsi:type='xsd:string'>World</firstName>
        </n:sayHello>
    </soap:Body>
</soap:Envelope>

LOG.SOAP: response from http://207.237.201.187:8080/soap/servlet/rpcrouter
<?xml version='1.0' encoding='UTF-8'?>
<SOAP-ENV:Envelope
    xmlns:SOAP-ENV='http://schemas.xmlsoap.org/soap/envelope/'
    xmlns:xsi='http://www.w3.org/1999/XMLSchema-instance'
    xmlns:xsd='http://www.w3.org/1999/XMLSchema'>
    <SOAP-ENV:Body>
        <ns1:sayHelloResponse
            xmlns:ns1='urn:examples:helloservice'
            SOAP-ENV:encodingStyle=
                'http://schemas.xmlsoap.org/soap/encoding/'>
            <return xsi:type='xsd:string'>Hello, World!</return>
        </ns1:sayHelloResponse>
    </SOAP-ENV:Body>
</SOAP-ENV:Envelope>

result = Hello, World!
```

To view additional HTTP information, just set electric.logging to SOAP,HTTP.

SOAP::Lite for Perl

SOAP::Lite for Perl, written by Paul Kulchenko, also provides limited support for WSDL. The package is available at *http://www.soaplite.com*.

Example 6-2 provides a complete Perl program for invoking the HelloService.

Example 6-2. Hello_Service.pl

```
use SOAP::Lite;

print "Connecting to Hello Service...\n";
print SOAP::Lite
    -> service('http://localhost:8080/wsdl/HelloService.wsdl')
    -> sayHello ('World');
```

The program generates the following output:

```
Connecting to Hello Service...
Hello, World!
```

IBM Web Services Invocation Framework (WSIF)

Finally, IBM has recently released WSIF. The package is available at *http://www.alphaworks.ibm.com/tech/wsif*.

Much like GLUE, WSIF provides a simple command-line option for automatically invoking WSDL services. For example, the following command:

```
java clients.DynamicInvoker http://localhost:8080/wsdl/HelloService.wsdl
    sayHello World
```

generates the following output:

```
Reading WSDL document from 'http://localhost:8080/wsdl/HelloService.wsdl'
Preparing WSIF dynamic invocation
Executing operation sayHello
Result:
greeting=Hello, World!

Done!
```

Basic WSDL Example: XMethods eBay Price Watcher Service

Before moving on to more complicated WSDL examples, let's examine another relatively simple one. Example 6-3 provides a WSDL file for the XMethods eBay Price Watcher Service. The service takes an existing eBay auction ID, and returns the value of the current bid.

Example 6-3. eBayWatcherService.wsdl (reprinted with permission of XMethods, Inc.)

```xml
<?xml version="1.0"?>
<definitions name="eBayWatcherService"
   targetNamespace=
      "http://www.xmethods.net/sd/eBayWatcherService.wsdl"
   xmlns:tns="http://www.xmethods.net/sd/eBayWatcherService.wsdl"
   xmlns:xsd="http://www.w3.org/2001/XMLSchema"
   xmlns:soap="http://schemas.xmlsoap.org/wsdl/soap/"
   xmlns="http://schemas.xmlsoap.org/wsdl/">

   <message name="getCurrentPriceRequest">
      <part name="auction_id" type = "xsd:string"/>
   </message>
   <message name="getCurrentPriceResponse">
      <part name="return" type = "xsd:float"/>
   </message>

   <portType name="eBayWatcherPortType">
      <operation name="getCurrentPrice">
         <input
            message="tns:getCurrentPriceRequest"
            name="getCurrentPrice"/>
         <output
            message="tns:getCurrentPriceResponse"
            name="getCurrentPriceResponse"/>
      </operation>
   </portType>

   <binding name="eBayWatcherBinding" type="tns:eBayWatcherPortType">
      <soap:binding
         style="rpc"
         transport="http://schemas.xmlsoap.org/soap/http"/>
      <operation name="getCurrentPrice">
         <soap:operation soapAction=""/>
         <input name="getCurrentPrice">
            <soap:body
               use="encoded"
               namespace="urn:xmethods-EbayWatcher"
               encodingStyle="http://schemas.xmlsoap.org/soap/encoding/"/>
         </input>
         <output name="getCurrentPriceResponse">
            <soap:body
               use="encoded"
               namespace="urn:xmethods-EbayWatcher"
               encodingStyle="http://schemas.xmlsoap.org/soap/encoding/"/>
         </output>
      </operation>
   </binding>

   <service name="eBayWatcherService">
      <documentation>
```

Example 6-3. eBayWatcherService.wsdl (reprinted with permission of XMethods, Inc.) (continued)

```
        Checks current high bid for an eBay auction
      </documentation>
      <port name="eBayWatcherPort" binding="tns:eBayWatcherBinding">
        <soap:address
          location="http://services.xmethods.net:80/soap/servlet/rpcrouter"/>
      </port>
    </service>
</definitions>
```

Here is an overview of the main WSDL elements:

messages

Two messages are defined: getCurrentPriceRequest and getCurrentPriceResponse. The request message contains a single string parameter; the response message contains a single float parameter.

portType

A single operation, getCurrentPrice, is defined. Again, we see the request/response operation pattern.

binding

The binding element specifies HTTP SOAP as the transport. The soapAction attribute is left as an empty string ("").

service

This element specifies that the service is available at *http://services. xmethods.net:80/soap/servlet/rpcrouter*.

To access the eBay watcher service, you can use any of the WSDL invocation tools defined earlier. For example, the following call to GLUE:

```
invoke http://www.xmethods.net/sd/2001/EBayWatcherService.wsdl
    getCurrentPrice 1271062297
```

retrieves the current bid price for a Handspring Visor Deluxe:

```
result = 103.5
```

The XMethods web site (*http://www.xmethods.net*) provides dozens of sample SOAP and .NET services. Nearly all of these services include WSDL files and therefore provide an excellent opportunity for learning WSDL in detail. As you browse the XMethods directory, try interfacing with the specified services via any of the WSDL invocation tools described here. Quite likely, you will be amazed at how easy it is to integrate and invoke new services.

WSDL Invocation Tools, Part II

Our initial discussion of WSDL invocation tools focused on programming and command-line invocation tools. We now move on to even simpler tools that are entirely driven by a web-based interface.

The GLUE Console

In addition to supporting a number of command-line tools, the GLUE platform also supports a very intuitive web interface for deploying new services and connecting to existing services.

To start the GLUE console, just type:

```
console
```

This will automatically start the GLUE console on the default port 8100. Open a web browser and you will see the GLUE console home page. (See Figure 6-5.)

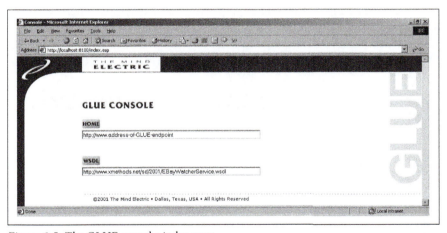

Figure 6-5. The GLUE console: index page

In the text box entitled WSDL, you can enter the URL for any WSDL file. For example, try entering the URL for the eBay Price Watcher Service, *http:// www.xmethods.net/sd/2001/EBayWatcherService.wsdl*.

Click the WSDL button, and you will see the Web Service overview page. (See Figure 6-6.) This page includes a description of the specified service (extracted from the WSDL document element) and a list of public operations. In the case of the eBay service, you should see a single getCurrentPrice method.

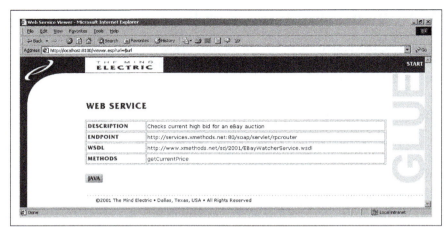

Figure 6-6. The GLUE console: Web Service overview page for the eBay Price Watcher Service

Click the getCurrentPrice method, and you will see the Web Method overview page. (See Figure 6-7.) This page includes a text box where you can specify the input auction ID.

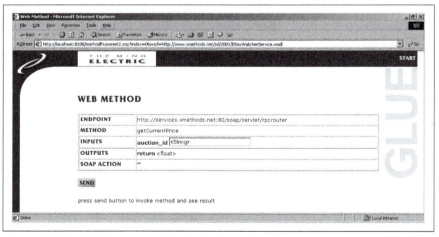

Figure 6-7. The GLUE console: Web Method overview page for the getCurrentPrice method

Enter an auction ID, click the Send button, and GLUE will automatically invoke the remote method and display the results at the bottom of the page. For example, Figure 6-8 shows the current bid price for the Handspring Visor Deluxe. Note that the price has already gone up $10 since invoking the service via the GLUE command-line tool!

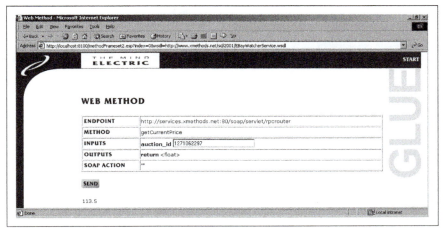

Figure 6-8. The GLUE console: invoking the getCurrentPrice method (results of the invocation are displayed at the bottom of the screen)

SOAPClient.com

If you would like to try out a web-based interface similar to GLUE, but don't want to bother downloading the GLUE package, consider the Generic SOAP Client available at SOAPClient.com.

Figure 6-9 shows the opening screen to the Generic SOAP Client. Much like the GLUE console, you can specify the address for a WSDL file in this screen.

Specify the same eBay Price Watcher Service WSDL file, and the SOAP Client will display a text box for entering the auction ID. (See Figure 6-10.)

Figure 6-11 displays the result of the eBay service invocation. The Handspring Visor is up another $4!

Automatically Generating WSDL Files

One of the best aspects of WSDL is that you rarely have to create WSDL files from scratch. A whole host of tools currently exists for transforming existing services into WSDL descriptions. You can then choose to use these WSDL files as is or manually tweak them with your favorite text editor. In the discussion that follows, we explore the WSDL generation tool provided by GLUE.

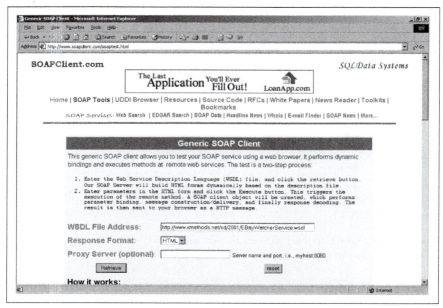

Figure 6-9. The Generic SOAP Client, available from SOAPClient.com

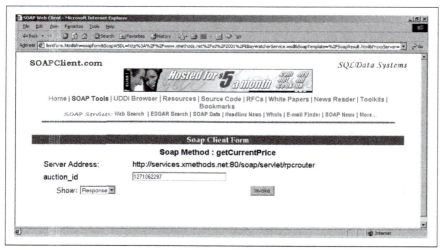

Figure 6-10. The Generic SOAP Client: Displaying information on the XMethods eBay Price Watcher Service

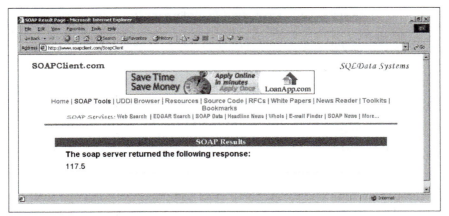

Figure 6-11. The Generic SOAP Client: Response from the XMethods eBay Price Watcher Service

If you create WSDL files from scratch or tweak WSDL files generated by a tool, it is a good idea to validate your final WSDL documents. You can download a WSDL validator from *http://pocketsoap.com/wsdl/*. This package requires that you have an XSLT engine and the zvonSchematron (*http://www.zvon.org*), but installation only takes a few minutes. Once installed, the validator is well worth the effort and creates nicely formatted HTML reports indicating WSDL errors and warnings.

GLUE java2wsdl Tool

The GLUE platform includes a java2wsdl command-line tool for transforming Java services into WSDL descriptions. The command-line usage is as follows:

```
usage: java2wsdl <arguments>
```

```
where valid arguments are:
  classname             name of java class
  -d directory          output directory
  -e url                endpoint of service
  -g                    include GET/POST binding
  -m map-file           read mapping instructions
  -n namespace          namespace for service
  -r description        description of service
  -s                    include SOAP binding
  -x command-file       command file to execute
```

Complete information on each argument is available online within the GLUE User Guide at *http://www.themindelectric.com/products/glue/releases/GLUE-1.1/docs/guide/index.html*. For now, we will focus on the most basic arguments.

For example, consider the PriceService class in Example 6-4. The service provides a single getPrice( ) method.

Example 6-4. PriceService.java

```
package com.ecerami.soap.examples;

import java.util.Hashtable;
/**
 * A Sample SOAP Service
 * Provides Current Price for requested Stockkeeping Unit (SKU)
 */
public class PriceService {
  protected Hashtable products;

  /**
   * Zero Argument Constructor
   * Load product database with two sample products
   */
  public PriceService ( ) {
    products = new Hashtable( );
    //  Red Hat Linux
    products.put("A358185", new Double (54.99));
    //  McAfee PGP Personal Privacy
    products.put("A358565", new Double (19.99));
  }

  /**
   *  Provides Current Price for requested SKU
   *  In a real-setup, this method would connect to
   *  a price database.  If SKU is not found, method
   *  will throw a PriceException.
   */
  public double getPrice (String sku)
    throws ProductNotFoundException {
    Double price = (Double) products.get(sku);
    if (price == null) {
      throw new ProductNotFoundException ("SKU: "+sku+" not found");
    }
    return price.doubleValue( );
  }
}
```

To generate a WSDL file for this class, run the following command:

```
java2wsdl com.ecerami.soap.examples.PriceService -s -e http://localhost:
8080/soap/servlet/rpcrouter -n urn:examples:priceservice
```

The -s option directs GLUE to create a SOAP binding; the -e option specifies the address of our service; and the -n option specifies the namespace URN for the service. GLUE will generate a *PriceService.wsdl* file. (See Example 6-5.)

 If your service is defined via a Java interface and you include your source files within your CLASSPATH, GLUE will extract your Javadoc comments, and turn these into WSDL documentation elements.

Example 6-5. PriceService.wsdl (automatically generated by GLUE)

```
<?xml version='1.0' encoding='UTF-8'?>
<!--generated by GLUE-->
<definitions name='com.ecerami.soap.examples.PriceService'
   targetNamespace='http://www.themindelectric.com/wsdl/com.ecerami.soap.
      examples.PriceService/'

   xmlns:tns='http://www.themindelectric.com/wsdl/com.ecerami.soap.
      examples.PriceService/'
   xmlns:electric='http://www.themindelectric.com/'
   xmlns:soap='http://schemas.xmlsoap.org/wsdl/soap/'
   xmlns:http='http://schemas.xmlsoap.org/wsdl/http/'
   xmlns:mime='http://schemas.xmlsoap.org/wsdl/mime/'
   xmlns:xsd='http://www.w3.org/2001/XMLSchema'
   xmlns:soapenc='http://schemas.xmlsoap.org/soap/encoding/'
   xmlns:wsdl='http://schemas.xmlsoap.org/wsdl/'
   xmlns='http://schemas.xmlsoap.org/wsdl/'>
<message name='getPriceOSoapIn'>
  <part name='sku' type='xsd:string'/>
</message>
<message name='getPriceOSoapOut'>
  <part name='Result' type='xsd:double'/>
</message>
<portType name='com.ecerami.soap.examples.PriceServiceSoap'>
  <operation name='getPrice' parameterOrder='sku'>
    <input name='getPriceOSoapIn' message='tns:getPriceOSoapIn'/>
    <output name='getPriceOSoapOut' message='tns:getPriceOSoapOut'/>
  </operation>
</portType>
<binding name='com.ecerami.soap.examples.PriceServiceSoap'
    type='tns:com.ecerami.soap.examples.PriceServiceSoap'>
  <soap:binding style='rpc'
    transport='http://schemas.xmlsoap.org/soap/http'/>
  <operation name='getPrice'>
    <soap:operation soapAction='getPrice' style='rpc'/>
    <input name='getPriceOSoapIn'>
      <soap:body use='encoded'
        namespace='urn:examples:priceservice'
        encodingStyle='http://schemas.xmlsoap.org/soap/encoding/'/>
    </input>
```

```
      <output name='getPrice0SoapOut'>
        <soap:body use='encoded'
        namespace='urn:examples:priceservice'
        encodingStyle='http://schemas.xmlsoap.org/soap/encoding/'/>
      </output>
    </operation>
  </binding>
  <service name='com.ecerami.soap.examples.PriceService'>
    <port name='com.ecerami.soap.examples.PriceServiceSoap'
      binding='tns:com.ecerami.soap.examples.PriceServiceSoap'>
      <soap:address location='http://207.237.201.187:8080
          /soap/servlet/ rpcrouter'/>
    </port>
  </service>
</definitions>
```

You can then invoke the service via SOAP::Lite:

```
use SOAP::Lite;

print "Connecting to Price Service...\n";
print SOAP::Lite
    -> service('http://localhost:8080/wsdl/PriceService.wsdl')
    -> getPrice ('A358185');
```

Hopefully, this example illustrates the great promise of web service interoperability. We have a WSDL file generated by GLUE, a server running Java, and a client running Perl, and they all work seamlessly together.

```
Connecting to Price Service...
54.99
```

The IBM Web Services Toolkit (available at *http://www. alphaworks.ibm.com/tech/webservicestoolkit*) provides a WSDL generation tool called wsdlgen. This tool can take existing Java classes, Enterprise JavaBeans, and Microsoft COM objects and automatically generate corresponding WSDL files. However, as this book goes to press, the wsdlgen tool creates files based on the 1999 version of the W3C XML Schema. The WSDL files are therefore incompatible with other WSDL invocation tools, such as SOAP::Lite and GLUE. If you choose to use the IBM tool, make sure to manually update your WSDL files to reflect the latest version of XML Schema (*http://www.w3.org/2001/XMLSchema*).

XML Schema Data Typing

In order for a SOAP client to communicate effectively with a SOAP server, the client and server must agree on a data type system. By default, XML 1.0

does not provide a data type system. In contrast, every programming language provides some basic facility for declaring data types, such as integers, floats, doubles, and strings. One of the greatest challenges in building web services is therefore creating a common data type system that can be used by a diverse set of programming languages running on a diverse set of operating systems.

WSDL does not aim to create a standard for XML data typing. In fact, WSDL is specifically designed for maximum flexibility and is therefore not tied exclusively to any one data type system. Nonetheless, WSDL does default to the W3C XML Schema specification. The XML Schema specification is also currently the most widely used specification for data typing.

The more you know about XML Schemas, the better you can understand complex WSDL files. A full discussion of XML Schemas is beyond the scope of this chapter. However, two facts are crucially important.

First, the XML Schema specification includes a basic type system for encoding most data types. This type system includes a long list of built-in simple types, including strings, floats, doubles, integers, time, and date. This list, shown in Table 6-1, is excerpted from the XML Schema Part 0: Primer (*http://www.w3org/TR/2000/WD=xmlschema=0=20000407/*). If your application sticks to these simple data types, there is no need to include the WSDL types element, and the resulting WSDL file is extremely simple. For example, our first two WSDL files use only strings and floats.

Table 6-1. A list of the main XML Schema built-in simple types

Simple type	Example(s)
string	Web Services
Boolean	true, false, 1, 0
float	-INF, -1E4, -0, 0, 12.78E-2, 12, INF, NaN
double	-INF, -1E4, -0, 0, 12.78E-2, 12, INF, NaN
decimal	-1.23, 0, 123.4, 1000.00
binary	100010
integer	-126789, -1, 0, 1, 126789
nonPositiveInteger	-126789, -1, 0
negativeInteger	-126789, -1
long	-1, 12678967543233
int	-1, 126789675
short	-1, 12678
byte	-1, 126
nonNegativeInteger	0, 1, 126789

Table 6-1. A list of the main XML Schema built-in simple types (continued)

Simple type	Example(s)
unsignedLong	0, 12678967543233
unsignedInt	0, 1267896754
unsignedShort	0, 12678
unsignedByte	0, 126
positiveInteger	1, 126789
date	1999-05-31
time	13:20:00.000, 13:20:00.000-05:00

Second, the XML Schema specification provides a facility for creating *new* data types. This is important if you want to create data types that go beyond what is already defined within the Schema. For example, a service might return an array of floats or a more complex stock quote object containing the high, low, and volume figures for a specific stock. Whenever your service goes beyond the simple XML Schema data types, you must declare these new data types within the WSDL types element.

In the next two sections of this chapter, we present two specific examples of using XML Schemas to create new data types. The first focuses on arrays; the second focuses on a more complex data type for encapsulating product information.

Arrays

Example 6-6, shown later in this section, is a sample WSDL file that illustrates the use of arrays. This is the Price List Service we created in Chapter 5. The service has one public method, called getPriceList, which expects an array of string SKU values and returns an array of double price values.

The WSDL file now includes a types element. Inside this element, we have defined two new complex types. Very broadly, the XML Schema defines simple types and complex types. Simple types cannot have element children or attributes, whereas complex types can have element children and attributes. We have declared complex types in our WSDL file, because an array may have multiple elements, one for each value in the array.

The XML Schema requires that any new type you create be based on some existing data type. This existing base type is specified via the base attribute. You can then choose to modify this base type using one of two main methods: extension or restriction. Extension simply means that your new data type will have all the properties of the base type plus some extra functionality. Restriction means that your new data type will have all the properties of the base data type, but may have additional restrictions placed on the data.

In Example 6-6, we'll create two new complex types via restriction. For example:

```
<complexType name="ArrayOfString">
  <complexContent>
    <restriction base="soapenc:Array">
      <attribute ref="soapenc:arrayType"
        wsdl:arrayType="string[]"/>
    </restriction>
  </complexContent>
</complexType>
```

Example 6-6. PriceListService.wsdl

```
<?xml version="1.0" encoding="UTF-8"?>
<definitions name="PriceListService"
  targetNamespace="http://www.ecerami.com/wsdl/PriceListService.wsdl"
  xmlns="http://schemas.xmlsoap.org/wsdl/"
  xmlns:soap="http://schemas.xmlsoap.org/wsdl/soap/"
  xmlns:tns="http://www.ecerami.com/wsdl/PriceListService.wsdl"
  xmlns:xsd="http://www.w3.org/2001/XMLSchema"
  xmlns:xsd1="http://www.ecerami.com/schema">

  <types>
    <schema xmlns="http://www.w3.org/2001/XMLSchema"
        targetNamespace="http://www.ecerami.com/schema"
        xmlns:wsdl="http://schemas.xmlsoap.org/wsdl/"
        xmlns:soapenc="http://schemas.xmlsoap.org/soap/encoding/">

        <complexType name="ArrayOfString">
          <complexContent>
            <restriction base="soapenc:Array">
              <attribute ref="soapenc:arrayType"
                wsdl:arrayType="string[]"/>
            </restriction>
          </complexContent>
        </complexType>
        <complexType name="ArrayOfDouble">
          <complexContent>
            <restriction base="soapenc:Array">
              <attribute ref="soapenc:arrayType"
                wsdl:arrayType="double[]"/>
            </restriction>
          </complexContent>
        </complexType>
    </schema>
  </types>

  <message name="PriceListRequest">
    <part name="sku_list" type="xsd1:ArrayOfString"/>
  </message>
```

Example 6-6. PriceListService.wsdl (continued)

```
<message name="PriceListResponse">
    <part name="price_list" type="xsd1:ArrayOfDouble"/>
</message>

<portType name="PriceList_PortType">
    <operation name="getPriceList">
        <input message="tns:PriceListRequest"/>
        <output message="tns:PriceListResponse"/>
    </operation>
</portType>

<binding name="PriceList_Binding" type="tns:PriceList_PortType">
<soap:binding style="rpc" transport="http://schemas.xmlsoap.org/soap/http"/>
    <operation name="getPriceList">
    <soap:operation soapAction="urn:examples:pricelistservice"/>
        <input>
            <soap:body
                encodingStyle="http://schemas.xmlsoap.org/soap/encoding/"
                namespace="urn:examples:pricelistservice"
                use="encoded"/>
        </input>
        <output>
            <soap:body
                encodingStyle="http://schemas.xmlsoap.org/soap/encoding/"
                namespace="urn:examples:pricelistservice" use="encoded"/>
        </output>
    </operation>
</binding>

<service name="PriceList_Service">
    <port name="PriceList_Port" binding="tns:PriceList_Binding">
        <soap:address location="http://localhost:8080/soap/servlet/rpcrouter"/>
    </port>
</service>
</definitions>
```

The WSDL specification requires that arrays be based on the SOAP 1.1 encoding schema. It also requires that arrays use the name ArrayOfXXX, where XXX is the type of item in the array. The previous example therefore creates a new type called ArrayOfString. This new type is based on the SOAP array data type, but it is restricted to holding only string values. Likewise, the ArrayOfDouble data type creates a new array type containing only double values.

When using the WSDL types element, you need to be particularly aware of XML namespace issues. First, note that the root schema element must include a namespace declaration for the SOAP encoding specification (*http:// schemas.xmlsoap.org/soap/encoding/*). This is required because our new data types extend the array definition specified by SOAP.

Second, the root schema element must specify a targetNamespace attribute. Any newly defined elements, such as our new array data types, will belong to the specified targetNamespace. To reference these data types later in the document, you must refer back to the same targetNamespace. Hence, our definitions element includes a new namespace declaration:

```
xmlns:xsd1="http://www.ecerami.com/schema">
```

xsd1 matches the targetNamespace and therefore enables us to reference the new data types later in the document. For example, the message element references the xsd1:ArrayOfString data type:

```
<message name="PriceListRequest">
    <part name="sku_list" type="xsd1:ArrayOfString"/>
</message>
```

 For an excellent and concise overview of W3C Schema complex types and their derivation via extension and restriction, see Donald Smith's article on "Understanding W3C Schema Complex Types." The article is available online at *http://www.xml.com/pub/a/2001/08/22/easyschema.html*.

Automatically invoking array services

Once you move beyond basic data types, the simple WSDL invocation methods described previously in this chapter no longer work quite as easily. For example, you cannot simply open the GLUE console, pass an array of strings, and hope to receive back an array of doubles. Additional work is necessary, and some manual code is required. Nonetheless, the additional work is minimal, and the discussion that follows focuses on the GLUE platform. We have chosen to focus on the GLUE platform because it represents the most elegant platform for working with complex data types; other tools, such as the IBM Web Services Toolkit, do, however, provide similar functionality.

To get started, you should become familiar with the GLUE wsdl2java command-line tool. The tool takes in a WSDL file and generates a suite of Java class files to automatically interface with the specified service. You can then write your own Java class to invoke the specified service. Best of all, the code you write is minimally simple, and all SOAP-specific details are completely hidden from your view. (See Figure 6-12.)

Here is the wsdl2java command-line usage:

```
usage: wsdl2java <arguments>

where valid arguments are:
    http://host:port/filename      URL of WSDL
```

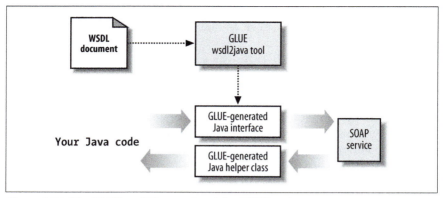

Figure 6-12. The GLUE wsdl2java tool and the GLUE architecture

```
-c                          checked exceptions
-d directory                output directory for files
-l user password realm      login credentials
-m map-file                 read mapping instructions
-p package                  set default package
-v                          verbose
-x command-file             command file to execute
```

Complete information on each argument is available online within the GLUE User Guide at *http://www.themindelectric.com/products/glue/releases/ GLUE-1.1/docs/guide/index.html*. For now, we will focus on the most basic arguments. For example, to generate Java class files for the *PriceListService. wsdl* file, first make sure that the WSDL file is available publicly on a web site or locally via a web server such as Tomcat. Then, issue the following command:

```
wsdl2java.bat http://localhost:8080/wsdl/PriceListService.wsdl -p com.
    ecerami.wsdl.glue
```

The first argument specifies the location of the WSDL file; the second argument specifies that the generated files should be placed in the package com. ecerami.wsdl.glue.

GLUE will automatically download the specified WSDL file and generate two Java class files:

```
write file IPriceList_Service.java
write file PriceList_ServiceHelper.java
```

The first file, *IPriceList_Service.java*, is shown in Example 6-7. This file represents a Java interface that mirrors the public methods exposed by the WSDL file. Specifically, the interface shows a getPriceList( ) method that receives an array of String values, and returns an array of double values.

Example 6-7. IPriceList_Service.java

```java
// generated by GLUE

package com.ecerami.wsdl.glue;

public interface IPriceList_Service
  {
  double[] getPriceList( String[] sku_list );
  }
```

The second file, *PriceList_ServiceHelper.java*, is shown in Example 6-8. This is known as a GLUE helper file, and it can dynamically bind to the service specified by the WSDL file. To access the service, simply call the static bind( ) method.

Example 6-8. PriceList_ServiceHelper.java

```java
// generated by GLUE

package com.ecerami.wsdl.glue;

import electric.registry.Registry;
import electric.registry.RegistryException;

public class PriceList_ServiceHelper
  {
  public static IPriceList_Service bind( ) throws RegistryException
    {
    return bind( "http://localhost:8080/wsdl/PriceListService.wsdl" );
    }

  public static IPriceList_Service bind( String url )
    throws RegistryException
    {
    return (IPriceList_Service)
       Registry.bind( url, IPriceList_Service.class );
    }
  }
```

Once GLUE has generated the interface and helper files, you just need to write your own class that actually invokes the service. Example 6-9 shows a sample application that invokes the Price List Service. The code first calls PriceList_ServiceHelper.bind( ), which then returns an IPriceList_Service object. All subsequent code behaves as if the Price List Service is a local object, and all SOAP-specific details are completely hidden from the developer.

Here is a sample output of the Invoke_PriceList application:

```
Product Catalog
SKU:  A358185 --> Price:  54.99
SKU:  A358565 --> Price:  19.99
```

Example 6-9. Invoke_PriceList.java

```
package com.ecerami.wsdl;

import com.ecerami.wsdl.glue.*;

/**
 * SOAP Invoker.  Uses the PriceListServiceHelper to invoke
 * SOAP service.  PriceListServiceHelper and IPriceListService
 * are automatically generated by GLUE.
 */
public class Invoke_PriceList {

  /**
   * Get Product List via SOAP
   */
  public double[] getPrices (String skus[]) throws Exception {
    IPriceList_Service priceListService = PriceList_ServiceHelper.bind( );
    double[] prices = priceListService.getPriceList(skus);
    return prices;
  }

  /**
   * Main Method
   */
  public static void main (String[] args) throws Exception {
    Invoke_PriceList invoker = new Invoke_PriceList( );
    System.out.println ("Product Catalog");
    String skus[] = {"A358185", "A358565" };
    double[] prices = invoker.getPrices (skus);
    for (int i=0; i<prices.length; i++) {
      System.out.print ("SKU:  "+skus[i]);
      System.out.println (" --> Price:  "+prices[i]);
    }
  }
}
```

Complex Types

Our final topic is the use of complex data types. For example, consider a home monitoring service that provides a concise update on your home. The data returned could include multiple data elements, such as the current temperature, security status, and whether the garage door is open or closed. Encoding this data into WSDL requires additional knowledge of XML Schemas, which reinforces the main precept that the more you know about XML Schemas, the better you will understand complex WSDL files.

To explore complex types, consider the WSDL file in Example 6-10. This WSDL file describes our Product Service from Chapter 5. The complex types are indicated in bold.

Example 6-10. ProductService.wsdl

```
<?xml version="1.0" encoding="UTF-8"?>
<definitions name="ProductService"
  targetNamespace="http://www.ecerami.com/wsdl/ProductService.wsdl"
  xmlns="http://schemas.xmlsoap.org/wsdl/"
  xmlns:soap="http://schemas.xmlsoap.org/wsdl/soap/"
  xmlns:tns="http://www.ecerami.com/wsdl/ProductService.wsdl"
  xmlns:xsd="http://www.w3.org/2001/XMLSchema"
  xmlns:xsd1="http://www.ecerami.com/schema">

  <types>
    <xsd:schema
        targetNamespace="http://www.ecerami.com/schema"
        xmlns="http://www.w3.org/2001/XMLSchema">
        <xsd:complexType name="product">
            <xsd:sequence>
                <xsd:element name="name" type="xsd:string"/>
                <xsd:element name="description" type="xsd:string"/>
                <xsd:element name="price" type="xsd:double"/>
                <xsd:element name="SKU" type="xsd:string"/>
            </xsd:sequence>
        </xsd:complexType>
    </xsd:schema>
  </types>

  <message name="getProductRequest">
    <part name="sku" type="xsd:string"/>
  </message>

  <message name="getProductResponse">
    <part name="product" type="xsd1:product"/>
  </message>

  <portType name="Product_PortType">
    <operation name="getProduct">
      <input message="tns:getProductRequest"/>
      <output message="tns:getProductResponse"/>
    </operation>
  </portType>

  <binding name="Product_Binding" type="tns:Product_PortType">
    <soap:binding style="rpc"
        transport="http://schemas.xmlsoap.org/soap/http"/>
    <operation name="getProduct">
      <soap:operation soapAction="urn:examples:productservice"/>
      <input>
        <soap:body
            encodingStyle="http://schemas.xmlsoap.org/soap/encoding/"
            namespace="urn:examples:productservice"
            use="encoded"/>
      </input>
      <output>
```

Example 6-10. ProductService.wsdl (continued)

```
          <soap:body
              encodingStyle="http://schemas.xmlsoap.org/soap/encoding/"
              namespace="urn:examples:productservice" use="encoded"/>
        </output>
      </operation>
    </binding>

    <service name="Product_Service">
      <port name="Product_Port" binding="tns:Product_Binding">
        <soap:address location="http://localhost:8080/soap/servlet/rpcrouter"/>
      </port>
    </service>
</definitions>
```

The service in Example 6-10 describes a getProduct operation that returns a complex *product* type for encapsulating product information, including product name, description, price, and SKU number.

The new product type is defined in much the same manner as the array definition from the previous example. The main difference is that we are now using the sequence element. The sequence element specifies a list of subelements and requires that these elements appear in the order specified. XML Schemas also enable you to specify cardinality via the minOccurs and maxOccurs attributes. If these attributes are absent (as in our example), they default to 1, requiring that each subelement must occur exactly one time.

Each subelement can also have its own data type, and you can see that we have mixed and matched string data types with double data types in our example.

Automatically invoking complex type services

To automatically invoke the Product Service, we return to the GLUE wsdl2java tool. This time around, GLUE will generate a Java interface class and a Java helper class, along with two additional files for handling the new complex type.

For example, the following command:

```
wsdl2java.bat http://localhost:8080/wsdl/ProductService.wsdl -p com.ecerami.
    wsdl.glue
```

generates the following output:

```
write file IProduct_Service.java
write file Product_ServiceHelper.java
write file product.java
write file Product_Service.map
```

The first two files in the output listing are familiar. The first file is a Java interface mirroring the service; the second file is a helper class for dynamically binding to the specified service. (See Example 6-11 and Example 6-12.)

Example 6-11. IProduct_Service.java

```
// generated by GLUE

package com.ecerami.wsdl.glue;

public interface IProduct_Service
  {
  product getProduct( String sku );
  }
```

Example 6-12. Product_ServiceHelper.java

```
// generated by GLUE

package com.ecerami.wsdl.glue;

import electric.registry.Registry;
import electric.registry.RegistryException;

public class Product_ServiceHelper
  {
  public static IProduct_Service bind( ) throws RegistryException
    {
    return bind( "http://localhost:8080/wsdl/ProductService.wsdl" );
    }

  public static IProduct_Service bind( String url )
   throws RegistryException
    {
    return (IProduct_Service)
      Registry.bind( url, IProduct_Service.class );
    }
  }
```

The third file in the output listing, *product.java*, represents a simple container class for encapsulating product data. (See Example 6-13.) GLUE essentially takes all the complex types defined within the WSDL file and creates a container class for each type. Each subelement is then transformed into a public variable for easy access. For example, the product class has four public variables, name, description, price, and SKU, corresponding to our new complex data type. Note also that the public variables match the XML Schema types specified within the WSDL file; for example, name is declared as a String, whereas price is declared as a double.

Example 6-13. product.java

```
// generated by GLUE

package com.ecerami.wsdl.glue;

public class product
  {
  public java.lang.String name;

  public java.lang.String description;

  public double price;

  public java.lang.String SKU;
  }
```

Finally, GLUE generates a Java-to-XML Schema mapping file. (See Example 6-14.) The file itself is extremely concise and is responsible for converting Java to XML Schema types and vice versa. (See Figure 6-13.) The root complexType element indicates that elements of type product should be transformed into the product class located in com.ecerami.wsdl.glue. Inside the root complex type, there is a one-to-one mapping between the XML Schema type and the public Java variable. For example, the element name is mapped to the product.name variable, and the type is specified as string. Likewise, the element price is mapped to the product.price variable, and the type is specified as double.

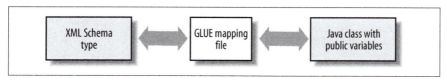

Figure 6-13. The GLUE Java-to-XML Schema mapping file

Example 6-14. Product_Service.map

```
<?xml version='1.0' encoding='UTF-8'?>
<!--generated by GLUE-->
<mappings xmlns='http://www.themindelectric.com/schema/'>
 <schema
  xmlns='http://www.w3.org/2001/XMLSchema'
  targetNamespace='http://www.ecerami.com/schema'
  xmlns:electric='http://www.themindelectric.com/schema/'>
  <complexType name='product' electric:class='com.ecerami.wsdl.glue.product'>
   <sequence>
    <element name='name' electric:field='name' type='string'/>
    <element name='description'
       electric:field='description' type='string'/>
    <element name='price' electric:field='price' type='double'/>
```

Example 6-14. Product_Service.map (continued)

```
    <element name='SKU' electric:field='SKU' type='string'/>
    </sequence>
  </complexType>
 </schema>
</mappings>
```

To invoke the Product Service, you must first explicitly load the mapping file via the GLUE Mappings class:

```
Mappings.readMappings("Product_Service.map");
```

You can then access the service just like in the previous example. See Example 6-15 for the complete invocation program. Here is some sample output:

```
Product Service
Name:  Red Hat Linux
Description:  Red Hat Linux Operating System
Price:  54.99
```

Example 6-15. Invoke_Product.java

```java
package com.ecerami.wsdl;

import java.io.IOException;
import electric.xml.io.Mappings;
import electric.xml.ParseException;
import electric.registry.RegistryException;
import com.ecerami.wsdl.glue.*;

/**
 * SOAP Invoker.  Uses the Product_ServiceHelper to invoke the Product
 * SOAP service.  All other .java files are automatically generated
 * by GLUE.
 */
public class Invoke_Product {

  /**
   * Get Product via SOAP Service
   */
  public product getProduct (String sku) throws Exception {
    // Load Java <--> XML Mapping
    Mappings.readMappings("Product_Service.map");
    // Invoke Service
    IProduct_Service service = Product_ServiceHelper.bind( );
    product prod = service.getProduct(sku);
    return prod;
  }

  /**
   * Main Method
   */
```

Example 6-15. Invoke_Product.java (continued)

```
public static void main (String[] args) throws Exception {
  Invoke_Product invoker = new Invoke_Product( );
  System.out.println ("Product Service");
  product prod = invoker.getProduct("A358185");
  System.out.println ("Name:  "+prod.name);
  System.out.println ("Description:  "+prod.description);
  System.out.println ("Price:  "+prod.price);
 }
}
```

This is a very small amount of code, but it is capable of doing very real work. Be sure to check The Mind Electric web site (*http://themindelectric. com*) for new releases of the GLUE product.

PART V

UDDI

CHAPTER 7

UDDI Essentials

UDDI is a technical specification for describing, discovering, and integrating web services. UDDI is therefore a critical part of the emerging web service protocol stack, enabling companies to both publish and find web services. This chapter provides a complete overview of UDDI and covers the following topics:

- The main concepts and history of UDDI
- The main uses of UDDI, such as its potential impact within the field of supply-chain management
- The technical aspects of UDDI, including a detailed explanation of the UDDI data model
- How to search UDDI via a web-based interface and how to use the UDDI programmatic API
- How to publish new companies and services to UDDI
- Popular UDDI implementations for Java, Perl, and Microsoft COM

Introduction to UDDI

At its core, UDDI consists of two parts. First, UDDI is a technical specification for building a distributed directory of businesses and web services. Data is stored within a specific XML format, and the UDDI specification includes API details for searching existing data and publishing new data. Second, the UDDI Business Registry (also frequently referred to as the UDDI "cloud services") is a fully operational implementation of the UDDI specification. Launched in May 2001 by Microsoft and IBM, the UDDI registry now enables anyone to search existing UDDI data. It also enables any company to register itself and its services.

The data captured within UDDI is divided into three main categories:

White pages
> This includes general information about a specific company—for example, business name, business description, contact information, address and phone numbers. It can also include unique business identifiers, such as a Dun & Bradstreet D-U-N-S® Number.

Yellow pages
> This includes general classification data for either the company or the service offered. For example, this data may include industry, product, or geographic codes based on standard taxonomies.

Green pages
> This category contains technical information about a web service. Generally, this includes a pointer to an external specification and an address for invoking the web service. UDDI is not restricted to describing web services based on SOAP. Rather, UDDI can be used to describe any service, from a single web page or email address all the way up to SOAP, CORBA, and Java RMI services.

A Brief History of UDDI

UDDI 1.0 was originally announced by Microsoft, IBM, and Ariba in September 2000. Since the initial announcement, the UDDI initiative has grown to include more than 280 companies. (A complete list of UDDI members is available at *http://www.uddi.org/community.html*.)

In May 2001, Microsoft and IBM launched the first UDDI operator sites and turned the UDDI registry live. In June 2001, UDDI announced Version 2.0. New features include:

- Improved support for internationalization. For example, businesses can describe themselves and their services in multiple languages.

- Improved support for describing complex organizations. For example, a business can publish business units, departments, or divisions and tie them together under one umbrella.

- An improved set of search options.

As of this writing, the Microsoft and IBM sites implement the 1.0 specification and plan 2.0 support in the near future. According to the original plan, the UDDI group will release three versions of UDDI and then turn the specification over to an appropriate standards body.

Why UDDI?

At first glance, UDDI appears extremely simple. Nonetheless, it includes some subtle points that are easily overlooked. Let's therefore begin by examining the future impact of UDDI within a specific industry.

To make the concepts as concrete as possible, consider the semiconductor industry. Currently, approximately 400 companies in the information technology, electronic component, and semiconductor manufacturing industries are members of an industry consortium called RosettaNet. RosettaNet is focused on creating standard processes and interfaces for e-business and supply-chain management. One of RosettaNet's main accomplishments is the creation of Partner Interface Processes (PIPs). PIPs are XML-based interfaces that enable two trading partners to exchange data. Dozens of PIPs already exist. For example:

PIP2A2
> Enables a partner to query another for product information

PIP3A2
> Enables a partner to query the price and availability of specific products

PIP3A4
> Enables a partner to submit an electronic purchase order and receive acknowledgment of the order

PIP3A3
> Enables a partner to transfer the contents of an electronic shopping cart

PIP3B4
> Enables a partner to query status on a specific shipment

By accelerating the adoption of PIPs, RosettaNet will dramatically increase interoperability between trading partners and enable more flexible supply-chain management. This increases overall efficiency and drives down costs. Each of the participating companies therefore has a direct incentive to adhere to the PIP standards.

Additional information regarding RosettaNet is available at *http://www.rosettanet.org*.

In April 2001, RosettaNet registered 83 individual PIPs within UDDI. Let's consider two fictional companies and examine how each may leverage UDDI in the near future.

Scenario 1: Publishing to UDDI

First, consider Acme Parts, a supplier of generic semiconductor widgets. Acme is a member of the RosettaNet consortium and has recently upgraded its e-business services to adhere to a subset of the RosettaNet specification. For example, Acme now enables partners to query for specific product information, product availability, and pricing. It also enables partners to submit electronic purchase orders and to constantly track the status of those orders.

Acme is eager to integrate into existing supply chains. It therefore registers itself within UDDI. It also registers each of its e-business services. For each service, it notes the technical specification implemented. For example, the Acme Parts: Submit Purchase Order is noted to adhere to RosettaNet PIP3A4.

By registering within UDDI, Acme advertises its services and enables buyers to easily discover the technical standards used. In the future, you can also imagine that Acme will purchase new UDDI-aware e-commerce software. The software will know the UDDI protocol and will be able to automatically register the company and its services.

Scenario 2: Searching UDDI

Next, consider United Semiconductor, a buyer of parts from Acme Parts and dozens of other suppliers. To drive down costs, United wants to integrate all its suppliers into one coherent system.

United has two options. First, let's assume that United and Acme are already well-established partners. United can therefore look up Acme within the UDDI Business Registry, determine which services are available from Acme, and determine whether those services adhere to the same RosettaNet standards. For each service, United can also determine the exact *binding points*. For example, the Acme Parts: Submit Purchase Order service is available at *http://www.acmeparts.com/services/po*. United therefore has all the information necessary to seamlessly add Acme to its supply chain and immediately start submitting electronic purchase orders.

As a second option, United could also look up other suppliers. Or it could look up all companies that implement the specific PIP for submitting electronic purchase orders.

UDDI Technical Overview

The UDDI technical architecture consists of three parts:

UDDI data model
> An XML Schema for describing businesses and web services. The data model is described in detail in the "UDDI Data Model" section, later in this chapter.

UDDI API
> A SOAP-based API for searching and publishing UDDI data.

UDDI cloud services
> Operator sites that provide implementations of the UDDI specification and synchronize all data on a scheduled basis.

UDDI cloud services are currently provided by Microsoft and IBM. Ariba had originally planned to offer an operator as well, but has since backed away from the commitment. Additional operators from other companies, including Hewlett-Packard, are planned for the near future. (For an updated list of operator sites, go to *http://www.uddi.org/register.html*.)

The current cloud services provide a logically centralized, but physically distributed, directory. This means that data submitted to one root node will automatically be replicated across all the other root nodes. Currently, data replication occurs every 24 hours.

It is also possible to set up private UDDI registries. For example, a large company may set up its own private UDDI registry for registering all internal web services. As these registries are not automatically synchronized with the root UDDI nodes, they are not considered part of the UDDI cloud.

UDDI Data Model

UDDI includes an XML Schema that describes four core types of information:

- businessEntity
- businessService
- bindingTemplate
- tModel

These core data elements are described in the following sections. Figure 7-1 illustrates the containment hierarchy. (This diagram is based on Figure 1 from the "UDDI Data Structure Reference V1.0", available at *http://www. uddi.org/pubs/DataStructure-V1.00-Open-20000930_2.doc*.) You may be tempted to rush ahead and try the web-based UDDI interface, but taking the time to understand these core elements now will help immensely when you're trying to make sense of both the web-based interface and the programmatic API.

 The actual UDDI XML Schemas are available online at the following URLs: *http://www.uddi.org/schema/2001/uddi_v1. xsd* (UDDI 1.0) and *http://www.uddi.org/schema/uddi_v2.xsd* (UDDI 2.0).

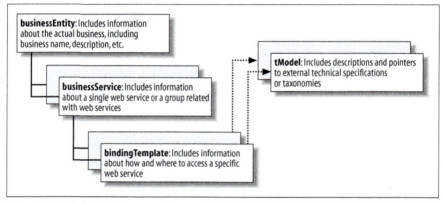

Figure 7-1. The UDDI data model

The businessEntity

The businessEntity element includes information about the actual business. This includes business name, description, address, and contact information. For example, here is an excerpt from the Microsoft businessEntity record:

```
<businessEntity
    businessKey="0076b468-eb27-42e5-ac09-9955cff462a3"
    operator="Microsoft Corporation" authorizedName="Martin Kohlleppel">
    <name>Microsoft Corporation</name>
    <description xml:lang="en">Empowering people through great software
    - any time, any place and on any device is Microsoft's vision. As the
    worldwide leader in software for personal and business computing, we
    strive to produce innovative products and services that meet our
    customer's...
```

```
    </description>
    <contacts>
        <contact useType="Corporate Addresses and telephone">
            <description xml:lang="en">Corporate Mailing Addresses</
                description>
            <personName />
            <phone useType="Corporate Headquarters">(425) 882-8080</phone>
            <address sortCode="~" useType="Corporate Headquarters">
            <addressLine>Microsoft Corporation</addressLine>
                <addressLine>One Microsoft Way</addressLine>
                <addressLine>Redmond, WA 98052-6399</addressLine>
                <addressLine>USA</addressLine>
            </address>
        </contact>
        <contact useType="Technical Contact - Corporate UD">
            <description xml:lang="en">World Wide Operations</description>
                <personName>Martin Kohlleppel</personName>
                <email>martink@microsoft.com</email>
        </contact>
    </contacts>
    <identifierBag>
        <keyedReference
        tModelKey="uuid:8609c81e-ee1f-4d5a-b202-3eb13ad01823"
        keyName="D-U-N-S" keyValue="08-146-6849" />
    </identifierBag>
    <categoryBag>
        <keyedReference
        tModelKey="uuid:c0b9fe13-179f-413d-8a5b-5004db8e5bb2"
        keyName="NAICS: Software Publisher" keyValue="51121" />
    </categoryBag>
</businessEntity>
```

Upon registering, each business receives a unique businessKey value. For example, the businessKey for Microsoft is 0076b468-eb27-42e5-ac09-9955cff462a3. As we shall soon see, the key is used to tie a business to its published services.

In addition to basic contact information, the businessEntity record can include optional business identifiers and business categories. Identifiers can represent any unique value that identifies the company. For example, UDDI is currently set up to accept both Dun & Bradstreet D-U-N-S® Numbers and Thomas Registry Supplier IDs. (See Table 7-1 and Table 7-2 for details.)

Table 7-1. Dun & Bradstreet D-U-N-S® Number

Name	dnb-com:D-U-N-S
Description	Dun & Bradstreet D-U-N-S® Number
UUID	uuid:8609C81E-EE1F-4D5A-B202-3EB13AD01823
Details	The Dun & Bradstreet D-U-N-S® (Data Universal Numbering System) Number is a nine-digit identification number used to identify businesses and subsidiaries. Over 62 million D-U-N-S numbers currently exist. Information is available at *http://www.dnb.com/english/duns/*.

Table 7-2. Thomas Register Supplier ID

Name	thomasregister-com:supplierID
Description	Thomas Register Supplier ID
UUID	uuid:B1B1BAF5-2329-43E6-AE13-BA8E97195039
Details	The Thomas Register of American Manufacturers provides a unique supplier ID for over 168,000 American and Canadian companies. Information is available at *http://www.thomasregister.com/*.

As you can see from our first example, the Microsoft businessEntity record includes the Microsoft D&B D-U-N-S® Number. To include multiple values, note that the businessEntity element includes an element named identifierBag. Here, the term "bag" indicates a generic container of multiple values, and enables a company to register multiple business identifiers.

Businesses can also register multiple business categories. This can include industry, product, service, or geographic codes based on standard taxonomies. UDDI is currently prepopulated with the following three business categories:

NAICS

> The North American Industry Classification System (NAICS) provides industry classification. (See Table 7-3 for details.)

UNSPSC

> The Universal Standard Products and Service Classification (UNSPSC) provides product and service classification. (See Table 7-4 for details.)

ISO 3166

> The International Organization for Standardization (ISO) maintains ISO 3166, a standard taxonomy for world geography. (See Table 7-5 for details.)

As you can see from our first example, the Microsoft record includes an NAICS classification for "NAICS: Software Publisher".

Table 7-3. NAICS

Name	ntis-gov:naics:1997
Description	Business Taxonomy: NAICS (1997 Release)
UUID	uuid:C0B9FE13-179F-413D-8A5B-5004DB8E5BB2
Details	NAICS provides a six-digit industry code for more than 19,000 industries. NAICS was created jointly by the governments of Canada, Mexico, and the U.S. to provide a standard system for statistical reporting throughout the North American Free Trade Association (NAFTA). Beginning in 1997, NAICS replaced the previous Standard Industry Classification (SIC). Additional information is available at *http://www.naics.com/*. To look up your NAICS code, go to *http://www.naics.com/search.htm*.

Table 7-4. UNSPSC

Name	unspsc-org:unspsc:3-1
Description	Product Taxonomy: UNSPSC (Version 3.1)
UUID	uuid:DB77450D-9FA8-45D4-A7BC-04411D14E384
Details	UNSPSC provides standard codes for classifying products and services. The standard was developed in 1998 and is currently maintained by the nonprofit Electronic Commerce Code Management Association (ECCMA). UNSPSC provides coverage of 54 industries and includes over 12,000 codes for every product and service imaginable. For example: the code 50131601 denotes "Fresh eggs", whereas the code 50131602 denotes "Egg substitutes"! Additional information is available at *http://www.unspsc.org*.

Table 7-5. ISO 3166

Name	uddi-org:iso-ch:3166:1999
Description	UDDI Geographic Taxonomy, ISO 3166
UUID	uuid:61668105-B6B6-425C-914B-409FB252C36D
Details	ISO maintains ISO 3166, a list of 237 country codes. For example, China has the code CN, whereas the U.S. has the code US. By using ISO 3166, companies registered with UDDI can identify their geographic headquarters or their main geographic areas of business. ISO 3166 is also used for top-level Internet domain country codes. Additional information is available at *http://www.din.de/gremien/nas/nabd/iso3166ma/index.html*.

The businessService

The businessService element includes information about a single web service or a group of related web services. This includes name, description, and an optional list of bindingTemplates (described in the next section of this chapter). For example, here is a sample businessService record for the XMethods.net Delayed Stock Quote Service:

```
<businessService
    serviceKey="d5921160-3e16-11d5-98bf-002035229c64"
    businessKey="ba744ed0-3aaf-11d5-80dc-002035229c64">
    <name>XMethods Delayed Stock Quotes</name>
    <description xml:lang="en">20-minute delayed stock quotes</description>
    <bindingTemplates>
        <bindingTemplate
            serviceKey="d5921160-3e16-11d5-98bf-002035229c64"
            bindingKey="d594a970-3e16-11d5-98bf-002035229c64">
        <description xml:lang="en">
            SOAP binding for delayed stock quotes service
        </description>
        <accessPoint URLType="http">
            http://services.xmethods.net:80/soap
        </accessPoint>
        <tModelInstanceDetails>
            <tModelInstanceInfo
            tModelKey="uuid:0e727db0-3e14-11d5-98bf-002035229c64" />
```

```
        </tModelInstanceDetails>
      </bindingTemplate>
    </bindingTemplates>
  </businessService>
```

Like the businessEntity, each businessService has a unique serviceKey.

The bindingTemplate

The bindingTemplate element includes information about how and where to access a specific web service. For example, in the previous XMethods record above, we can see that the Stock Quote Service is available via SOAP at *http://services.xmethods.net:80/soap*. Bindings need not refer only to HTTP-based services. In fact, UDDI bindings can point to email-based services, fax-based services, FTP-based services, or even telephone-based services. (See Table 7-6 for details.)

Table 7-6. UDDI binding options

Name	Description	UUID	Details
uddi-org:smtp	Email-based service	uuid:93335D49-3EFB-48A0-ACEA-EA102B60DDC6	Identifies a service that is invoked via SMTP email. For example, this could specify a person's email address or an SMTP-based SOAP service.
uddi-org:fax	Fax-based service	uuid:1A2B00BE-6E2C-42F5-875B-56F32686E0E7	Identifies a service that is invoked via fax transmissions.
uddi-org:ftp	FTP-based service	uuid:1A2B00BE-6E2C-42F5-875B-56F32686E0E7	Identifies a service that is invoked via FTP.
uddi-org:telephone	Telephone-based service	uuid:38E12427-5536-4260-A6F9-B5B530E63A07	Identifies a service that is invoked via a telephone call. This could include interaction by voice and/or touch-tone.
uddi-org:http	HTTP-based service	uuid:68DE9E80-AD09-469D-8A37-088422BFBC36	Identifies a web service that is invoked via the HTTP protocol. This could reference a simple web page or a more complex HTTP-based SOAP application.
uddi-org:homepage	HTTP web homepage URL	uuid:4CEC1CEF-1F68-4B23-8CB7-8BAA763AEB89	Identifies a web home page.

The tModel

The tModel is the last core data type, but potentially the most difficult to grasp. tModel stands for technical model. tModels are primarily used to provide pointers to external technical specifications. For example, the bindingTemplate for the XMethods Stock Quote Service provides information about where to access the SOAP binding, but it does not provide information about how to interface with it. The tModel element fills this gap by providing a pointer to an external specification. For example, here is the tModel referenced by the XMethods Stock Quote binding:

```
<tModel
    tModelKey="uuid:0e727db0-3e14-11d5-98bf-002035229c64"
    operator="www.ibm.com/services/uddi" authorizedName="0100001QS1">
    <name>XMethods Simple Stock Quote</name>
    <description xml:lang="en">Simple stock quote interface</description>
    <overviewDoc>
        <description xml:lang="en">wsdl link</description>
        <overviewURL>
            http://www.xmethods.net/tmodels/SimpleStockQuote.wsdl
        </overviewURL>
    </overviewDoc>
    <categoryBag>
        <keyedReference
            tModelKey="uuid:c1acf26d-9672-4404-9d70-39b756e62ab4"
            keyName="uddi-org:types" keyValue="wsdlSpec" />
    </categoryBag>
</tModel>
```

The overview document provides the pointer to the external specification. In this record, XMethods has followed the best practice of specifying the SOAP interface using WSDL, and has provided a pointer to the actual WSDL file. You need not always specify a WSDL file; you can, for example, specify a generic web page with detailed instructions on interfacing with the service.

 The terms tModel and *service type* are frequently used interchangeably. For example, the Microsoft UDDI site enables one to "search service type by name." This is equivalent to searching tModels by name.

tModels are vitally important because they enable you to identify the technical specifications implemented. More importantly, if two companies reference the same tModel, you can be assured that both companies implement the same specification.

As a final note, it is important to mention that tModels are not reserved for technical specifications of web services. In fact, tModels are used whenever it is necessary to point to *any* external specification. For example, all the previously described business identifiers and classifications have been registered as tModels. Specifically, the D&B D-U-N-S® Number references an external standard created by Dun & Bradstreet and has therefore been registered as a unique tModel (uuid:8609C81E-EE1F-4D5A-B202-3EB13AD01823).

tModels can also reference other tModels. For example, the XMethods tModel references the tModel for uddi-org:types. The types tModel provides a mechanism to categorize specifications; in our case, XMethods has identified the wsdlSpec category.

Searching UDDI

With a firm grasp of the UDDI data model, we now turn to the mechanics of searching the UDDI Business Registry. Most users who are new to UDDI are likely to begin with the web-based UDDI interface. The following section therefore traces a sample search on the Microsoft UDDI Operator site. We'll then retrace the same search via the programmatic UDDI API.

Web-Based Searching

There are three options for searching UDDI:

- Internet Explorer now supports UDDI name resolution via the Real Names Keyword System. Just type "uddi" in the Internet Explorer address bar, followed by the name of the target company. For example, type "uddi ariba".
- You may also go directly to the Microsoft UDDI site at *http://uddi. microsoft.com*.
- Or you can go directly to the IBM UDDI site at *http://www-3.ibm.com/ services/uddi/*.

A sample screenshot of the Microsoft UDDI site is displayed in Figure 7-2. The Search box in the upper left enables you to search by business name.

To explore each of the core UDDI data types, let us consider a common search path. We'll begin by searching for a specific business, selecting a business service, drilling down to a binding template, and finally retrieving the tModel technical specification. The search path is summarized as follows:

```
BusinessEntity
    →  BusinessService
      →  BindingTemplate
        →  tModel record
```

To begin, type "XMethods" in the Search box. A list of matching results is displayed in Figure 7-3.

Figure 7-2. The Microsoft UDDI home page; note the Search box in the upper left corner

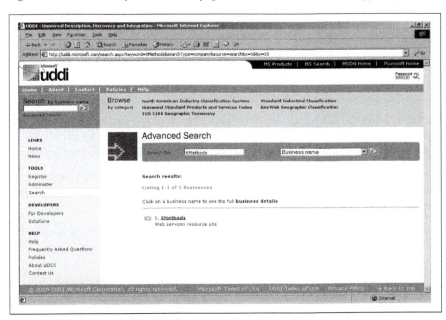

Figure 7-3. Searching for XMethods

When you click on the XMethods link, the complete XMethods businessEntity record is displayed, as shown in Figure 7-4.

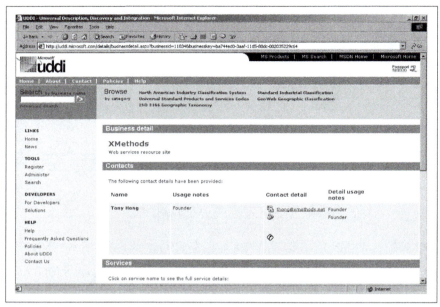

Figure 7-4. The XMethods businessEntity record

If you scroll down the page, you will see a complete listing of all services offered by XMethods. Click the link for XMethods Delayed Stock Quotes. Figure 7-5 displays the full businessService record.

Figure 7-5 displays a single bindingTemplate, and we can see the URL for accessing the Stock Quote Service. If you click the Details link under Bindings, Figure 7-6 will display additional details regarding the bindingTemplate.

Under Specification signature, we can see that the binding references a tModel named XMethods Simple Stock Quote. Click on the tModel record, and the results are displayed in Figure 7-7.

From Figure 7-7, you can now retrieve the XMethods WSDL specification file.

As an alternative to the Microsoft UDDI browser, try the UDDI browser available at Soapclient.com (*http://www. soapclient.com/uddisearch.html*). This service enables you to search the Microsoft and IBM sites and to intuitively drill all the way down to the tModel record.

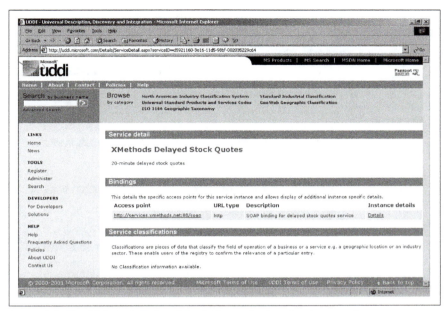

Figure 7-5. The XMethods Delayed Stock Quotes businessService record

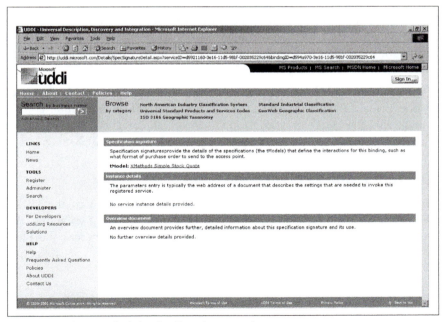

Figure 7-6. The XMethods bindingTemplate record

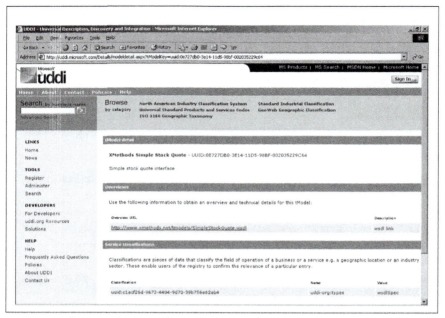

Figure 7-7. The "XMethods Simple Stock Quote" tModel record

It is important to note that the Microsoft Advanced Search enables you to search by multiple criteria, including NAICS code, UNSPSC code, or ISO 3166 country code. For example, Figure 7-8 shows a sample search for the NAICS code for software publishers.

If you are curious to browse the UDDI registry from a different perspective, try the Visual UDDI Map provided by Antarcti.ca (*http://uddi.antarcti.ca*). The visual map enables you to drill down by category. For example, Figure 7-9 and Figure 7-10 demonstrate drilling down by NAICS code.

The UDDI Inquiry API

The UDDI API is a SOAP-based protocol for interfacing with the UDDI Business Registry. Very broadly, the API is divided into two parts: the Inquiry API provides search and retrieval functionality, whereas the Publisher API provides insert and update functionality.

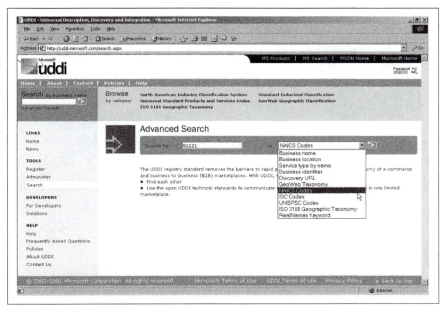

Figure 7-8. Advanced search: searching by NAICS code

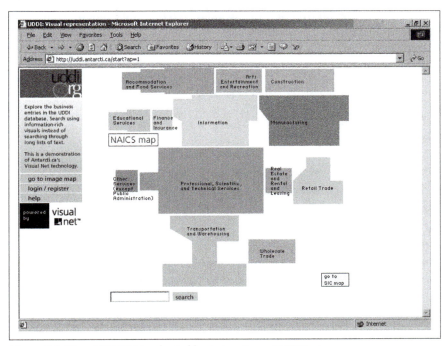

Figure 7-9. Visual UDDI Map hosted by Antarcti.ca—NAICS view

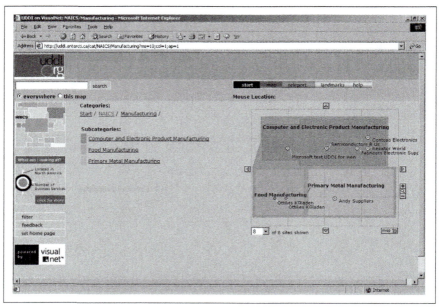

Figure 7-10. Visual UDDI Map hosted by Antarcti.ca—NAICS Manufacturing view

Table 7-7 provides an overview of the main UDDI inquiry functions. Inquiry functions are further subdivided into two groups: *find_xxx* functions provide general search functionality, whereas *get_xxx* functions retrieve full records based on unique key values.

Table 7-7. Main functions of the UDDI Inquiry API

Function name	Description
find_xxx Functions	
find_binding	Searches for bindings associated with a specified service
find_business	Searches for businesses that match the specified criteria
find_service	Searches for services associated with a specified business
find_tModel	Searches for tModels that match the specified criteria
get_xxx Functions	
get_bindingDetail	Retrieves a complete bindingTemplate record
get_businessDetail	Retrieves a complete businessEntity record
get_serviceDetail	Retrieves a complete businessService record
get_tModelDetail	Retrieves a complete tModel record

Inquiry interfaces are provided at the following URLs:

- Microsoft: *http://uddi.microsoft.com/inquire*
- IBM: *http://www-3.ibm.com/services/uddi/inquiryapi*

To send inquiry functions, you can send a SOAP request directly to either of these URLs. Alternatively, you can try one of the UDDI implementations described later in this chapter.

To learn the mechanics of the UDDI API, the simplest option is to set up a web-based interface for submitting UDDI queries directly. To facilitate this, I have set up a UDDI test bed at *http://ecerami.com/uddi/*. Figure 7-11 provides a screenshot of this test bed. You can enter any UDDI function in the text box on the right. When you click Submit, your query is routed to the Microsoft site, and the XML results are displayed. If you do not want to type the full query, you can select one of the links for a predefined query. Predefined queries are available for each of the query functions that were described earlier in Table 7-7.

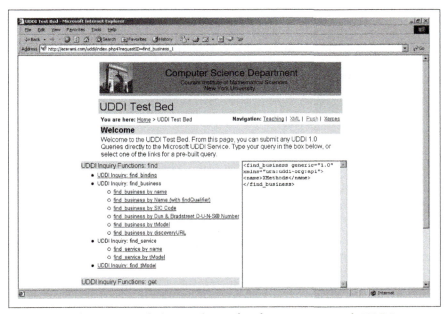

Figure 7-11. The UDDI test bed: a simple interface for trying out sample UDDI queries

Given the table of query functions, let's try to retrace the search path described in the web-based searching interface shown in Figure 7-11. For each of the following examples, we have included a sample request and response. To keep the examples more concise, we have also stripped out the SOAP-specific details.

The find_business function

Let's begin with the *find_business* function. The complete API specification for this and all other inquiry functions is provided in Chapter 8. Here is a sample *find_business* query to search for XMethods:

```
<find_business generic="1.0" xmlns="urn:uddi-org:api">
    <name>XMethods</name>
</find_business>
```

Note that the request specifies UDDI Version 1.0, as indicated by the generic attribute. Within the *find_business* function, we specify a name element, set to the value XMethods. By default, UDDI will ignore case, and perform a strict left-to-right lexical search. Use the % character to specify wildcard options; for example, %data% will find all companies containing the word "data".

Microsoft returns the following response:

```
<businessList generic="1.0" operator="Microsoft Corporation"
    truncated="false" xmlns="urn:uddi-org:api">
    <businessInfos>
        <businessInfo businessKey="ba744ed0-3aaf-11d5-80dc-002035229c64">
            <name>XMethods</name>
            <description xml:lang="en">Web services resource site</description>
            <serviceInfos>
                <serviceInfo
                    serviceKey="d5b180a0-4342-11d5-bd6c-002035229c64"
                    businessKey="ba744ed0-3aaf-11d5-80dc-002035229c64">
                    <name>XMethods Barnes and Noble Quote</name>
                </serviceInfo>
                <serviceInfo
                    serviceKey="ed85f000-4345-11d5-bd6c-002035229c64"
                    businessKey="ba744ed0-3aaf-11d5-80dc-002035229c64">
                    <name>XMethods Pacific Bell SMS Service</name>
                </serviceInfo>
                <serviceInfo
                    serviceKey="d5921160-3e16-11d5-98bf-002035229c64"
                    businessKey="ba744ed0-3aaf-11d5-80dc-002035229c64">
                    <name>XMethods Delayed Stock Quotes</name>
                </serviceInfo>
                <serviceInfo
                    serviceKey="618167a0-3e64-11d5-98bf-002035229c64"
                    businessKey="ba744ed0-3aaf-11d5-80dc-002035229c64">
                    <name>XMethods Currency Exchange Rates</name>
                </serviceInfo>
            </serviceInfos>
        </businessInfo>
    </businessInfos>
</businessList>
```

The response includes a root businessList element, and one businessInfo element for each matching company. If the UDDI operator returns only a partial list of matching results, the businessList element's truncated attribute will be set to true. If no matches are found, a businessList element with zero sub-elements is returned. In our case, Microsoft has identified one match for XMethods and has indicated its unique businessKey.

The get_businessDetail function

Having obtained the unique businessKey, we can query Microsoft again for the complete businessEntity record. This is accomplished via the *get_businessDetail* function:

```
<get_businessDetail generic="1.0" xmlns="urn:uddi-org:api">
    <businessKey>ba744ed0-3aaf-11d5-80dc-002035229c64</businessKey>
</get_businessDetail>
```

This method retrieves the complete businessEntity record for each specified businessKey. (You can specify multiple businessKeys, if you like.)

Microsoft responds as follows:

```
<businessDetail generic="1.0" operator="Microsoft Corporation"
    truncated="false" xmlns="urn:uddi-org:api">
    <businessEntity
        businessKey="ba744ed0-3aaf-11d5-80dc-002035229c64"
        operator="www.ibm.com/services/uddi" authorizedName="0100001QS1">
        <discoveryURLs>
            <discoveryURL useType="businessEntity">
                http://www.ibm.com/services/uddi/uddiget?
                businessKey=BA744ED0-3AAF-11D5-80DC-002035229C64
            </discoveryURL>
        </discoveryURLs>
        <name>XMethods</name>
        <description xml:lang="en">Web services resource site</description>
        <contacts>
            <contact useType="Founder">
                <description xml:lang="en" />
                <personName>Tony Hong</personName>
                <phone useType="Founder" />
                <email useType="Founder">thong@xmethods.net</email>
                <address>
                    <addressLine />
                    <addressLine />
                    <addressLine />
                    <addressLine />
                    <addressLine />
                </address>
            </contact>
        </contacts>
```

```
      <businessServices>
         [... Information about Business Services goes here...]
      </businessServices>
   </businessEntity>
</businessDetail>
```

The response includes a root businessDetail element, and one businessEntity element for each matching business. If no matches are found, an E_invalidKeyPassed error is returned. (Error handling will be discussed shortly.)

The find_service function

Given a businessKey, one can also query for all of its associated services. This is accomplished via the *find_service* function:

```
<find_service generic="1.0" xmlns="urn:uddi-org:api"
   businessKey="ba744ed0-3aaf-11d5-80dc-002035229c64">
</find_service>
```

Microsoft responds as follows:

```
<serviceList generic="1.0" operator="Microsoft Corporation"
   truncated="false" xmlns="urn:uddi-org:api">
   <serviceInfos>
      <serviceInfo
         serviceKey="618167a0-3e64-11d5-98bf-002035229c64"
         businessKey="ba744ed0-3aaf-11d5-80dc-002035229c64">
         <name>XMethods Currency Exchange Rates</name>
      </serviceInfo>
      <serviceInfo
         serviceKey="d5921160-3e16-11d5-98bf-002035229c64"
         businessKey="ba744ed0-3aaf-11d5-80dc-002035229c64">
         <name>XMethods Delayed Stock Quotes</name>
      </serviceInfo>
      <serviceInfo
         serviceKey="ed85f000-4345-11d5-bd6c-002035229c64"
         businessKey="ba744ed0-3aaf-11d5-80dc-002035229c64">
         <name>XMethods Pacific Bell SMS Service</name>
      </serviceInfo>
      <serviceInfo
         serviceKey="d5b180a0-4342-11d5-bd6c-002035229c64"
         businessKey="ba744ed0-3aaf-11d5-80dc-002035229c64">
         <name>XMethods Barnes and Noble Quote</name>
      </serviceInfo>
   </serviceInfos>
</serviceList>
```

The response includes a root serviceList element, and one serviceInfo element for each matching company. If no matches are found, a serviceList element with zero subelements is returned.

If you want to narrow your search, you can specify an optional name element. For example, the following query searches for all XMethods services containing the word "Quote".

```
<find_service generic="1.0" xmlns="urn:uddi-org:api"
    businessKey="ba744ed0-3aaf-11d5-80dc-002035229c64">
    <name>%Quote%</name>
</find_service>
```

The get_serviceDetail function

Given a unique serviceKey, one can retrieve the complete businessService record. This is accomplished via the *get_serviceDetail* function. For example, the following query retrieves the XMethods Delayed Stock Quotes Service:

```
<get_serviceDetail generic="1.0" xmlns="urn:uddi-org:api">
    <serviceKey>d5921160-3e16-11d5-98bf-002035229c64</serviceKey>
</get_serviceDetail>
```

Microsoft responds as follows:

```
<serviceDetail generic="1.0" operator="Microsoft Corporation"
    truncated="false" xmlns="urn:uddi-org:api">
    <businessService
        serviceKey="d5921160-3e16-11d5-98bf-002035229c64"
        businessKey="ba744ed0-3aaf-11d5-80dc-002035229c64">
        <name>XMethods Delayed Stock Quotes</name>
        <description xml:lang="en">
            20-minute delayed stock quotes
        </description>
        <bindingTemplates>
            <bindingTemplate
                serviceKey="d5921160-3e16-11d5-98bf-002035229c64"
                bindingKey="d594a970-3e16-11d5-98bf-002035229c64">
                <description xml:lang="en">
                    SOAP binding for delayed stock quotes service
                </description>
                <accessPoint URLType="http">
                    http://services.xmethods.net:80/soap
                </accessPoint>
                <tModelInstanceDetails>
                    <tModelInstanceInfo
                        tModelKey="uuid:0e727db0-3e14-11d5-98bf-002035229c64" />
                </tModelInstanceDetails>
            </bindingTemplate>
        </bindingTemplates>
    </businessService>
</serviceDetail>
```

The response includes a root serviceDetail element and one businessService element for each matching service. If no matches are found, an E_invalidKeyPassed error is returned.

The get_bindingDetail function

You may have noticed that the *get_serviceDetail* function returns complete details regarding all bindingTemplates. (See the example response in the previous section.) If you only want binding details, you can use the *get_bindingDetail* function. For example, the following query retrieves the SOAP binding for the XMethods Stock Quote service:

```
<get_bindingDetail generic="1.0" xmlns="urn:uddi-org:api">
    <bindingKey>d594a970-3e16-11d5-98bf-002035229c64</bindingKey>
</get_bindingDetail>
```

Here, you can specify one or more unique bindingKey values. Microsoft returns the full bindingTemplate record:

```
<bindingDetail generic="1.0" operator="Microsoft Corporation"
    truncated="false" xmlns="urn:uddi-org:api">
    <bindingTemplate
        serviceKey="d5921160-3e16-11d5-98bf-002035229c64"
        bindingKey="d594a970-3e16-11d5-98bf-002035229c64">
        <description xml:lang="en">
            SOAP binding for delayed stock quotes service
        </description>
        <accessPoint URLType="http">
            http://services.xmethods.net:80/soap
        </accessPoint>
        <tModelInstanceDetails>
            <tModelInstanceInfo
                tModelKey="uuid:0e727db0-3e14-11d5-98bf-002035229c64" />
        </tModelInstanceDetails>
    </bindingTemplate>
</bindingDetail>
```

Querying for a live binding via a programmatic API represents one of the potential strengths of UDDI. For example, consider a UDDI-aware software application that attempts to connect to a web service. If access fails, the software can query UDDI for fresh binding information and attempt to reconnect at a new access point. This may be particularly useful for disaster recovery or connecting to backup systems.

The get_tModelDetail function

Finally, given a tModelKey, one can retrieve the full tModel record. This is accomplished via the *get_tModelDetail* function. For example, the following query retrieves the tModel record referenced by the XMethods SOAP bindingTemplate:

```
<get_tModelDetail generic="1.0" xmlns="urn:uddi-org:api">
    <tModelKey>uuid:0e727db0-3e14-11d5-98bf-002035229c64</tModelKey>
</get_tModelDetail>
```

Microsoft returns the following response:

```
<tModelDetail generic="1.0" operator="Microsoft Corporation"
    truncated="false" xmlns="urn:uddi-org:api">
    <tModel
        tModelKey="uuid:0e727db0-3e14-11d5-98bf-002035229c64"
        operator="www.ibm.com/services/uddi" authorizedName="0100001QS1">
        <name>XMethods Simple Stock Quote</name>
        <description xml:lang="en">Simple stock quote interface</description>
        <overviewDoc>
            <description xml:lang="en">wsdl link</description>
            <overviewURL>
                http://www.xmethods.net/tmodels/SimpleStockQuote.wsdl
            </overviewURL>
        </overviewDoc>
        <categoryBag>
            <keyedReference
                tModelKey="uuid:c1acf26d-9672-4404-9d70-39b756e62ab4"
                keyName="uddi-org:types" keyValue="wsdlSpec" />
        </categoryBag>
    </tModel>
</tModelDetail>
```

The response includes a root tModelDetail element, and one tModel element for each matching tModel. If no matches are found, an E_invalidKeyPassed error is returned.

Error handling

In the event of an error, the UDDI operator will return a *disposition report*. The disposition report includes specific details on the cause of the error. For example, the following query is invalid because it references an illegal company element, instead of the expected name element:

```
<find_business generic="1.0" xmlns="urn:uddi-org:api">
    <company>XMethods</company>
</find_business>
```

Microsoft responds by returning a full disposition report:

```
<?xml version="1.0" encoding="utf-8"?>
<soap:Envelope xmlns:soap="http://schemas.xmlsoap.org/soap/envelope/">
   <soap:Body>
      <soap:Fault>
         <faultcode>soap:Client</faultcode>
         <faultstring>System.Web.Services.Protocols.SoapException ---&gt;
         System.Xml.Schema.XmlSchemaException: Element 'urn:uddi-org:api:
         find_business' has invalid content. Expected 'urn:uddi-org:api:
         findQualifiers urn:uddi-org:api:name urn:uddi-org:api:identifierBag
         urn:uddi-org:api:categoryBag urn:uddi-org:api:tModelBag
         urn:uddi-org:api:discoveryURLs'. An error occurred at (4, 2).
         at System.Xml.XmlValidatingReader.InternalValidationCallback
         (Object sender, ValidationEventArgs e)
         [Full Stack Trace here...]
         <detail>
            <dispositionReport
               xmlns:xsi="http://www.w3.org/2001/XMLSchema-instance"
               xmlns:xsd="http://www.w3.org/2001/XMLSchema" generic="1.0"
               operator="Microsoft Corporation" xmlns="urn:uddi-org:api">
               <result errno="10500">
                  <errInfo errCode="E_fatalError">
                     Element 'urn:uddi-org:api:find_business' has
                     invalid content.  Expected 'urn:uddi-org:api:
                     findQualifiers urn:uddi-org:api:name urn:uddi-org:
                     api:identifierBag urn:uddi-org:api:categoryBag
                     urn:uddi-org:api:tModelBag urn:uddi-org:api:
                     discoveryURLs'. An error occurred at (4, 2).
                  </errInfo>
               </result>
            </dispositionReport>
         </detail>
      </soap:Fault>
   </soap:Body>
</soap:Envelope>
```

The UDDI operator uses the SOAP Fault element to return errors, and inserts the disposition report inside the SOAP detail element. This follows the general SOAP error-handling pattern. (See Chapter 3 for details).

Publishing to UDDI

Having covered the details of searching UDDI, the next step is publishing to UDDI. Again, you have the option of using a web-based interface or a programmatic API. Both Microsoft and IBM provide test registries where you can experiment with publishing new data. It is highly recommended that you experiment with these test registries first, prior to publishing data to live servers.

Web-Based Publishing

To access the web-based test registries, use the following URLs:

- Microsoft: *https://test.uddi.microsoft.com*
- IBM: *https://www-3.ibm.com/services/uddi/testregistry*

For the production registries, use the same URLs referenced in the "Searching UDDI" section, earlier in this chapter.

Security and user authentication

All inserts and updates to the UDDI registry require user authentication and must be transported via SSL. According to the UDDI specification, however, each operator site is free to implement its own user authentication scheme. Because of this, each business must select one operator site for all publishing transactions. Data from this site will always propagate to other root nodes, but all updates and inserts must be performed at the originally selected site.

Microsoft provides user authentication via Microsoft Passport. See Figure 7-12 for a sample login screen. To publish UDDI data, you can either register a new Passport account or enter the login and password for an existing Passport account.

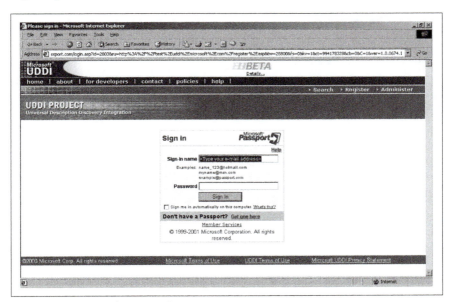

Figure 7-12. Microsoft Passport login screen

Publishing a business entity

In the sample screenshots that follow, we return to the case of Acme Parts, which was discussed earlier in this chapter. To recap, Acme Parts has just released its Acme Parts: Submit Purchase Order Service. The service adheres to RosettaNet PIP3A4, and Acme wants to register its business and its new service within UDDI.

Once you have logged in via Microsoft Passport, you will see the general UDDI administration screen. See Figure 7-13 for a sample screenshot. To add a new business, click the Add a New Business link.

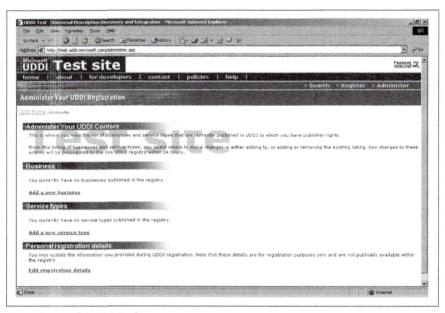

Figure 7-13. The UDDI administration screen

Figure 7-14 shows the initial fields required for publishing a new business entity. Fill in the name and description for Acme Parts and click the Save button.

Figure 7-15 shows the Edit Business page. From the Edit Business page, you can add contact information, business identifiers, and business classifications.

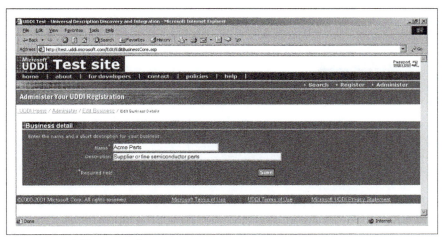

Figure 7-14. Adding a new business

Figure 7-15. The Edit Business page

For example, if you click Add a classification, you can drill down to your specific business classification. See Figure 7-16 for a sample screenshot.

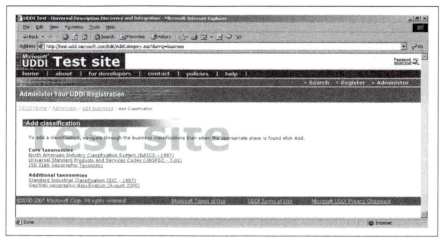

Figure 7-16. Adding a business classification

Microsoft provides drill-down support for the core UDDI taxonomies: NAICS, UNSPSC, and ISO 3166. It also provides support for two additional taxonomies: the Standard Industry Classification (SIC) and the Microsoft GeoWeb geographic classification. Figure 7-17 shows a sample screenshot of the NAICS drill-down functionality.

Figure 7-17. Adding an NAICS code

Once you have added any contacts, identifications, or classifications, make sure to select the Publish button. Your data will not be saved to the registry without this final step.

Publishing a business service

To add a business service, return to the administration home page. You should now see your published business entity. (See Figure 7-18.) To add a service, select Edit business, then click Add a Service.

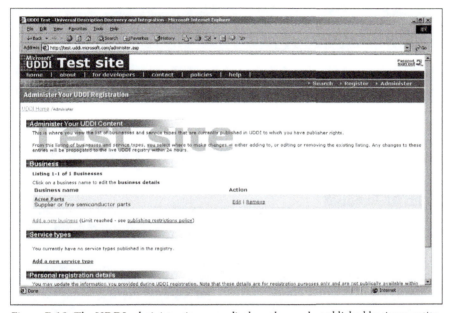

Figure 7-18. The UDDI administration page displays the newly published business entity

Figure 7-19 shows the initial fields required for publishing a new service. Enter the service name and description, and click the Continue button.

Figure 7-20 shows the Edit Service page. From the Edit Service page, click Define new binding.

Figure 7-21 shows the initial fields required to create a new binding. For each binding, you must enter an access point, a URL type (HTTP, HTTPS, FTP, mailto, fax, phone, or other), and an optional description.

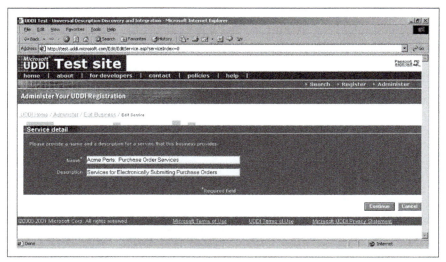

Figure 7-19. Adding a new service

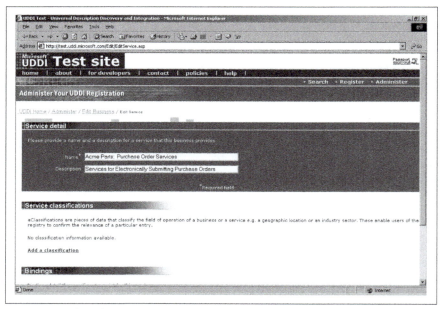

Figure 7-20. The Edit Service page

In the case of Acme Parts, I have entered a fictional URL for a SOAP binding interface. Click the Continue button and the Edit Bindings page will be refreshed with a new section for adding specification signatures. See Figure 7-22 for details.

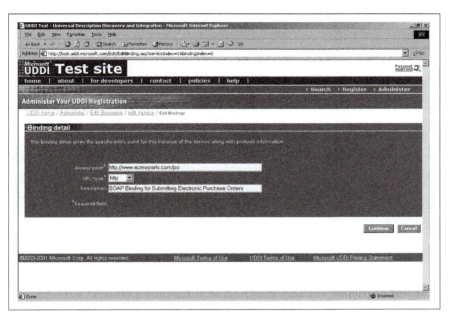

Figure 7-21. The Edit Bindings page

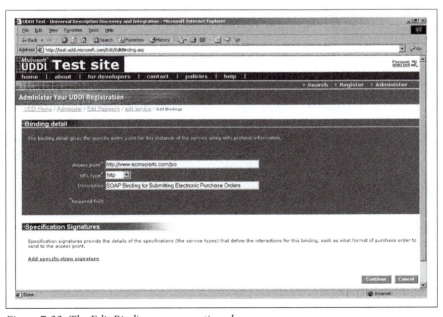

Figure 7-22. The Edit Bindings page, continued

The final step is to add your specification signature. Unfortunately, there is not much consistency in labeling tModel records—on the Microsoft site, the terms service type and specification signature both refer to tModel records. In the case of Acme Parts, we want to reference the RosettaNet PIP3A4. To begin, click the link for Add Specification Signature.

You will be prompted with a Find dialog screen for searching all registered tModel records. See Figure 7-23 for details. Enter the word "RosettaNet" and click Continue. Figure 7-24 shows a list of matching results. .

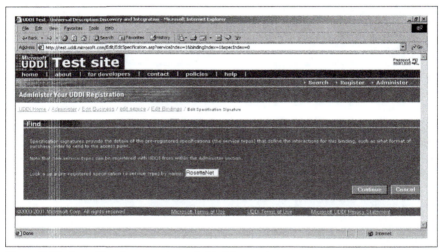

Figure 7-23. Searching for preregistered tModel records

Unfortunately, RosettaNet has not registered all of its PIPs within the test registry. If this were the production registry, you could scroll down and find an exact match for PIP3A4. For now, select the closest match, and click on the first item named RosettaNet.Order.Management. Click Continue. Figure 7-25 shows the Edit Specification Signature page.

All the fields on this page are optional. However, if you wish to add additional details for this tModel record, you may do so here. Then, click the Continue button several times, until you reach the Publish button. Just like when adding a new business record, your record will not be saved until you actually choose to publish it.

Publishing a tModel record

The most difficult aspect of publishing a new service is determining which technical specification it implements. The most useful web services will be those that implement public specifications. For example, your e-commerce

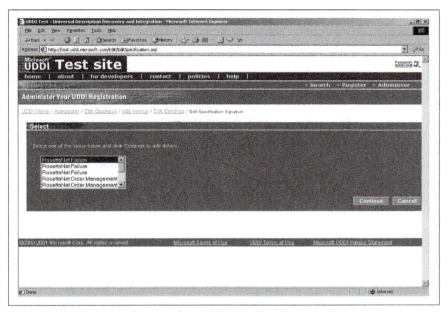

Figure 7-24. tModel search results for "RosettaNet"

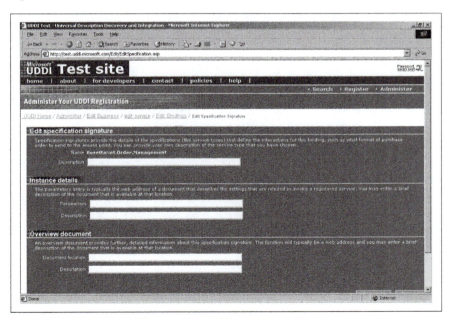

Figure 7-25. The Edit Specification Signature page

service may implement a RosettaNet standard or an OAGIS standard. (See the sidebar "Open Applications Group," later in this chapter.) As web services mature, more and more standards bodies will define interfaces for a diverse set of applications. Perhaps there will one day be standards for financial transactions, weather information, sports updates, headline news distribution, and online auctions.

When building a web service, the first step is to determine if any standards exist for your application and whether it makes sense to implement any of these standards. If no such standards exist or you want to publish your own specification, you will need to register your own tModel record. For example, Acme Parts may offer a Product Availability Service. This specific implementation is not covered by RosettaNet, and Acme Parts has decided to publish a WSDL file describing the interface.

To add a new service type, go back to the main administration page, and select Add a New Service Type. Figure 7-26 shows the required fields.

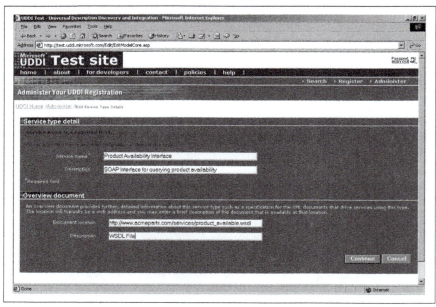

Figure 7-26. Adding a new service type

In the case of Acme Parts, I have added a reference to a sample WSDL file that describes the SOAP binding.

Open Applications Group

The Open Applications Group (OAG) is a nonprofit consortium focused on e-business integration. Much like RosettaNet, OAG has published its own specification, the Open Applications Group Integration Specification (OAGIS). A sampling of OAGIS interfaces includes:

get_catalog
> Enables catalog synchronization between two partners

get_pricelist
> Enables one partner to request a current price list from another partner

get_prodavail
> Enables one partner to query for product availability

sync_exchangerate
> Enables two partners to synchronize foreign exchange rates

Like RosettaNet, the OAGIS specification has been registered with UDDI. Additional information is available at *http://www.openapplications.org.*

The UDDI Publishing API

Publishing to UDDI usually takes place via a web-based interface. Nonetheless, there are certain instances when you may want direct access to the publishing API. For example, you may be building web services software that automatically registers new web services, or you may need an automatic method of updating binding access URLs, in the event of disaster recovery.

Publishing requests must be sent to a secure URL that is distinct from the Inquiry API URL. To publish to the test registries, use the following URLs:

- Microsoft: *https://test.uddi.microsoft.com/publish*
- IBM: *https://www.ibm.com/services/uddi/testregistry/protect/publish*

To publish to the production registries, use these URLs:

- Microsoft: *https://uddi.microsoft.com/publish*
- IBM: *https://www.ibm.com/services/uddi/protect/publish*

Table 7-8 provides an overview of the main UDDI publishing functions. The publishing API is divided into three main subsections: authenticating users, saving data, and deleting data. In the sections that follow, we will see examples from each of the three subsections.

Table 7-8. Main functions of the UDDI publishing API

Function name	Description
Authentication functions	
get_authToken	Requests an authentication token from the operator site. An authentication token is required for all subsequent *save_xxx* and *delete_xxx* functions.
discard_authToken	Requests that the specified authentication token be discarded and invalidated.
save_xxx functions	
save_binding	Inserts or updates a bindingTemplate record.
save_business	Inserts or updates a businessEntity record.
save_service	Inserts or updates a businessService record.
save_tModel	Inserts or updates a tModel record.
delete_xxx functions	
delete_binding	Deletes the bindingTemplate record specified by the bindingKey.
delete_business	Deletes the businessEntity record specified by the businessKey.
delete_service	Deletes the businessService record specified by the serviceKey.
delete_tModel	Hides the tModel record specified by the tModelKey. A hidden tModel record can still be referenced by another UDDI record (e.g., a bindingTemplate record), but it will be excluded from search results generated by the *find_tModel* function. tModel records cannot be deleted.

Authenticating users

Publishing UDDI data can only be performed by authorized users. As indicated previously, each operator site is free to implement its own user authentication scheme.

When sending save or delete requests, the UDDI API requires that the request include an authentication token. To obtain a token, you must first make a *get_authToken* request. The function requires that you specify a user ID and password. For example, the following request attempts to authenticate a user at Acme Parts:

```
<get_authToken generic="1.0" xmlns="urn:uddi-org:api"
    userID="boss@acmeparts.com" cred="theBoss ">
</get_authToken>
```

If the user is not recognized, the operator site will return an E_unknownUser error. Otherwise, the operator site will return an authentication token. For example, Microsoft returns the following response:

```
<authToken generic="1.0" xmlns="urn:uddi-org:api"
operator="http://uddi.microsoft.com">
    <authInfo>1BAAAAAAHmykB2ylo*pV*pnrFoS4a*IblrgZSlpa
    jYC853wq9HIfsbaozLxYpG2Bo;1AAAAAAAAKZi8QkOJ8BJfnMc
    *HeQCtOTHvu3TDkPEogcauDpvtHyxQGczEEOcj9bdl7C48RRyrK
    H7ReaF8OHivQEMltSEhgD8RNhmtOrHFdZoWkANFe*uSLmab4VvA
    FKLHFouvDh3MJ*9VK9YMLl4dg$$
    </authInfo>
</authToken>
```

All subsequent calls to save or delete data will require the use of this token. When you have completed your publishing requests, you have the option of discarding the token by calling the *discard_authToken* function. For example:

```
<discard_authToken generic="1.0" xmlns="urn:uddi-org:api">
    <authInfo>1BAAAAAAHmykB2ylo*pV*pnrFoS4a*IblrgZSlpa
    jYC853wq9HIfsbaozLxYpG2Bo;1AAAAAAAAKZi8QkOJ8BJfnMc
    *HeQCtOTHvu3TDkPEogcauDpvtHyxQGczEEOcj9bdl7C48RRyrK
    H7ReaF8OHivQEMltSEhgD8RNhmtOrHFdZoWkANFe*uSLmab4VvA
    FKLHFouvDh3MJ*9VK9YMLl4dg$$
    </authInfo>
</discard_authToken>
```

If successful, the operator site will return an E_success status code. For example:

```
<dispositionReport generic="1.0"
    operator="Microsoft Corporation" xmlns="urn:uddi-org:api">
    <result errno="0">
        <errInfo errCode="E_success"></errInfo>
    </result>
</dispositionReport>
```

If you do decide to discard an authorization token, you can always get a new one by calling the *get_authToken* function again.

Saving UDDI data

The publishing API enables you to insert new data or update existing data. For example, let's say that we have already registered our business but want to update the business description. To save general business entity data, use the *save_business* function. For example:

```
<save_business generic="1.0" xmlns="urn:uddi-org:api">
    <authInfo>1BAAAAAAHmykB2ylo*pV*pnrFoS4a*IblrgZSlpa
    jYC853wq9HIfsbaozLxYpG2Bo;1AAAAAAAAKZi8QkOJ8BJfnMc
    *HeQCtOTHvu3TDkPEogcauDpvtHyxQGczEEOcj9bdl7C48RRyrK
    H7ReaF8OHivQEMltSEhgD8RNhmtOrHFdZoWkANFe*uSLmab4VvA
    FKLHFouvDh3MJ*9VK9YMLl4dg$$
    </authInfo>
```

```
<businessEntity
    businessKey="03754729-3D3C-48E0-854A-1C1FD576CA5B">
    <name>Acme Parts</name>
    <description xml:lang="en">
        Supplier of fine semiconductor parts and Integrated Circuits
    </description>
</businessEntity>
</save_business>
```

In this example, note the use of the authorization token. Also note the updated business description. In general, the value of the unique key—in this case, the businessKey—determines whether this is an update or an insert. If the unique key is specified as an empty string (e.g., businessKey=""), this is an insert for a new record. Otherwise, this is a request to update the record indicated by the unique key.

In response, the UDDI operator will echo back the newly saved data. For example, Microsoft returns the following:

```
<businessDetail generic="1.0" operator="Microsoft Corporation"
truncated="false" xmlns="urn:uddi-org:api">
    <businessEntity
        authorizedName="Ethan Cerami"
        businessKey="03754729-3D3C-48E0-854A-1C1FD576CA5B"
        operator="Microsoft Corporation">
        <discoveryURLs>
            <discoveryURL useType="businessEntity">
                http://test.uddi.microsoft.com/discovery?businessKey=0375
                4729-3D3C-48E0-854A-1C1FD576CA5B
            </discoveryURL>
        </discoveryURLs>
        <name>Acme Parts</name>
        <description xml:lang="en">
            Supplier of fine semiconductor parts and Integrated Circuits
        </description>
    </businessEntity>
</businessDetail>
```

To insert an entirely new record, consider using the *save_tModel* function:

```
<save_tModel generic="1.0" xmlns="urn:uddi-org:api">
    <authInfo>1BAAAAAAHmykB2ylo*pV*pnrFoS4a*IblrgZSlpa
jYC853wq9HIfsbaozLxYpG2Bo;1AAAAAAAAKZi8QkOJ8BJfnMc
*HeQCtOTHvu3TDkPEogcauDpvtHyxQGczEEOcj9bdl7C48RRyrK
H7ReaF8OHivQEMltSEhgD8RNhmtOrHFdZoWkANFe*uSLmab4VvA
FKLHFouvDh3MJ*9VK9YML14dg$$
    </authInfo>
    <tModel tModelKey="">
        <name>Price Query Interface</name>
        <description xml:lang="en">
            SOAP Interface for querying product prices
        </description>
        <overviewDoc>
```

```
        <description xml:lang="en">
            WSDL File
        </description>
        <overviewURL>
            http://www.acmeparts.com/services/query_price.wsdl
        </overviewURL>
    </overviewDoc>
  </tModel>
</save_tModel>
```

Here, we have registered a new tModel record for the Acme Price Query interface. Because the tModelKey is set to the empty string, the UDDI operator considers this an insert. Microsoft returns the following response:

```
<tModelDetail generic="1.0" operator="Microsoft Corporation"
truncated="false" xmlns="urn:uddi-org:api">
    <tModel authorizedName="Ethan Cerami" operator="Microsoft Corporation"
    tModelKey="uuid:01EBBD03-324D-4D7C-97EA-79B9C396D6EA">
        <name>Price Query Interface</name>
        <description xml:lang="en">
            SOAP Interface for querying product prices
        </description>
        <overviewDoc>
            <description xml:lang="en">WSDL File</description>
            <overviewURL>
                http://www.acmeparts.com/services/query_price.wsdl
            </overviewURL>
        </overviewDoc>
    </tModel>
</tModelDetail>
```

Note that the tModel record has now been assigned its own unique ID.

Deleting/hiding UDDI data

Deleting data is generally very straightforward and only requires that you specify the unique key value. For example, the following request hides the newly created tModel record:

```
<delete_tModel generic="1.0" xmlns="urn:uddi-org:api">
    <authInfo>1BAAAAAAHmykB2ylo*pV*pnrFoS4a*IblrgZSlpa
jYC853wq9HIfsbaozLxYpG2Bo;1AAAAAAAAKZi8QkOJ8BJfnMc
*HeQCtOTHvu3TDkPEogcauDpvtHyxQGczEEOcj9bdl7C48RRyrK
H7ReaF8OHivQEMltSEhgD8RNhmtOrHFdZoWkANFe*uSLmab4VvA
FKLHFouvDh3MJ*9VK9YMLl4dg$$</authInfo>
    <tModelKey>uuid:01EBBD03-324D-4D7C-97EA-79B9C396D6EA"</tModelKey>
</delete_tModel>
```

A hidden tModel record can still be referenced by another UDDI record (e.g., a bindingTemplate record), but it will be excluded from search results generated by the *find_tModel* function. Therefore, unlike businessEntity, businessService, or bindingTemplate records, tModel records cannot actually be deleted.

UDDI Implementations

A number of UDDI implementations are currently available. These implementations make it easier to search or publish UDDI data, without getting mired in the complexities of the UDDI API. Here is a brief synopsis of the main UDDI implementations available.

Java

There are two UDDI implementations for Java.

UDDI4J (UDDI for Java) (http://oss.software.ibm.com/developerworks/projects/uddi4j/)
    UDDI4J was originally created by IBM. In January 2001, IBM turned over the code to its own open source site. Details are available in Chapter 9.

jUDDI (http://www.juddi.org/)
    jUDDI is an open source Java implementation of a UDDI registry and a toolkit for accessing UDDI services. Initially developed by Bowstreet, Inc., jUDDI is now hosted on the SourceForge open source development site.

Microsoft COM

There is one UDDI implementation for Microsoft.com.

UDDI Software Development Kit (SDK) (http://uddi.microsoft.com/developer/)
    The Microsoft UDDI Software Development Kit (SDK) provides a COM-based API for accessing UDDI services.

Perl

There is one UDDI implementation for Perl.

SOAP::Lite (http://www.soaplite.com)
    SOAP::Lite provides a basic UDDI client for inquiry and publishing.

Web Resources

For additional details regarding UDDI, the following web resources are extremely useful.

http://www.uddi.org/
> The official UDDI site. The site includes a useful UDDI technical white paper, a list of participating UDDI organizations, press releases, a complete archive of all technical specifications, and the official UDDI FAQ.

http://groups.yahoo.com/group/uddi-technical
> A UDDI technical newsgroup. The newsgroup provides an active forum for UDDI technical issues and the UDDI API. For the general UDDI newsgroup, go to *http://groups.yahoo.com/group/uddi-general*.

http://www.uddicentral.com
> A web site devoted to UDDI information and news.

CHAPTER 8

UDDI Inquiry API: Quick Reference

This chapter provides a quick reference to the UDDI Inquiry API. The Inquiry API enables you to search existing data or retrieve specific records from a UDDI operator site. For an overview of the API and the UDDI Data Model, refer to Chapter 7.

A snapshot of each UDDI inquiry function is provided in Table 8-1. Later in this chapter, we examine the functions in detail, providing the following information about each function:

- A brief description
- The language syntax for UDDI 1.0 and 2.0
- Descriptions of all function arguments
- A list of possible error values

When possible, we also include one or more UDDI 1.0 examples for each function. Each of the examples was verified against the Microsoft UDDI Operator site. The chapter concludes with a brief overview of the UDDI find qualifiers, which enable more precise search criteria.

Table 8-1. The UDDI Inquiry API

Inquiry API	Description	UDDI version
find_binding	Searches for template bindings associated with a specified service	1.0, 2.0
find_business	Searches for businesses that match the specified criteria	1.0, 2.0
find_relatedBusinesses	Discovers businesses that have been related via the *uddi-org: relationships* model	2.0
find_service	Searches for services associated with a specified business	1.0, 2.0
find_tModel	Searches for tModel records that match the specified criteria	1.0, 2.0
get_bindingDetail	Retrieves the complete bindingTemplate for each specified bindingKey	1.0, 2.0

Table 8-1. The UDDI Inquiry API (continued)

Inquiry API	Description	UDDI version
get_businessDetail	Retrieves the complete businessEntity for each specified businessKey	1.0, 2.0
get_businessDetailExt	Retrieves the extended businessEntity for each specified businessKey	1.0, 2.0
get_serviceDetail	Retrieves the businessService record for each specified serviceKey	1.0, 2.0
get_tModelDetail	Retrieves the tModel record for each specified tModelKey	1.0, 2.0

The UDDI Inquiry API

find_bindings

The *find_bindings* function searches for template binding records associated with a specified service and the specified tModel record(s). The response includes a root bindingDetail element and one bindingTemplate element for each matching binding. If the UDDI operator returns only a partial list of matching results, the bindingDetail element's truncated attribute will be set to true. If no matches are found, a bindingDetail element with zero subelements is returned.

Version: 1.0 and 2.0

1.0 syntax:

```
<find_binding serviceKey="uuid_key" generic="1.0"
    [maxRows="nn"] xmlns="urn:uddi-org:api">
    [<findQualifiers/>]
    <tModelBag/>
</find_binding>
```

2.0 syntax:

```
<find_binding serviceKey="uuid_key" [maxRows="nn"] generic="2.0"
    xmlns="urn:uddi-org:api_v2">
    [<findQualifiers/>]
    <tModelBag/>
</find_binding>
```

Arguments:

serviceKey

Required uuid_key attribute specifying the associated businessService.

maxRows

Optional attribute to specify the maximum number of rows to be returned; if maxRows is exceeded, the bindingDetail element's truncated attribute will be set to true.

findQualifiers
    Optional element to override the default search functionality. For additional details, see the "Find Qualifiers" section, later in this chapter.

tModelBag
    Required uuid_key element to specify tModel records. If more than one tModel is specified, the search is performed via a logical AND.

Example:

The following UDDI 1.0 example searches for all SOAP bindings associated with the XMethods Delayed Stock Quote Service. The XMethods Stock Quote Service is specified by the serviceKey d5921160-3e16-11d5-98bf-002035229c64, and the WSDL specification for the SOAP interface is referenced by the tModel record uuid:0e727db0-3e14-11d5-98bf-002035229c64.

```
<find_binding serviceKey="d5921160-3e16-11d5-98bf-002035229c64" generic="1.0"
    xmlns="urn:uddi-org:api">
    <tModelBag>
        <tModelKey>
            uuid:0e727db0-3e14-11d5-98bf-002035229c64
        </tModelKey>
    </tModelBag>
</find_binding>
```

Here is a response to the query:

```
<bindingDetail generic="1.0" operator="Microsoft Corporation"
    truncated="false" xmlns="urn:uddi-org:api">
    <bindingTemplate serviceKey="d5921160-3e16-11d5-98bf-002035229c64"
        bindingKey="d594a970-3e16-11d5-98bf-002035229c64">
        <description xml:lang="en">
            SOAP binding for delayed stock quotes service
        </description>
        <accessPoint URLType="http">
            http://services.xmethods.net:80/soap
        </accessPoint>
        <tModelInstanceDetails>
            <tModelInstanceInfo
                tModelKey="uuid:0e727db0-3e14-11d5-98bf-002035229c64" />
        </tModelInstanceDetails>
    </bindingTemplate>
</bindingDetail>
```

Errors:

E_invalidKeyPassed
    An invalid serviceKey attribute was specified.

E_tooManyOptions
    Too many search options were specified (UDDI 1.0 only).

E_unsupported
    The specified findQualifier is not supported.

find_business

The *find_business* function searches for businesses that match the specified criteria. The response includes a root businessList element, and one businessInfo element for each matching company. If the UDDI operator returns only a partial list of matching results, the businessList element's truncated attribute will be set to true. If no matches are found, a businessList element with zero subelements is returned.

Version: 1.0 and 2.0

1.0 syntax:

```
<find_business generic="1.0" [maxRows="nn"]
    xmlns="urn:uddi-org:api">
    [<findQualifiers/>]
    [<name/>]
    [<identifierBag/>]
    [<categoryBag/>]
    [<tModelBag/>]
    [<discoveryURLs>]
</find_business>
```

2.0 syntax:

```
<find_business generic="2.0" [maxRows="nn"]
    xmlns="urn:uddi-org:api_v2">
    [<findQualifiers/>]
    [<name/> [<name/>]...]
    [<discoveryURLs/>]
    [<identifierBag/>]
    [<categoryBag/>]
    [<tModelBag/>]
</find_business>
```

Arguments:

maxRows

Optional attribute to specify the maximum number of rows to be returned; if maxRows is exceeded, the businessList element's truncated attribute will be set to true.

findQualifiers

Optional element to override the default search functionality. For example, the find qualifier exactNameMatch will match exact business names. For details, see the "Find Qualifiers" section, later in this chapter.

name

The full or partial name of the business. UDDI 2.0 enables you to specify up to five business names. The default behavior is to perform an exact left-to-right lexical search. Use % to specify wildcard options; for example, %data% will find all companies containing the word "data".

discoveryURLs

Optional element to search by discovery URLs. If more than one discoveryURL is specified, the search is performed via a logical OR.

identifierBag

Optional element to search by identifier. For example, you can search by Dun & Bradstreet D-U-N-S® Number. If more than one identifier is specified, the search is performed via a logical OR.

categoryBag

Optional element to search by category. For example, you can search by NAICS codes. If more than one category is specified, the search is performed via a logical AND.

tModelBag

Optional element to search by tModel records. If more than one tModel is specified, the search is performed via a logical AND.

Examples:

Here are three example 1.0 queries:

- Search for all businesses beginning with the word "XMethods":

```
<find_business generic="1.0" xmlns="urn:uddi-org:api">
    <name>XMethods</name>
</find_business>
```

- Search for all businesses with the specified Dun & Bradstreet D-U-N-S® number:

```
<find_business generic="1.0" xmlns="urn:uddi-org:api">
    <identifierBag>
    <keyedReference tModelKey="uuid:8609c81e-ee1f-4d5a-b202-3eb13ad01823"
      keyName="dnb-com:D-U-N-S" keyValue="04-693-3052" />
    </identifierBag>
</find_business>
```

- Search for all businesses registered with the NAICS code for Advertising:

```
<find_business generic="1.0" xmlns="urn:uddi-org:api">
    <categoryBag>
        <keyedReference tModelKey="uuid:70a80f61-77bc-4821-a5e2-
            2a406acc35dd"
        keyName="Advertising" keyValue="7310" />
    </categoryBag>
</find_business>
```

Here is a response to the first example query (search for the word "XMethods"):

```
<businessList generic="1.0" operator="Microsoft Corporation"
    truncated="false" xmlns="urn:uddi-org:api">
    <businessInfos>
        <businessInfo businessKey="ba744ed0-3aaf-11d5-80dc-002035229c64">
            <name>XMethods</name>
```

```
    <description xml:lang="en">Web services resource site</description>
    <serviceInfos>
        <serviceInfo serviceKey="d5b180a0-4342-11d5-bd6c-002035229c64"
            businessKey="ba744ed0-3aaf-11d5-80dc-002035229c64">
            <name>XMethods Barnes and Noble Quote</name>
        </serviceInfo>
        <serviceInfo serviceKey="ed85f000-4345-11d5-bd6c-002035229c64"
            businessKey="ba744ed0-3aaf-11d5-80dc-002035229c64">
            <name>XMethods Pacific Bell SMS Service</name>
        </serviceInfo>
        <serviceInfo serviceKey="d5921160-3e16-11d5-98bf-002035229c64"
            businessKey="ba744ed0-3aaf-11d5-80dc-002035229c64">
            <name>XMethods Delayed Stock Quotes</name>
        </serviceInfo>
        <serviceInfo serviceKey="618167a0-3e64-11d5-98bf-002035229c64"
            businessKey="ba744ed0-3aaf-11d5-80dc-002035229c64">
            <name>XMethods Currency Exchange Rates</name>
        </serviceInfo>
    </serviceInfos>
    </businessInfo>
    </businessInfos>
</businessList>
```

Errors:

E_nameTooLong

The business name is too long.

E_unsupported

The specified findQualifier is not supported.

E_tooManyOptions

Too many search options were specified.

find_relatedBusinesses

The *find_relatedBusinesses* function searches for businesses related to the specified businessKey. UDDI 2.0 provides improved support for describing complex organizations. For example, a business can publish business units, departments, or divisions and tie them together under one umbrella. Business relationships are created via the uddi-org:relationships tModel record (uuid:807A2C6A-EE22-470D-ADC7-E0424A337C03). UDDI 2.0 supports three relationship values:

parent-child

Used to indicate a parent-child relationship. For example, a holding company that owns a subsidiary may choose to publish a parent-child relationship.

peer-peer

Used to indicate two peer entities. For example, two divisions within one company may choose to publish a peer-peer relationship.

identity

Used to indicate that two entities represent the same organization.

The *find_relatedBusinesses* function is used to discover businesses that have been related via the uddi-org:relationships model. The response includes a root relatedBusinessesList element. If the UDDI operator returns only a partial list of matching results, the relatedBusinessesList element's truncated attribute will be set to true. If no matches are found, a relatedBusinessesList element with zero subelements is returned.

Version: 2.0

2.0 syntax:

```
<find_relatedBusinesses generic="2.0" xmlns="urn:uddi-org:api_v2">
  [<findQualifiers/>]
  <businessKey/>
  [<keyedReference/>]
</find_relatedBusinesses>
```

Arguments:

findQualifiers

Optional element to override the default search functionality. For additional details, see the "Find Qualifiers" section, later in this chapter.

businessKey

Required uuid_key specifying the businessEntity.

keyedReference

Optional element used to specify a uddi-org:relationship value. A keyedReference requires three attributes: tModelKey, keyName, and keyValue. For example, to retrieve businesses entity records that have a peer-peer relationship with the specified businessKey, use the following keyedReference:

```
<keyedReference
   tModelKey="uuid:807A2C6A-EE22-470D-ADC7-E0424A337C03"
   keyName="uddi-org:relationships"
   keyValue="peer-peer" />
```

Errors:

E_invalidKeyPassed

An invalid businessKey attribute was specified.

E_unsupported

The specified findQualifier is not supported.

find_service

The *find_service* function searches for services associated with a specified business. The response includes a root serviceList element, and one serviceInfo element for each matching company. If the UDDI operator returns only a partial list of matching results, the serviceList element's truncated attribute will be set to true. If no matches are found, a serviceList element with zero subelements is returned.

Version: 1.0 and 2.0

1.0 syntax:

```
<find_service businessKey="uuid_key" generic="1.0" [maxRows="nn"]
    xmlns="urn:uddi-org:api">
    [<findQualifiers/>]
    [<name/>]
    [<categoryBag/>]
    [<tModelBag/>]
</find_service>
```

2.0 syntax:

```
<find_service businessKey="uuid_key" generic="2.0" [maxRows="nn"]
    xmlns="urn:uddi-org:api_v2">
    [<findQualifiers/>]
    [<name/> [<name/>]...]
    [<categoryBag/>]
    [<tModelBag/>]
</find_service>
```

Arguments:

businessKey

Required uuid_key attribute specifying the associated businessEntity.

maxRows

Optional attribute to specify the maximum number of rows to be returned. If maxRows is exceeded, the serviceList element's truncated attribute will be set to true.

findQualifiers

Optional element to override the default search functionality. For example, the find qualifier exactNameMatch will match exact service names. For additional details, see the "Find Qualifiers" section, later in this chapter.

name

> The full or partial name of the service. UDDI 2.0 allows you to specify up to five service names. The default behavior is to perform an exact left-to-right lexical search. Use % to specify wildcard options; for example, %quote% will find all services containing the word "quote".

categoryBag

> Optional element to search by category. If more than one category is specified, the search is performed via a logical AND.

tModelBag

> Optional element to search by tModels. If more than one tModel is specified, the search is performed via a logical AND.

Examples:

Here are two example 1.0 queries:

- Search for all services provided by XMethods:

```
<find_service generic="1.0" xmlns="urn:uddi-org:api"
    businessKey="ba744ed0-3aaf-11d5-80dc-002035229c64">
</find_service>
```

- Search for all services provided by XMethods that contain the word "quote":

```
<find_service generic="1.0" xmlns="urn:uddi-org:api"
    businessKey="ba744ed0-3aaf-11d5-80dc-002035229c64">
    <name>%Quote%</name>
</find_service>
```

Here is a response to the second example query:

```
<serviceList generic="1.0" operator="Microsoft Corporation"
    truncated="false" xmlns="urn:uddi-org:api">
    <serviceInfos>
        <serviceInfo serviceKey="d5921160-3e16-11d5-98bf-002035229c64"
            businessKey="ba744ed0-3aaf-11d5-80dc-002035229c64">
            <name>XMethods Delayed Stock Quotes</name>
        </serviceInfo>
        <serviceInfo serviceKey="d5b180a0-4342-11d5-bd6c-002035229c64"
            businessKey="ba744ed0-3aaf-11d5-80dc-002035229c64">
            <name>XMethods Barnes and Noble Quote</name>
        </serviceInfo>
    </serviceInfos>
</serviceList>
```

Errors:

E_invalidKeyPassed

> An invalid businessKey attribute was specified.

E_nameTooLong

> The service name is too long.

E_tooManyOptions

Too many search options were specified (UDDI 1.0 only).

E_unsupported

The specified findQualifier is not supported.

find_tModel

The *find_tModel* function searches for tModel records that match the specified criteria. The response includes a root tModelList element and one tModelInfo element for each matching company. If the UDDI operator returns only a partial list of matching results, the tModelList element's truncated attribute will be set to true. If no matches are found, a tModelList element with zero subelements is returned.

Version: 1.0 and 2.0

1.0 syntax:

```
<find_tModel generic="1.0" [maxRows="nn"] xmlns="urn:uddi-org:api">
    [<findQualifiers/>]
    [<name/>]
    [<identifierBag/>]
    [<categoryBag/>]
</find_tModel>
```

2.0 syntax:

```
<find_tModel generic="2.0" [maxRows="nn"] xmlns="urn:uddi-org:api_v2">
    [<findQualifiers/>]
    [<name/>]
    [<identifierBag/>]
    [<categoryBag/>]
</find_tModel>
```

Arguments:

maxRows

Optional attribute to specify the maximum number of rows to be returned. If maxRows is exceeded, the tModelList element's truncated attribute will be set to true.

findQualifiers

Optional element to override the default search functionality. For example, the find qualifier exactNameMatch will match exact tModel names. For additional details, see the "Find Qualifiers" section, later in this chapter.

name

> The full or partial name of the `tModel`. The default behavior is to perform an exact left-to-right lexical search. Use % to specify wildcard options; for example, `%shipping%` will find all `tModels` containing the word "shipping".

identifierBag

> Optional element to search by identifier. If more than one identifier is specified, the search is performed via a logical OR.

categoryBag

> Optional element to search by category. If more than one category is specified, the search is performed via a logical AND.

Examples:

Here are two example 1.0 queries:

- Search for all `tModel` records registered with OAGIS:

  ```
  <find_tModel generic="1.0" xmlns="urn:uddi-org:api">
      <name>OAGIS%</name>
  </find_tModel>
  ```

- Search for all `tModel` records that are registered with the RosettaNet specification and that contain the word "Shipment".

  ```
  <find_tModel generic="1.0" xmlns="urn:uddi-org:api">
      <name>RosettaNet%Shipment%</name>
  </find_tModel>
  ```

Here is a response to the second example query:

```
<tModelList generic="1.0" operator="Microsoft Corporation"
    truncated="false" xmlns="urn:uddi-org:api">
    <tModelInfos>
        <tModelInfo tModelKey="uuid:e13fbf58-f69a-4c8a-a2f5-aecc5cca75e1">
            <name>Rosettanet-org:PIP4B2:NotifyOfShipmentReceipt:v1.0</name>
        </tModelInfo>
        <tModelInfo tModelKey="uuid:7b15e1a7-bbe7-4c32-8f44-64662a555b7c">
            <name>Rosettanet-org:PIP3B5:ChangeShipment:v01.00.00</name>
        </tModelInfo>
        <tModelInfo tModelKey="uuid:87c133f5-f521-420a-8316-9ff37e292796">
            <name>Rosettanet-org:PIP3B4:QueryShipmentStatus:v01.00.00</name>
        </tModelInfo>
        <tModelInfo tModelKey="uuid:cf073d7c-e297-470f-b7de-4ae18bd72ca9">
            <name>Rosettanet-org:PIP3B3:DistributeShipmentStatus:v01.00.00</name>
        </tModelInfo>
        <tModelInfo tModelKey="uuid:7c60881c-ad6c-4520-955b-49fe75b71d53">
            <name>Rosettanet-org:PIP3B2:NotifyOfAdvanceShipment:v01.00.00</name>
        </tModelInfo>
        <tModelInfo tModelKey="uuid:05b548d8-0c23-4249-8a68-b653f7c97d8a">
            <name>Rosettanet-org:PIP3B2:NotifyOfAdvanceShipment:v01.01.00</name>
        </tModelInfo>
    </tModelInfos>
</tModelList>
```

For more information on OAGIS or RosettaNet, refer to Chapter 7.

Errors:

E_nameTooLong
> The tModel name is too long.

E_tooManyOptions
> Too many search options were specified (UDDI 1.0 only).

E_unsupported
> The specified findQualifier is not supported.

---

get_bindingDetail

The *get_bindingDetail* function retrieves the complete bindingTemplate for each specified bindingKey. The response includes a root bindingDetail element, and one bindingTemplate element for each matching binding. If the UDDI operator returns only a partial list of matching results, the bindingDetail element's truncated attribute will be set to true. If no matches are found, an E_invalidKeyPassed error is returned.

Version: 1.0 and 2.0

1.0 syntax:

```
<get_bindingDetail  generic="1.0" xmlns="urn:uddi-org:api">
    <bindingKey/>
    [<bindingKey/> ...]
</get_bindingDetail>
```

2.0 syntax:

```
<get_bindingDetail generic="2.0" xmlns="urn:uddi-org:api_v2" >
    <bindingKey/>
    [<bindingKey/> ...]
</get_bindingDetail>
```

Argument:

bindingKey
> Required uuid_key specifying the bindingTemplate

Example:

The following UDDI 1.0 example retrieves a bindingTemplate associated with the XMethods Stock Quote Service:

```
<get_bindingDetail generic="1.0" xmlns="urn:uddi-org:api">
    <bindingKey>d594a970-3e16-11d5-98bf-002035229c64</bindingKey>
</get_bindingDetail>
```

Here is a response to the query:

```
<bindingDetail generic="1.0" operator="Microsoft Corporation"
```

```
    truncated="false" xmlns="urn:uddi-org:api">
    <bindingTemplate serviceKey="d5921160-3e16-11d5-98bf-002035229c64"
        bindingKey="d594a970-3e16-11d5-98bf-002035229c64">
        <description xml:lang="en">
            SOAP binding for delayed stock quotes service
        </description>
        <accessPoint URLType="http">
            http://services.xmethods.net:80/soap
        </accessPoint>
        <tModelInstanceDetails>
            <tModelInstanceInfo
                tModelKey="uuid:0e727db0-3e14-11d5-98bf-002035229c64" />
        </tModelInstanceDetails>
    </bindingTemplate>
</bindingDetail>
```

Error:

E_invalidKeyPassed

> An invalid bindingKey was specified.

---

get_businessDetail

The *get_businessDetail* function retrieves the complete businessEntity for each
specified businessKey. The response includes a root businessDetail element, and
one businessEntity element for each matching business. If the UDDI operator
returns only a partial list of matching results, the businessDetail truncated
attribute will be set to true. If no matches are found, an E_invalidKeyPassed error
is returned.

Version: 1.0 and 2.0

1.0 Syntax:

```
<get_businessDetail generic="1.0" xmlns="urn:uddi-org:api">
    <businessKey/>
    [<businessKey/> ...]
</get_businessDetail>
```

2.0 Syntax:

```
<get_businessDetail generic="2.0" xmlns="urn:uddi-org:api_v2">
    <businessKey/>
    [<businessKey/> ...]
</get_businessDetail>
```

Argument:

businessKey

> Required uuid_key specifying the businessEntity. You can specify multi-
> ple businessKeys.

Example:

The following UDDI 1.0 example retrieves the businessEntity record for XMethods, Inc:

```
<get_businessDetail generic="1.0" xmlns="urn:uddi-org:api">
    <businessKey>ba744ed0-3aaf-11d5-80dc-002035229c64</businessKey>
</get_businessDetail>
```

Here is a complete response to the query:

```
<businessDetail generic="1.0" operator="Microsoft Corporation"
    truncated="false" xmlns="urn:uddi-org:api">
    <businessEntity
    businessKey="ba744ed0-3aaf-11d5-80dc-002035229c64"
    operator="www.ibm.com/services/uddi" authorizedName="0100001QS1">
    <discoveryURLs>
        <discoveryURL useType="businessEntity">
            http://www.ibm.com/services/uddi/uddiget?businessKey=
            BA744ED0-3AAF-11D5-80DC-002035229C64
        </discoveryURL>
    </discoveryURLs>
    <name>XMethods</name>
    <description xml:lang="en">Web services resource site</description>
        <contacts>
            <contact useType="Founder">
                <description xml:lang="en" />
                <personName>Tony Hong</personName>
                <phone useType="Founder" />
                <email useType="Founder">thong@xmethods.net</email>
                <address>
                    <addressLine />
                    <addressLine />
                    <addressLine />
                    <addressLine />
                    <addressLine />
                </address>
            </contact>
        </contacts>
        <businessServices>
            <businessService
                serviceKey="d5b180a0-4342-11d5-bd6c-002035229c64"
                businessKey="ba744ed0-3aaf-11d5-80dc-002035229c64">
            <name>XMethods Barnes and Noble Quote</name>
            <description xml:lang="en">
                Returns book price from Barnes and Noble online store, given
                ISBN
            </description>
            <bindingTemplates>
                <bindingTemplate
                    serviceKey="d5b180a0-4342-11d5-bd6c-002035229c64"
                    bindingKey="d5b61480-4342-11d5-bd6c-002035229c64">
                    <description xml:lang="en">
                        SOAP Binding for tmodel:XMethods Book Quote
```

```
        </description>
        <accessPoint URLType="http">
            http://services.xmethods.net:80/soap/servlet/rpcrouter
        </accessPoint>
        <tModelInstanceDetails>
            <tModelInstanceInfo
                tModelKey="uuid:26d3abd0-433d-11d5-bd6c-
                    002035229c64" />
        </tModelInstanceDetails>
      </bindingTemplate>
   </bindingTemplates>
</businessService>
<businessService serviceKey="ed85f000-4345-11d5-bd6c-002035229c64"
    businessKey="ba744ed0-3aaf-11d5-80dc-002035229c64">
    <name>XMethods Pacific Bell SMS Service</name>
    <description xml:lang="en">
        Sends a text message to a subscriber on the PacBell SMS
        network
    </description>
    <bindingTemplates>
        <bindingTemplate
            serviceKey="ed85f000-4345-11d5-bd6c-002035229c64"
            bindingKey="ed8d1bf0-4345-11d5-bd6c-002035229c64">
            <description xml:lang="en">
                SOAP Binding for tmodel:XMethods SMS
            </description>
            <accessPoint URLType="http">
                http://services.xmethods.net:80/perl/soaplite.cgi
            </accessPoint>
            <tModelInstanceDetails>
                <tModelInstanceInfo
                    tModelKey="uuid:33f24880-433d-11d5-bd6c-
                        002035229c64" />
            </tModelInstanceDetails>
        </bindingTemplate>
    </bindingTemplates>
</businessService>
<businessService
    serviceKey="d5921160-3e16-11d5-98bf-002035229c64"
    businessKey="ba744ed0-3aaf-11d5-80dc-002035229c64">
    <name>XMethods Delayed Stock Quotes</name>
    <description xml:lang="en">
        20-minute delayed stock quotes
    </description>
    <bindingTemplates>
        <bindingTemplate
            serviceKey="d5921160-3e16-11d5-98bf-002035229c64"
            bindingKey="d594a970-3e16-11d5-98bf-002035229c64">
            <description xml:lang="en">
                SOAP binding for delayed stock quotes service
            </description>
            <accessPoint URLType="http">
                http://services.xmethods.net:80/soap
```

```
        </accessPoint>
        <tModelInstanceDetails>
            <tModelInstanceInfo
                tModelKey="uuid:0e727db0-3e14-11d5-98bf-
                    002035229c64" />
        </tModelInstanceDetails>
    </bindingTemplate>
    </bindingTemplates>
</businessService>
<businessService
    serviceKey="618167a0-3e64-11d5-98bf-002035229c64"
    businessKey="ba744ed0-3aaf-11d5-80dc-002035229c64">
    <name>XMethods Currency Exchange Rates</name>
    <description xml:lang="en">
        Returns exchange rates between 2 countries' currencies
    </description>
    <bindingTemplates>
        <bindingTemplate
            serviceKey="618167a0-3e64-11d5-98bf-002035229c64"
            bindingKey="618474e0-3e64-11d5-98bf-002035229c64">
            <description xml:lang="en">
                SOAP binding for currency exchange rates service
            </description>
            <accessPoint URLType="http">
                http://services.xmethods.net:80/soap
            </accessPoint>
            <tModelInstanceDetails>
                <tModelInstanceInfo
                    tModelKey="uuid:e092f730-3e63-11d5-98bf-
                        002035229c64" />
            </tModelInstanceDetails>
        </bindingTemplate>
    </bindingTemplates>
</businessService>
    </businessServices>
</businessEntity>
</businessDetail>
```

Error:

E_invalidKeyPassed

An invalid businessKey was specified.

---

get_businessDetailExt

The *get_businessDetailExt* function retrieves the extended businessEntity for each specified businessKey. The response includes a root businessDetailExt element, and one businessEntityExt element for each matching business. If the operator returns only a partial list of matching results, the businessDetailExt element's truncated attribute will be set to true. If no matches are found, an E_invalidKeyPassed error is returned. This function is useful for querying external

UDDI registries that are not part of the UDDI cloud services and that may contain extra business registration information. When querying a UDDI operator site, this method returns the exact same results as *get_businessDetail*.

Version: 1.0 and 2.0

1.0 syntax:

```
<get_businessDetailExt generic="1.0" xmlns="urn:uddi-org:api" >
    <businessKey/>
    [<businessKey/> ...]
</get_businessDetailExt>
```

2.0 syntax:

```
<get_businessDetailExt generic="2.0" xmlns="urn:uddi-org:api_v2" >
    <businessKey/>
    [<businessKey/> ...]
</get_businessDetailExt>
```

Argument:

businessKey

> Required uuid_key specifying the businessEntity. You can specify multiple businessKeys.

Example:

The following UDDI 1.0 example retrieves the external businessEntity record for XMethods, Inc.

```
<get_businessDetailExt generic="1.0" xmlns="urn:uddi-org:api">
    <businessKey>ba744ed0-3aaf-11d5-80dc-002035229c64</businessKey>
</get_businessDetailExt>
```

When querying a UDDI Operator site, this query returns the exact same result noted in the *get_businessDetail* example earlier in this chapter.

Errors:

E_invalidKeyPassed

> An invalid businessKey was specified.

E_unsupported

> The query is not supported. If this occurs, use the get_businessDetail query.

get_serviceDetail

The *get_serviceDetail* function retrieves the businessService record for each specified serviceKey. The response includes a root serviceDetail element, and one businessService element for each matching service. If the UDDI operator returns only a partial list of matching results, the serviceDetail element's truncated attribute will be set to true. If no matches are found, an E_invalidKeyPassed error is returned.

Version: 1.0 and 2.0

1.0 syntax:

```
<get_serviceDetail  generic="1.0" xmlns="urn:uddi-org:api" >
    <serviceKey/>
    [<serviceKey/> ...]
</get_serviceDetail>
```

2.0 syntax:

```
<get_serviceDetail generic="2.0" xmlns="urn:uddi-org:api_v2">
    <serviceKey/>
    [<serviceKey/> ...]
</get_serviceDetail>
```

Argument:

serviceKey

Required uuid_key specifying the serviceDetail. You can specify multiple serviceKeys.

Example:

The following UDDI 1.0 example retrieves the service details for the XMethods Stock Quote service:

```
<get_serviceDetail generic="1.0" xmlns="urn:uddi-org:api">
    <serviceKey>d5921160-3e16-11d5-98bf-002035229c64</serviceKey>
</get_serviceDetail>
```

Here is a complete response to the query:

```
<serviceDetail generic="1.0" operator="Microsoft Corporation"
    truncated="false" xmlns="urn:uddi-org:api">
    <businessService
        serviceKey="d5921160-3e16-11d5-98bf-002035229c64"
        businessKey="ba744ed0-3aaf-11d5-80dc-002035229c64">
        <name>XMethods Delayed Stock Quotes</name>
        <description xml:lang="en">
            20-minute delayed stock quotes
        </description>
        <bindingTemplates>
            <bindingTemplate
                serviceKey="d5921160-3e16-11d5-98bf-002035229c64"
                bindingKey="d594a970-3e16-11d5-98bf-002035229c64">
                <description xml:lang="en">
                    SOAP binding for delayed stock quotes service
                </description>
                <accessPoint URLType="http">
                    http://services.xmethods.net:80/soap
                </accessPoint>
```

```
            <tModelInstanceDetails>
                <tModelInstanceInfo
                    tModelKey="uuid:0e727db0-3e14-11d5-98bf-002035229c64" />
            </tModelInstanceDetails>
          </bindingTemplate>
        </bindingTemplates>
      </businessService>
    </serviceDetail>
```

Error:

E_invalidKeyPassed

> An invalid serviceKey was specified.

---

get_tModelDetail

The *get_tModelDetail* function retrieves the tModel record for each specified tModelKey. The response includes a root tModelDetail element, and one tModel element for each matching tModel. If the UDDI operator returns only a partial list of matching results, the tModelDetail element's truncated attribute will be set to true. If no matches are found, an E_invalidKeyPassed error is returned.

Version: 1.0 and 2.0

1.0 syntax:

```
<get_tModelDetail generic="1.0" xmlns="urn:uddi-org:api">
    <tModelKey/>
    [<tModelKey/> ...]
</get_tModelDetail>
```

2.0 syntax:

```
<get_tModelDetail generic="2.0" xmlns="urn:uddi-org:api_v2">
    <tModelKey/>
    [<tModelKey/> ...]
</get_tModelDetail>
```

Argument:

tModelKey

> Required uuid_key specifying the tModel. You can specify multiple tModelKeys.

Example:

The following UDDI 1.0 example retrieves the tModel record for the RosettaNet Partner Interface Process (PIP) for "Query Shipment Status":

```
<get_tModelDetail generic="1.0" xmlns="urn:uddi-org:api">
    <tModelKey>uuid:87c133f5-f521-420a-8316-9ff37e292796</tModelKey>
</get_tModelDetail>
```

Following is a complete response to the query:

```
<tModelDetail generic="1.0" operator="Microsoft Corporation"
    truncated="false" xmlns="urn:uddi-org:api">
    <tModel tModelKey="uuid:87c133f5-f521-420a-8316-9ff37e292796"
        operator="Microsoft Corporation" authorizedName="Suhayl Masud">
        <name>Rosettanet-org:PIP3B4:QueryShipmentStatus:v01.00.00</name>
        <description xml:lang="en">
            Enables in-transit information users to query shipment status,
            and allows transport service providers to respond with shipment
            status notifications
        </description>
        <overviewDoc>
            <description xml:lang="en">
                This is the compressed file that contains the specification
                in a word document, the html message guideline document and
                the xml dtds
            </description>
            <overviewURL>
                http://www.rosettanet.org/rosettanet/Doc/0/
                CG0J24SOSBA13FCD0282FOPTD8/3B4_QueryShipment
                Status_R01_00_00.zip
            </overviewURL>
        </overviewDoc>
    </tModel>
</tModelDetail>
```

Errors:

E_invalidKeyPassed

    An invalid tModelKey was specified.

E_keyRetired

    The specified tModelKey is no longer active.

Find Qualifiers

Each of the *find* functions can take an optional list of UDDI find qualifiers,
which enable more precise search criteria. Table 8-2 provides a list of the
most frequently used UDDI find qualifiers.

Table 8-2. Most frequently used UDDI find qualifiers

Find qualifier	Description
exactNameMatch	Mandates an exact name match
caseSensitiveMatch	Mandates that the search be case-sensitive
sortByNameAsc	Sorts results by name in ascending alphabetic order
sortByNameDesc	Sorts results by name in descending alphabetic order
sortByDateAsc	Sorts results by date last updated in ascending chronological order
sortByDateDesc	Sorts results by date last updated in descending chronological order
soundex	Mandates a sound-alike search for the specified name (UDDI 2.0 only)

The following example illustrates the use of the exactNameMatch qualifier:

```
<find_business generic="1.0" xmlns="urn:uddi-org:api">
    <findQualifiers>
        <findQualifier>exactNameMatch</findQualifier>
    </findQualifiers>
    <name>Ariba, Inc</name>
</find_business>
```

UDDI's search facilities are fairly comprehensive and may be enhanced in future versions.

CHAPTER 9

UDDI 4J

UDDI for Java (UDDI4J) is a Java client toolkit for retrieving and publishing UDDI data. IBM originally created UDDI4J; in January 2001, it turned the code over to its own developerWorks open source site *(http://www-124. ibm.com/developerworks/oss/)*.

This chapter provides a complete overview of UDDI4J, including:

- The technical aspects of using the UDDI4J API
- Three sample applications, including two applications that use the UDDI Inquiry API and one that uses the UDDI Publishing API
- A quick-reference guide to the complete UDDI4J API

Getting Started

To get started, you must first download the UDDI4J distribution. The distribution is available at *http://oss.software.ibm.com/developerworks/projects/ uddi4j/*.

You will also need the following additional software:

- The complete Apache SOAP distribution, including the prerequisite software, such as the Xerces XML Parser and the JavaMail API. See Chapter 3 for complete details.
- The Java Secure Socket Extension (JSSE), available at *http://java.sun. com/products/jsse/index.html*. JSSE is required if you plan to publish UDDI data.

Technical Overview

The UDDI4J API provides a direct mapping of the UDDI Data Model and the UDDI Programming API. (See Chapter 7 for details.) The most important class is the UDDIProxy class. This class provides centralized access to all inquiry and publishing functions included in the UDDI 1.0 Programming API. To perform inquiry functions, you must provide an inquiry URL for a UDDI operator site via the setInquiryURL( ) method. To perform publishing functions, you must specify an HTTPS URL via the setPublishURL( ) method.

Each of the UDDI Programming API functions is directly available via the UDDIProxy class. For example, the UDDIProxy class has inquiry methods for find_business( ), get_businessDetail( ), get_TModelDetail( ), etc. It also has publishing methods for save_business(), save_service(), delete_business( ), etc.

Depending on the method call, the UDDIProxy object will generate a SOAP request, send the request to the specified UDDI operator site, and make the response data available via intermediate objects. Most of these intermediate objects are available in the com.ibm.uddi.datatype package. For example, the com.ibm.uddi.datatype.business package contains classes for extracting business entity information, such as the business name, description, and contact information.

In the event of an error, the UDDIProxy class will throw a UDDIException. Depending on the type of error, the UDDIException may contain a DispositionReport object containing detailed information about the cause of the error.

Finding and Retrieving UDDI Data

UDDI lets you search for information about businesses and business entities, using slightly different APIs.

Searching for Businesses

Our first example runs the UDDIProxy find_business( ) method and prints out the matching results. The program expects a single command-line argument, in which you specify the name of a business. For example, the following command line:

```
java com.ecerami.uddi.findBusiness Micro
```

generates the following output:

```
Searching for Businesses:  Micro
Microtrack, Inc.:  f53480ab-be29-4090-9239-f4c4a7cf71c6
Microform Reading Room:  622a4879-dcaa-4bab-9aec-6e6bfb858067
Micro Informatica LLC:  dce959cf-200d-4d9e-beee-ede770299212
Microsoft Corporation:  0076b468-eb27-42e5-ac09-9955cff462a3
Micromotor:  11bb5410-61d7-11d5-b286-002035229c64
MicroVideo Learning Systems:  8995b9f7-0043-4eb0-adaf-2aa81ad387e4
MicroApplications, Inc.:  a23c901e-834c-4b8a-bf38-3f96fedc349a
MicroLink LLC:  fb5783d6-4ba4-4bce-b181-4d3cd9f35e3d
MicroMain Corporation:  1e6c5410-00e7-4aee-acfb-fb59f3896322
Micro Motion Inc.:  d4e4b830-f19e-4edf-9f44-8936e53d9a33
```

The complete code is shown in Example 9-1. First, note that the findBusinessByName( ) method creates a new UDDIProxy object and specifies the inquiry URL for the Microsoft UDDI site. (For a complete list of inquiry and publishing URLs, refer to Chapter 7.)

The code then calls the proxy's find_business( ) method:

```
BusinessList businessList = proxy.find_business(businessName, null, 0);
```

This method expects three arguments: a business name, a FindQualifier object, and a maximum number of records to return. In our case, we have no find qualifiers and therefore pass a null value. (See the "Find Qualifiers" section later in this chapter for details regarding the use of find qualifiers.) We also specify a 0 value for maximum number of records; 0 is a reserved value that indicates no restrictions on the number of rows returned.

The find_business( ) method returns a BusinessList object. The code then navigates through the BusinessList object to obtain the matching businesses. For complete details on navigating through the business data hierarchy, refer to the com.ibm.uddi.datatype.business package in the Quick Reference API.

In the event of a UDDIException, the code attempts to extract the DispositionReport object and display the cause of the error.

Example 9-1. findBusiness.java

```
package com.ecerami.uddi;

import java.util.*;
import com.ibm.uddi.UDDIException;
import com.ibm.uddi.client.UDDIProxy;
import com.ibm.uddi.response.*;
import java.net.MalformedURLException;
import org.apache.soap.SOAPException;

/**
 * Sample UDDI Program:  searches for all companies that
```

Example 9-1. findBusiness.java (continued)

```
 * match the first command line argument.
 * Example usage:  java findBusiness XMethods
 */
public class findBusiness {

  /**
   *  Main method
   */
  public static void main (String args[]) {
    findBusiness inquiry = new findBusiness( );

    try {
      //  Search for Specified Business Name
      String businessName = args[0];
      System.out.println ("Searching for Businesses:  "+businessName);
      Vector businessInfoVector = inquiry.findBusinessByName (businessName);

      // Print name and business key for each matching business
      for (int i=0; i<businessInfoVector.size( ); i++) {
          BusinessInfo businessInfo =
            (BusinessInfo) businessInfoVector.elementAt(i);
          String name = businessInfo.getNameString( );
          String businessKey = businessInfo.getBusinessKey( );
          System.out.println (name+":  "+businessKey);
      }
    } catch (MalformedURLException e) {
      e.printStackTrace( );
    } catch (SOAPException e) {
      e.printStackTrace( );
    } catch (UDDIException e) {
      //  Extract UDDI Disposition Report
      DispositionReport dr = e.getDispositionReport( );
      if (dr!=null) {
        System.out.println("UDDIException faultCode:" +
          e.getFaultCode( ) +
          "\n errno:"    + dr.getErrno( ) +
          "\n errCode:"  + dr.getErrCode( ) +
          "\n errInfoText:" + dr.getErrInfoText( ));
      }
      e.printStackTrace( );
    }
  }

  /**
   *  Find Business by Name
   *  @param businessName Business Name Target
   *  @return Vector of BusinessInfo objects
   */
  public Vector findBusinessByName (String businessName)
    throws MalformedURLException, SOAPException, UDDIException {
    //  Create UDDI Proxy Object
```

Example 9-1. findBusiness.java (continued)

```
UDDIProxy proxy = new UDDIProxy( );

// Point to Microsoft Inquiry URL
proxy.setInquiryURL("http://uddi.microsoft.com/inquire");

// Find Matching Businesses
BusinessList businessList = proxy.find_business(businessName, null, 0);

// Process UDDI Response
BusinessInfos businessInfos = businessList.getBusinessInfos( );
Vector businessInfoVector = businessInfos.getBusinessInfoVector( );
return businessInfoVector;
  }
}
```

FindQualifiers

You can use the FindQualifiers object to specify more precise control over the search criteria. For example, the following code searches for exact name matches:

```
Vector fqs = new Vector( );
FindQualifiers findQualifiers = new FindQualifiers ( );
FindQualifier fq = new FindQualifier(FindQualifier.exactNameMatch);
fqs.addElement(fq);
findQualifiers.setFindQualifierVector(fqs);
BusinessList bl = proxy.find_business("Microsoft Corporation",
    findQualifiers, 0);
```

For more complete details, refer to the com.ibm.uddi.util package in the Quick Reference API.

IdentifierBag

You can use the IdentifierBag object to perform searches indexed by one or more UDDI identifiers. For example, the following code attempts to locate the business record associated with the specified Dun & Bradstreet D-U-N-S® Number:

```
Vector keyedReferenceVector = new Vector( );
KeyedReference keyedRef = new KeyedReference
    ("dnb-com:D-U-N-S", "04-693-3052");
keyedRef.setTModelKey ("uuid:8609c81e-ee1f-4d5a-b202-3eb13ad01823");
keyedReferenceVector.addElement (keyedRef);
IdentifierBag idBag = new IdentifierBag ( );
idBag.setKeyedReferenceVector(keyedReferenceVector);
BusinessList bl = proxy.find_business(idBag, null, 0);
```

For details regarding UDDI identifiers, refer to Chapter 7.

CategoryBag

You can use the CategoryBag object to perform searches indexed by one or more UDDI categorizations. For example, the following code searches for all businesses registered with the NAICS code for software publisher:

```
keyedReferenceVector = new Vector( );
keyedRef = new KeyedReference ("ntis-gov:naics:1997", "51121");
keyedRef.setTModelKey ("uuid:COB9FE13-179F-413D-8A5B-5004DB8E5BB2");
keyedReferenceVector.addElement (keyedRef);
CategoryBag categoryBag = new CategoryBag ( );
categoryBag.setKeyedReferenceVector(keyedReferenceVector);
BusinessList bl = proxy.find_business(categoryBag, null, 0);
```

For details regarding preregistered UDDI taxonomies and categorizations, refer to Chapter 7.

Retrieving a businessEntity Record

Our second example runs the proxy get_businessDetail( ) method and prints out portions of the full businessEntity record. The program expects a single command-line argument, in which you can specify the businessKey for a business.

For example, the following command line:

```
java com.ecerami.uddi.getBusinessDetail 0076b468-eb27-42e5-ac09-9955cff462a3
```

generates the following output:

```
Business Name:  Microsoft Corporation
Description:  Empowering people through great software - any time, any place
and on any device is Microsoft's vision. As the worldwide leader in software
for personal and business computing, we strive to produce innovative
products and services that meet our customer's
Contact:  Corporate Mailing Addresses
Address:  Microsoft Corporation
Address:  One Microsoft Way
Address:  Redmond, WA 98052-6399
Address:  USA
Contact:  World Wide Operations
Email:  martink@microsoft.com
```

The complete code is shown in Example 9-2. Note that the get_businessDetail( ) method returns a BusinessDetail object. You can then navigate through the BusinessDetail object to display any portion of the record you want. In this case, the code displays the business name, description, and contact information. For details on navigating through the BusinessDetail object, refer to the com.ibm.uddi.datatype.business package in the Quick Reference API (discussed in Chapter 8).

Example 9-2. getBusinessDetail.java

```
package com.ecerami.uddi;

/**
 * Sample UDDI Program:  retrieves the businessEntity
 * specified by the first command line argument.
 * Example usage:
 * java getBusinessDetail ba744ed0-3aaf-11d5-80dc-002035229c64
 */
import java.util.*;
import com.ibm.uddi.client.UDDIProxy;
import com.ibm.uddi.UDDIException;
import com.ibm.uddi.response.DispositionReport;
import com.ibm.uddi.response.BusinessDetail;
import com.ibm.uddi.datatype.business.*;
import java.net.MalformedURLException;
import org.apache.soap.SOAPException;

public class getBusinessDetail {

  /**
   * Main Method
   */
  public static void main (String args[]) {
    try {
      getBusinessDetail inquiry = new getBusinessDetail();
      BusinessDetail businessDetail = inquiry.getBusinessDetail (args[0]);
      inquiry.print_businessDetail (businessDetail);
    } catch (MalformedURLException e) {
      e.printStackTrace();
    } catch (SOAPException e) {
      e.printStackTrace();
    } catch (UDDIException e) {
      //  Extract UDDI Disposition Report
      DispositionReport dr = e.getDispositionReport();
      if (dr!=null) {
        System.out.println("UDDIException faultCode:" +
          e.getFaultCode() +
          "\n errno:"     + dr.getErrno() +
          "\n errCode:" + dr.getErrCode() +
          "\n errInfoText:" + dr.getErrInfoText());
      }
      e.printStackTrace();
    }
  }

  /**
   * Retrieve Business Detail Record
   * @param businessKey UDDI Business Key
   * @return UDDI Business Detail record
   */
  public BusinessDetail getBusinessDetail (String businessKey)
```

Example 9-2. getBusinessDetail.java (continued)

```java
    throws MalformedURLException, SOAPException, UDDIException {
    //  Create UDDI Proxy Object
    UDDIProxy proxy = new UDDIProxy();
    //  Point to Microsoft Inquiry URL
    proxy.setInquiryURL("http://uddi.microsoft.com/inquire");

    //  Retrieve BusinessDetail record
    BusinessDetail businessDetail = proxy.get_businessDetail(businessKey);
    return businessDetail;
}

/**
 * Print Business Entity Data
 * @param businessDetail UDDI Business Detail Record
 */
private void print_businessDetail (BusinessDetail businessDetail) {
  Vector businessEntityVector = businessDetail.getBusinessEntityVector();
  for (int i = 0; i < businessEntityVector.size(); i++) {
      BusinessEntity businessEntity =
        (BusinessEntity) businessEntityVector.elementAt(i);
      String name = businessEntity.getNameString();
      String description = businessEntity.getDefaultDescriptionString();
      System.out.println ("Business Name:  "+name);
      System.out.println ("Description:  "+description);
      Contacts contacts = businessEntity.getContacts();
      print_contacts (contacts);
    }
}

/**
 * Print Contact Data
 * @param contacts UDDI Contacts Information
 */
private void print_contacts (Contacts contacts) {
  Vector contactVector = contacts.getContactVector();
  for (int j=0; j< contactVector.size(); j++) {
    Contact contact = (Contact) contactVector.elementAt (j);
    String description = contact.getDefaultDescriptionString();
    Vector addressVector = contact.getAddressVector();
    Vector emailVector = contact.getEmailVector();
    System.out.println ("Contact:  "+ description);
    print_addressVector (addressVector);
    print_emailVector (emailVector);
  }
}

/**
 * Print Address Data
 * @param addressVector Vector of UDDI Address Records
 */
private void print_addressVector (Vector addressVector) {
```

Example 9-2. getBusinessDetail.java (continued)

```
    for (int i=0; i< addressVector.size( ); i++) {
      Address address = (Address) addressVector.elementAt(i);
      Vector addressLines = address.getAddressLineVector( );
      for (int j=0; j<addressLines.size( ); j++) {
        AddressLine addressLine = (AddressLine) addressLines.elementAt(j);
        String addressText = addressLine.getText( );
        System.out.println("Address:  "+addressText);
      }
    }
  }

  /**
   * Print Email Data
   * @param emailVector Vector of UDDI Email Objects
   */
  private void print_emailVector (Vector emailVector) {
    for (int i=0; i< emailVector.size( ); i++) {
      Email email = (Email) emailVector.elementAt(i);
      String emailText = email.getText( );
      System.out.println ("Email:  "+emailText);
    }
  }
}
```

Publishing UDDI Data

UDDI publishing requests must be sent via an SSL connection and are restricted to authorized users only. To specify an HTTPS URL, use the setPublishURL( ) method. To obtain user authorization, you must use the proxy get_authToken( ) method. This method requires a username and password and returns an authentication token, which must be passed to all subsequent publishing methods.

Our final example illustrates how to save a new businessEntity record, and also illustrates the generic technique for obtaining a user authentication token. The code creates a new businessEntity record for Acme Parts, then confirms that the record was published by extracting and displaying the new businessKey.

The program expects two command-line arguments, in which you can specify a username and password. For example, the following command line:

```
java com.ecerami.uddi.saveBusiness ethan@ecerami.com oreilly
```

generates the following output:

```
Saving New Business:  Acme Parts
Authentication Token:
1IbuzUmG2DuPzkcoUd1I6iy*BqWwxPhuFWf2!ggowk*6Kiznlu4sjQeJT
```

```
OnuL2c1Smm8m28aogU!I6ZL73yROf3Q$$;1IbuzUmG2AoqvPmRavvTeO1UsaVLQkOAmGYVyyxwk3
   2Kb4
c3jMROMo4Rlp7kaQYRCXu9!95wQ8FZTIjE!47uKC9NPCCryfOYh!IltwfYMCaPKTq*ROrTWMrzcg
   UWEt
!g859iKxlE*w7QPIx8n8aYWs8WCkAn7UHwyb
```
Published Business Key: 3deafa60-0023-4220-b3e0-0c87cb34526a

Example 9-3 includes a UDDIUtil class that is responsible for authenticating users. Note that the class specifies an SSL provider:

```
System.setProperty("java.protocol.handler.pkgs",
   "com.sun.net.ssl.internal.www.protocol");
Security.addProvider (new com.sun.net.ssl.internal.ssl.Provider());
```

These two lines are required for transferring information via SSL.

Note that the proxy get_authToken( ) method requires a username and password and returns an AuthToken object. The AuthToken object can then be used in all subsequent publishing requests.

The remainder of the code is shown in Example 9-3. Within this code, we save a new BusinessEntity object with a new name, description, and contact information. Note in particular the instantiation of the BusinessEntity object:

```
BusinessEntity businessEntity = new BusinessEntity("", "Acme Parts");
```

The code passes an empty businessKey string to the constructor, indicating that this is a new record. The proxy's save_business( ) method echoes back a BusinessDetail object, enabling us to extract the newly assigned businessKey value.

Example 9-3. saveBusiness.java

```java
package com.ecerami.uddi;

/**
 * UDDI Program:  publishes a new UDDI BusinessEntity
 * record.  Specify username and password on command line.
 * Example usage:
 * java saveBusiness ethan@ecerami.com password
 */
import com.ibm.uddi.*;
import com.ibm.uddi.client.*;
import com.ibm.uddi.datatype.business.*;
import com.ibm.uddi.response.*;
import java.util.Vector;
import java.net.MalformedURLException;
import org.apache.soap.SOAPException;

public class saveBusiness {
  private AuthToken token;
  private UDDIProxy proxy;
```

Example 9-3. saveBusiness.java (continued)

```java
/**
 * Main Method
 */
public static void main (String args[]) {
  saveBusiness publish = null;
  try {
      System.out.println("Saving New Business:  Acme Parts");
      AuthToken token = UDDIUtil.get_authentication_token(args[0], args[1]);
      System.out.println("Authentication Token:  "+token.getAuthInfoString());
      publish = new saveBusiness(token);
      String businessKey = publish.save_business();
      System.out.println("Published Business Key:  "+businessKey);
  } catch (MalformedURLException e) {
      e.printStackTrace();
  } catch (SOAPException e) {
      e.printStackTrace();
  } catch (UDDIException e) {
      DispositionReport dr = e.getDispositionReport();
      UDDIUtil.printDispositionReport (dr);
      e.printStackTrace();
  }
}

/**
 * Constructor
 * @param token UDDI Authentication Token
 */
public saveBusiness (AuthToken token) {
  this.token = token;
}

/**
 * Save New Business Entity
 */
public String save_business ()
  throws MalformedURLException, SOAPException, UDDIException {
  String businessKey = null;

  //  Point to Microsoft Test Publish URL (SSL)
  proxy = new UDDIProxy();
  proxy.setPublishURL("https://test.uddi.microsoft.com/publish");

  //  Create Sample Business Entity Record
  BusinessEntity businessEntity = create_business ();
  Vector businessEntityVector = new Vector();
  businessEntityVector.addElement(businessEntity);

  //  Publish new Business Record
  BusinessDetail businessDetail =
    proxy.save_business(token.getAuthInfoString(), businessEntityVector);
```

Example 9-3. saveBusiness.java (continued)

```java
    // Verify publication by extracting new business key
    Vector businessEntities = businessDetail.getBusinessEntityVector( );
    if (businessEntities.size( ) > 0) {
      BusinessEntity returnedBusinessEntity =
        (BusinessEntity)(businessEntities.elementAt(0));
      businessKey = returnedBusinessEntity.getBusinessKey( );
    }
    return businessKey;
  }

  /**
   * Create new sample Business Entity record
   */
  private BusinessEntity create_business( ) {
    Vector businessEntities = new Vector( );
    BusinessEntity businessEntity = new BusinessEntity("", "Acme Parts");

    // Set Business Description
    businessEntity.setDefaultDescriptionString
      ("Maker of fine semiconductor parts");

    // Set Contact Name and Email
    Contact contact = new Contact ("Ethan Cerami");
    Email email = new Email("cerami@cs.nyu.edu");
    Vector emailVector = new Vector( );
    emailVector.addElement(email);
    contact.setEmailVector(emailVector);
    Contacts contacts = new Contacts( );
    Vector contactVector = new Vector( );
    contactVector.addElement(contact);
    contacts.setContactVector(contactVector);
    businessEntity.setContacts(contacts);
    return businessEntity;
  }
}
```

UDDI4J Quick Reference API

This section includes a quick-reference guide to the UDDI4J API. All packages within the API are included except for com.ibm.uddi.request, which client applications do not typically use directly.

The com.ibm.uddi Package

com.ibm.uddi.UDDIElement

This is the base class for all UDDI elements.

Synopsis

```
public abstract class UDDIElement extends Object {
  // Constructors
    public UDDIElement( );
    public UDDIElement(Element el) throws UDDIException;
  // Field Summary
    protected Element base;
    public static String GENERIC;
    public static String XMLNS;
  // Public Methods
    public NodeList getChildElementsByTagName(Element el, String tag);
    abstract public void saveToXML(Element base);
  // Protected Methods
    protected String getText(Node el);
}
```

Hierarchy

```
java.lang.Object → com.ibm.uddi.UDDIElement
```

com.ibm.uddi.UDDIException

This class encapsulates UDDI related errors. A UDDIException object may include a DispositionReport object, containing detailed information about the cause of the error.

Synopsis

```
public class UDDIException extends Exception {
  // Constructors
    public UDDIException( );
    public UDDIException(Element el, boolean createDispositionReport);
  // Public Methods
    public String getDetail( );
    public Element getDetailElement( );
    public DispositionReport getDispositionReport( );
    public String getFaultActor( );
    public String getFaultCode( );
    public String getFaultString( );
```

```
     public boolean isValidElement(Element el);
     public String toString();
  // Protected Methods
     protected String getText(Node el);
}
```

Hierarchy

java.lang.Object → java.lang.Throwable → java.lang.Exception → com.ibm.
uddi.UDDIException

---

com.ibm.uddi.VectorNodeList

This utility class provides an implementation of the org.w3c.dom.NodeList interface, but it is not typically used directly by UDDI client code.

Synopsis

```
public class VectorNodeList extends Object implements NodeList {
  // Constructors
     public VectorNodeList(Vector v);
  // Public Methods
     public int getLength();
     public Vector getVector();
     public Node item(int index);
}
```

Hierarchy

java.lang.Object → com.ibm.uddi.VectorNodeList

The com.ibm.uddi.client Package

---

com.ibm.uddi.client.UDDIProxy

This class provides centralized access to all inquiry and publishing functions
provided by the UDDI 1.0 Programming API. To perform inquiry functions, you
must set the inquiry URL via the setInquiryURL() method; to perform publishing
functions, you must set an HTTPS URL via the setPublishURL() method. All
publishing requests, such as save_xxx() and delete_xxx(), require an authentication token; to obtain an authentication token, use the get_authToken() method
and specify a username and password.

Synopsis

```
public class UDDIProxy extends Object {
  // Constructors
     public UDDIProxy();
     public UDDIProxy(URL inquiryURL, URL publishURL,
       SOAPTransport transport);
```

```
// Public Methods
   public DispositionReport delete_binding(String authInfo,
      String bindingKey) throws UDDIException, SOAPException;
   public DispositionReport delete_binding(String authInfo,
      Vector bindingKeyStrings) throws UDDIException, SOAPException;
   public DispositionReport delete_business(String authInfo,
      String businessKey) throws UDDIException, SOAPException;
   public DispositionReport delete_business(String authInfo,
      Vector businessKeyStrings) throws UDDIException, SOAPException;
   public DispositionReport delete_service(String authInfo,
      String serviceKey) throws UDDIException, SOAPException;
   public DispositionReport delete_service(String authInfo,
      Vector serviceKeyStrings) throws UDDIException, SOAPException;
   public DispositionReport delete_tModel(String authInfo,
      String tModelKey) throws UDDIException, SOAPException;
   public DispositionReport delete_tModel(String authInfo,
      Vector tModelKeyStrings) throws UDDIException, SOAPException;
   public DispositionReport discard_authToken(AuthInfo authInfo)
      throws UDDIException, SOAPException;
   public BindingDetail find_binding(FindQualifiers findQualifiers,
      String serviceKey, TModelBag tmodelbag, int maxRows)
      throws UDDIException, SOAPException;
   public BusinessList find_business(CategoryBag bag, FindQualifiers
      findQualifiers, int maxRows) throws UDDIException, SOAPException;
   public BusinessList find_business(DiscoveryURLs bag, FindQualifiers
      findQualifiers, int maxRows) throws UDDIException, SOAPException;
   public BusinessList find_business(IdentifierBag bag, FindQualifiers
      findQualifiers, int maxRows) throws UDDIException, SOAPException;
   public BusinessList find_business(String name, FindQualifiers
      findQualifiers, int maxRows) throws UDDIException, SOAPException;
   public BusinessList find_business(TModelBag bag, FindQualifiers
      findQualifiers, int maxRows) throws UDDIException, SOAPException;
   public ServiceList find_service(String businessKey, CategoryBag bag,
      FindQualifiers findQualifiers, int maxRows) throws UDDIException,
      SOAPException;
   public ServiceList find_service(String businessKey, String name,
      FindQualifiers findQualifiers, int maxRows) throws UDDIException,
      SOAPException;
   public ServiceList find_service(String businessKey, TModelBag bag,
      FindQualifiers findQualifiers, int maxRows) throws UDDIException,
      SOAPException;
   public TModelList find_tModel(CategoryBag bag, FindQualifiers
      findQualifiers, int maxRows) throws UDDIException, SOAPException;
   public TModelList find_tModel(IdentifierBag identifierBag,
      FindQualifiers findQualifiers, int maxRows) throws UDDIException,
      SOAPException;
   public TModelList find_tModel(String name, FindQualifiers
      findQualifiers,int maxRows) throws UDDIException, SOAPException;
   public AuthToken get_authToken(String userid, String cred)
      throws UDDIException, SOAPException;
   public BindingDetail get_bindingDetail(String bindingKey)
      throws UDDIException, SOAPException;
   public BindingDetail get_bindingDetail(Vector bindingKeyStrings)
```

```java
    throws UDDIException, SOAPException;
public BusinessDetail get_businessDetail(String businessKey)
    throws UDDIException, SOAPException;
public BusinessDetail get_businessDetail(Vector businessKeyStrings)
    throws UDDIException, SOAPException;
public BusinessDetailExt get_businessDetailExt(String businessKey)
    throws UDDIException, SOAPException;
public BusinessDetailExt get_businessDetailExt(Vector
    businessKeyStrings) throws UDDIException, SOAPException;
public RegisteredInfo get_registeredInfo(String authInfo)
    throws UDDIException, SOAPException;
public ServiceDetail get_serviceDetail(String serviceKey)
    throws UDDIException, SOAPException;
public ServiceDetail get_serviceDetail(Vector serviceKeyStrings)
    throws UDDIException, SOAPException;
public TModelDetail get_tModelDetail(String tModelKey)
    throws UDDIException, SOAPException;
public TModelDetail get_tModelDetail(Vector tModelKeyStrings)
    throws UDDIException, SOAPException;
public BindingDetail save_binding(String authInfo,
    Vector bindingTemplates) throws UDDIException, SOAPException;
public BusinessDetail save_business(String authInfo,
    UploadRegister[] uploadRegisters) throws UDDIException,
    SOAPException;
public BusinessDetail save_business(String authInfo,
    Vector businessEntities) throws UDDIException, SOAPException;
public ServiceDetail save_service(String authInfo,
    Vector businessServices) throws UDDIException, SOAPException;
public TModelDetail save_tModel(String authInfo, UploadRegister[]
    uploadRegisters) throws UDDIException, SOAPException;
public TModelDetail save_tModel(String authInfo, Vector tModels)
    throws UDDIException, SOAPException;
public Element send(Element el, boolean inquiry)
    throws SOAPException;
public Element send(UDDIElement el, boolean inquiry)
    throws SOAPException;
public void setInquiryURL(String url) throws MalformedURLException;
public void setPublishURL(String url) throws MalformedURLException;
public void setTransport(SOAPTransport transport);
public DispositionReport validate_categorization(String tModelKey,
    String keyValueString, BusinessEntity businessEntity)
    throws UDDIException, SOAPException;
public DispositionReport validate_categorization(String tModelKey,
    String keyValueString, BusinessService businessService)
    throws UDDIException, SOAPException;
public DispositionReport validate_categorization(String tModelKey,
    String keyValueString, TModel tModel) throws UDDIException,
    SOAPException;
}
```

Hierarchy

java.lang.Object → com.ibm.uddi.client.UDDIProxy

The com.ibm.uddi.datatype Package

com.ibm.uddi.datatype.Description

This class encapsulates a textual description associated with multiple UDDI data type objects, including BindingTemplate, BusinessEntity, BusinessService, and TModel.

Synopsis

```
public class Description extends UDDIElement {
  // Constructors
    public Description();
    public Description(String value);
    public Description(Element base) throws UDDIException;
  // Field Summary
    protected Element base;
    public static final String UDDI_TAG;
  // Public Methods
    public String getLang();
    public String getText();
    public void saveToXML(Element parent);
    public void setLang(String s);
    public void setText(String s);
}
```

Hierarchy

```
java.lang.Object → com.ibm.uddi.UDDIElement → com.ibm.uddi.datatype.
Description
```

com.ibm.uddi.datatype.Name

This class encapsulates a textual name associated with multiple UDDI data type objects, including BusinessEntity, BusinessService, and TModel.

Synopsis

```
public class Name extends UDDIElement {
  // Constructors
    public Name();
    public Name(String value);
    public Name(Element base) throws UDDIException;
  // Field Summary
    protected Element base;
    public static final String UDDI_TAG;
  // Public Methods
    public String getText();
    public void saveToXML(Element parent);
    public void setText(String s);
}
```

Hierarchy

```
java.lang.Object → com.ibm.uddi.UDDIElement →
com.ibm.uddi.datatype.Name
```

com.ibm.uddi.datatype.OverviewDoc

This class encapsulates an external overview document associated with multiple
UDDI data type objects, including TModel and InstanceDetails.

Synopsis

```
public class OverviewDoc extends UDDIElement {
    // Constructors
      public OverviewDoc();
      public OverviewDoc(Element base) throws UDDIException;
    // Field Summary
      protected Element base;
      public static final String UDDI_TAG;
    // Public Methods
      public String getDefaultDescriptionString();
      public Vector getDescriptionVector();
      public OverviewURL getOverviewURL();
      public String getOverviewURLString();
      public void saveToXML(Element parent);
      public void setDefaultDescriptionString(String s);
      public void setDescriptionVector(Vector s);
      public void setOverviewURL(OverviewURL s);
      public void setOverviewURL(String s);
}
```

Hierarchy

```
java.lang.Object → com.ibm.uddi.UDDIElement → com.ibm.uddi.datatype.
OverviewDoc
```

com.ibm.uddi.datatype.OverviewURL

This class encapsulates the URL for an external overview document.

Synopsis

```
public class OverviewURL extends UDDIElement {
    // Constructors
      public OverviewURL();
      public OverviewURL(String value);
      public OverviewURL(Element base) throws UDDIException;
    // Field Summary
      protected Element base;
      public static final String UDDI_TAG;
    // Public Methods
```

```
    public String getText( );
    public void saveToXML(Element parent);
    public void setText(String s);
}
```

Hierarchy

```
java.lang.Object → com.ibm.uddi.UDDIElement → com.ibm.uddi.datatype.
OverviewURL
```

The com.ibm.uddi.datatype.binding Package

com.ibm.uddi.datatype.binding.AccessPoint

This class encapsulates information for a UDDI accessPoint record.

Synopsis

```
public class AccessPoint extends UDDIElement {
  // Constructors
    public AccessPoint( );
    public AccessPoint(String value, String URLType);
    public AccessPoint(Element base) throws UDDIException;
  // Field Summary
    protected Element base;
    public static final String UDDI_TAG;
  // Public Methods
    public String getText( );
    public String getURLType( );
    public void saveToXML(Element parent);
    public void setText(String s);
    public void setURLType(String s);
}
```

Hierarchy

```
java.lang.Object → com.ibm.uddi.UDDIElement → com.ibm.uddi.datatype.
binding.AccessPoint
```

com.ibm.uddi.datatype.binding.BindingTemplate

This class encapsulates information for a UDDI bindingTemplate record.

Synopsis

```
public class BindingTemplate extends UDDIElement {
  // Constructors
    public BindingTemplate( );
    public BindingTemplate(String bindingKey, TModelInstanceDetails
      tModelInstanceDetails);
```

```
    public BindingTemplate(Element base) throws UDDIException;
  // Field Summary
    protected Element base;
    public static final String UDDI_TAG;
  // Public Methods
    public AccessPoint getAccessPoint( );
    public String getBindingKey( );
    public String getDefaultDescriptionString( );
    public Vector getDescriptionVector( );
    public HostingRedirector getHostingRedirector( );
    public String getServiceKey( );
    public TModelInstanceDetails getTModelInstanceDetails( );
    public void saveToXML(Element parent);
    public void setAccessPoint(AccessPoint s);
    public void setBindingKey(String s);
    public void setDefaultDescriptionString(String s);
    public void setDescriptionVector(Vector s);
    public void setHostingRedirector(HostingRedirector s);
    public void setServiceKey(String s);
    public void setTModelInstanceDetails(TModelInstanceDetails s);
}
```

Hierarchy

```
java.lang.Object → com.ibm.uddi.UDDIElement → com.ibm.uddi.datatype.
binding.BindingTemplate
```

---

com.ibm.uddi.datatype.binding.BindingTemplates

This class encapsulates multiple BindingTemplate objects.

Synopsis

```
public class BindingTemplates extends UDDIElement {
  // Constructors
    public BindingTemplates( );
    public BindingTemplates(Element base) throws UDDIException;
  // Field Summary
    protected Element base;
    public static final String UDDI_TAG;
  // Public Methods
    public Vector getBindingTemplateVector( );
    public void saveToXML(Element parent);
    public void setBindingTemplateVector(Vector s);
}
```

Hierarchy

```
java.lang.Object → com.ibm.uddi.UDDIElement → com.ibm.uddi.datatype.
binding.BindingTemplates
```

com.ibm.uddi.datatype.binding.HostingRedirector

This class encapsulates information for a UDDI hostingRedirector record.

Synopsis

```
public class HostingRedirector extends UDDIElement {
  // Constructors
    public HostingRedirector( );
    public HostingRedirector(String bindingKey);
    public HostingRedirector(Element base) throws UDDIException;
  // Field Summary
    protected Element base;
    public static final String UDDI_TAG;
  // Public Methods
    public String getBindingKey( );
    public void saveToXML(Element parent);
    public void setBindingKey(String s);
}
```

Hierarchy

```
java.lang.Object → com.ibm.uddi.UDDIElement → com.ibm.uddi.datatype.
binding.HostingRedirector
```

com.ibm.uddi.datatype.binding.InstanceDetails

This class encapsulates information for the instance details of a bindingTemplate record.

Synopsis

```
public class InstanceDetails extends UDDIElement {
  // Constructors
    public InstanceDetails( );
    public InstanceDetails(Element base) throws UDDIException;
  // Field Summary
    protected Element base;
    public static final String UDDI_TAG;
  // Public Methods
    public String getDefaultDescriptionString( );
    public Vector getDescriptionVector( );
    public InstanceParms getInstanceParms( );
    public OverviewDoc getOverviewDoc( );
    public void saveToXML(Element parent);
    public void setDefaultDescriptionString(String s);
    public void setDescriptionVector(Vector s);
    public void setInstanceParms(InstanceParms s);
    public void setOverviewDoc(OverviewDoc s);
}
```

Hierarchy

```
java.lang.Object → com.ibm.uddi.UDDIElement → com.ibm.uddi.datatype.
binding.InstanceDetails
```

com.ibm.uddi.datatype.binding.InstanceParms

This class encapsulates information for the settings file or the instance
parameters of a bindingTemplate record.

Synopsis

```
public class InstanceParms extends UDDIElement {
  // Constructors
    public InstanceParms( );
    public InstanceParms(String value);
    public InstanceParms(Element base) throws UDDIException;
  // Field Summary
    protected Element base;
    public static final String UDDI_TAG;
  // Public Methods
    public String getText( );
    public void saveToXML(Element parent);
    public void setText(String s);
}
```

Hierarchy

```
java.lang.Object → com.ibm.uddi.UDDIElement → com.ibm.uddi.datatype.
binding.InstanceParms
```

com.ibm.uddi.datatype.binding.TModelInstanceDetails

This class encapsulates multiple TModelInstanceInfo objects.

Synopsis

```
public class TModelInstanceDetails extends UDDIElement {
  // Constructors
    public TModelInstanceDetails( );
    public TModelInstanceDetails(Element base) throws UDDIException;
  // Field Summary
    protected Element base;
    public static final String UDDI_TAG;
  // Public Methods
    public Vector getTModelInstanceInfoVector( );
    public void saveToXML(Element parent);
    public void setTModelInstanceInfoVector(Vector s);
}
```

```
java.lang.Object → com.ibm.uddi.UDDIElement → com.ibm.uddi.datatype.
binding.TModelInstanceDetails
```

com.ibm.uddi.datatype.binding.TModelInstanceInfo

This class encapsulates information for the instance details of a UDDI
tModel record.

Synopsis

```
public class TModelInstanceInfo extends UDDIElement {
  // Constructors
    public TModelInstanceInfo( );
    public TModelInstanceInfo(String tModelKey);
    public TModelInstanceInfo(Element base) throws UDDIException;
  // Field Summary
    protected Element base;
    public static final String UDDI_TAG;
  // Public Methods
    public String getDefaultDescriptionString( );
    public Vector getDescriptionVector( );
    public InstanceDetails getInstanceDetails( );
    public String getTModelKey( );
    public void saveToXML(Element parent);
    public void setDefaultDescriptionString(String s);
    public void setDescriptionVector(Vector s);
    public void setInstanceDetails(InstanceDetails s);
    public void setTModelKey(String s);
}
```

Hierarchy

```
java.lang.Object → com.ibm.uddi.UDDIElement → com.ibm.uddi.datatype.
binding.TModelInstanceInfo
```

The com.ibm.uddi.datatype.business Package

com.ibm.uddi.datatype.business.Address

This class encapsulates information about a business address. Refer also to the
com.ibm.uddi.datatype.business.AddressLine class, which is discussed in the
following section.

Synopsis

```
public class Address extends UDDIElement {
  // Constructors
    public Address( );
```

```
    public Address(Element base) throws UDDIException;
  // Field Summary
    protected Element base;
    public static final String UDDI_TAG;
  // Public Methods
    public Vector getAddressLineStrings( );
    public Vector getAddressLineVector( );
    public String getSortCode( );
    public String getUseType( );
    public void saveToXML(Element parent);
    public void setAddressLineStrings(Vector s);
    public void setAddressLineVector(Vector s);
    public void setSortCode(String s);
    public void setUseType(String s);
}
```

Hierarchy

```
java.lang.Object → com.ibm.uddi.UDDIElement → com.ibm.uddi.datatype.
business.Address
```

---

com.ibm.uddi.datatype.business.AddressLine

This class encapsulates a single line within a business address.

Synopsis

```
public class AddressLine extends UDDIElement {
  // Constructors
    public AddressLine( );
    public AddressLine(String value);
    public AddressLine(Element base) throws UDDIException;
  // Field Summary
    protected Element base;
    public static final String UDDI_TAG;
  // Public Methods
    public String getText( );
    public void saveToXML(Element parent);
    public void setText(String s);
}
```

Hierarchy

```
java.lang.Object → com.ibm.uddi.UDDIElement → com.ibm.uddi.datatype.
business.AddressLine
```

com.ibm.uddi.datatype.business.BusinessEntity

This class encapsulates all information for a UDDI businessEntity record. This includes the business name, description, contacts, businessKey, and any business identifiers or business taxonomy categorizations.

Synopsis

```
public class BusinessEntity extends UDDIElement {
  // Constructors
    public BusinessEntity( );
    public BusinessEntity(String businessKey, String name);
    public BusinessEntity(Element base) throws UDDIException;
  // Field Summary
    protected Element base;
    public static final String UDDI_TAG;
  // Public Methods
    public String getAuthorizedName( );
    public String getBusinessKey( );
    public BusinessServices getBusinessServices( );
    public CategoryBag getCategoryBag( );
    public Contacts getContacts( );
    public String getDefaultDescriptionString( );
    public Vector getDescriptionVector( );
    public DiscoveryURLs getDiscoveryURLs( );
    public IdentifierBag getIdentifierBag( );
    public Name getName( );
    public String getNameString( );
    public String getOperator( );
    public void saveToXML(Element parent);
    public void setAuthorizedName(String s);
    public void setBusinessKey(String s);
    public void setBusinessServices(BusinessServices s);
    public void setCategoryBag(CategoryBag s);
    public void setContacts(Contacts s);
    public void setDefaultDescriptionString(String s);
    public void setDescriptionVector(Vector s);
    public void setDiscoveryURLs(DiscoveryURLs s);
    public void setIdentifierBag(IdentifierBag s);
    public void setName(Name s);
    public void setName(String s);
    public void setOperator(String s);
}
```

Hierarchy

```
java.lang.Object → com.ibm.uddi.UDDIElement → com.ibm.uddi.datatype.
business.BusinessEntity
```

com.ibm.uddi.datatype.business.Contact

This class encapsulates information about a business contact. This includes the person's name, one or more business addresses, email addresses, and telephone numbers.

Synopsis

```java
public class Contact extends UDDIElement {
  // Constructors
    public Contact( );
    public Contact(String personName);
    public Contact(Element base) throws UDDIException;
  // Field Summary
    protected Element base;
    public static final String UDDI_TAG;
  // Public Methods
    public Vector getAddressVector( );
    public String getDefaultDescriptionString( );
    public Vector getDescriptionVector( );
    public Vector getEmailVector( );
    public PersonName getPersonName( );
    public String getPersonNameString( );
    public Vector getPhoneVector( );
    public String getUseType( );
    public void saveToXML(Element parent);
    public void setAddressVector(Vector s);
    public void setDefaultDescriptionString(String s);
    public void setDescriptionVector(Vector s);
    public void setEmailVector(Vector s);
    public void setPersonName(PersonName s);
    public void setPersonName(String s);
    public void setPhoneVector(Vector s);
    public void setUseType(String s);
}
```

Hierarchy

```
java.lang.Object → com.ibm.uddi.UDDIElement → com.ibm.uddi.datatype.
business.Contact
```

com.ibm.uddi.datatype.business.Contacts

This class encapsulates multiple Contact objects.

Synopsis

```java
public class Contacts extends UDDIElement {
  // Constructors
    public Contacts( );
    public Contacts(Element base) throws UDDIException;
```

```
// Field Summary
  protected Element base;
  public static final String UDDI_TAG;
// Public Methods
  public Vector getContactVector( );
  public void saveToXML(Element parent);
  public void setContactVector(Vector s);
}
```

Hierarchy

```
java.lang.Object → com.ibm.uddi.UDDIElement → com.ibm.uddi.datatype.
business.Contacts
```

com.ibm.uddi.datatype.business.Email

This class encapsulates a single email address.

Synopsis

```
public class Email extends UDDIElement {
  // Constructors
    public Email( );
    public Email(String value);
    public Email(Element base) throws UDDIException;
  // Field Summary
    protected Element base;
    public static final String UDDI_TAG;
  // Public Methods
    public String getText( );
    public String getUseType( );
    public void saveToXML(Element parent);
    public void setText(String s);
    public void setUseType(String s);
}
```

Hierarchy

```
java.lang.Object → com.ibm.uddi.UDDIElement → com.ibm.uddi.datatype.
business.Email
```

com.ibm.uddi.datatype.business.PersonName

This class encapsulates a single person's name.

Synopsis

```
public class PersonName extends UDDIElement {
  // Constructors
    public PersonName( );
    public PersonName(String value);
```

```
      public PersonName(Element base) throws UDDIException;
    // Field Summary
      protected Element base;
      public static final String UDDI_TAG;
    // Public Methods
      public String getText( );
      public void saveToXML(Element parent);
      public void setText(String s);
  }
```

Hierarchy

```
java.lang.Object → com.ibm.uddi.UDDIElement → com.ibm.uddi.datatype.
business.PersonName
```

com.ibm.uddi.datatype.business.Phone

This class encapsulates a single telephone number.

Synopsis

```
public class Phone extends UDDIElement {
    // Constructors
      public Phone( );
      public Phone(String value);
      public Phone(Element base) throws UDDIException;
    // Field Summary
      protected Element base;
      public static final String UDDI_TAG;
    // Public Methods
      public String getText( );
      public String getUseType( );
      public void saveToXML(Element parent);
      public void setText(String s);
      public void setUseType(String s);
  }
```

Hierarchy

```
java.lang.Object → com.ibm.uddi.UDDIElement → com.ibm.uddi.datatype.
business.Phone
```

The com.ibm.uddi.datatype.service Package

com.ibm.uddi.datatype.service.BusinessService

This class encapsulates all information for a UDDI businessService record.

Synopsis

```
public class BusinessService extends UDDIElement {
  // Constructors
    public BusinessService( );
    public BusinessService(String serviceKey, String name,
      BindingTemplates bindingTemplates);
    public BusinessService(Element base) throws UDDIException;
  // Field Summary
    protected Element base;
    public static final String UDDI_TAG;
  // Public Methods
    public BindingTemplates getBindingTemplates( );
    public String getBusinessKey( );
    public CategoryBag getCategoryBag( );
    public String getDefaultDescriptionString( );
    public Vector getDescriptionVector( );
    public Name getName( );
    public String getNameString( );
    public String getServiceKey( );
    public void saveToXML(Element parent);
    public void setBindingTemplates(BindingTemplates s);
    public void setBusinessKey(String s);
    public void setCategoryBag(CategoryBag s);
    public void setDefaultDescriptionString(String s);
    public void setDescriptionVector(Vector s);
    public void setName(Name s);
    public void setName(String s);
    public void setServiceKey(String s);
}
```

Hierarchy

```
java.lang.Object → com.ibm.uddi.UDDIElement → com.ibm.uddi.datatype.
service.BusinessService
```

com.ibm.uddi.datatype.service.BusinessServices

This class encapsulates multiple BusinessService objects.

Synopsis

```
public class BusinessServices extends UDDIElement {
  // Constructors
    public BusinessServices( );
    public BusinessServices(Element base) throws UDDIException;
  // Field Summary
    protected Element base;
    public static final String UDDI_TAG;
```

```
    // Public Methods
      public Vector getBusinessServiceVector( );
      public void saveToXML(Element parent);
      public void setBusinessServiceVector(Vector s);
  }
```

Hierarchy

```
    java.lang.Object → com.ibm.uddi.UDDIElement → com.ibm.uddi.datatype.
    service.BusinessServices
```

The com.ibm.uddi.datatype.tmodel Package

com.ibm.uddi.datatype.tmodel.TModel

This class encapsulates all information for a UDDI tModel record.

Synopsis

```
    public class TModel extends UDDIElement {
      // Constructors
      public TModel( );
      public TModel(String tModelKey, String name);
      public TModel(Element base) throws UDDIException;
      // Field Summary
      protected Element base;
      public static final String NAICS_TMODEL_KEY;
      public static final String UDDI_TAG;
      public static final String UNSPSC_TMODEL_KEY;
      // Public Methods
      public String getAuthorizedName( );
      public CategoryBag getCategoryBag( );
      public String getDefaultDescriptionString( );
      public Vector getDescriptionVector( );
      public IdentifierBag getIdentifierBag( );
      public Name getName( );
      public String getNameString( );
      public String getOperator( );
      public OverviewDoc getOverviewDoc( );
      public String getTModelKey( );
      public void saveToXML(Element parent);
      public void setAuthorizedName(String s);
      public void setCategoryBag(CategoryBag s);
      public void setDefaultDescriptionString(String s);
      public void setDescriptionVector(Vector s);
      public void setIdentifierBag(IdentifierBag s);
      public void setName(Name s);
      public void setName(String s);
      public void setOperator(String s);
      public void setOverviewDoc(OverviewDoc s);
      public void setTModelKey(String s);
  }
```

Hierarchy

```
java.lang.Object → com.ibm.uddi.UDDIElement → com.ibm.uddi.datatype.
tmodel.TModel
```

The com.ibm.uddi.response Package

com.ibm.uddi.response.AuthToken

This class encapsulates the UDDI operator response for a get_authToken( ) query.
Use the getAuthInfoString( ) method to retrieve the actual authentication token
value.

Synopsis

```
public class AuthToken extends UDDIElement {
  // Constructors
    public AuthToken( );
    public AuthToken(String operator, String authInfo);
    public AuthToken(Element base) throws UDDIException;
  // Field Summary
    protected Element base;
    public static final String UDDI_TAG;
  // Public Methods
    public AuthInfo getAuthInfo( );
    public String getAuthInfoString( );
    public String getOperator( );
    public void saveToXML(Element parent);
    public void setAuthInfo(AuthInfo s);
    public void setAuthInfo(String s);
    public void setOperator(String s);
}
```

Hierarchy

```
java.lang.Object → com.ibm.uddi.UDDIElement → com.ibm.uddi.response.
AuthToken
```

com.ibm.uddi.response.BindingDetail

This class encapsulates the UDDI operator response for a get_bindingDetail( )
query, a find_binding( ) query, or a save_binding( ) publishing request. Use the
getBindingTemplateVector( ) method to extract a Vector of BindingTemplate
objects.

Synopsis

```
public class BindingDetail extends UDDIElement {
  // Constructors
    public BindingDetail( );
```

```
    public BindingDetail(String operator);
    public BindingDetail(Element base) throws UDDIException;
  // Field Summary
    protected Element base;
    public static final String UDDI_TAG;
  // Public Methods
    public Vector getBindingTemplateVector( );
    public String getOperator( );
    public String getTruncated( );
    public boolean getTruncatedBoolean( );
    public void saveToXML(Element parent);
    public void setBindingTemplateVector(Vector s);
    public void setOperator(String s);
    public void setTruncated(boolean s);
    public void setTruncated(String s);
}
```

Hierarchy

```
java.lang.Object → com.ibm.uddi.UDDIElement → com.ibm.uddi.response.
BindingDetail
```

com.ibm.uddi.response.BusinessDetail

This class encapsulates the UDDI operator response for a get_businessDetail( )
query or a save_business( ) publishing request. Use the getBusinessEntityVector( )
method to extract a Vector of BusinessEntity objects.

Synopsis

```
public class BusinessDetail extends UDDIElement {
  // Constructors
    public BusinessDetail( );
    public BusinessDetail(String operator);
    public BusinessDetail(Element base) throws UDDIException;
  // Field Summary
    protected Element base;
    public static final String UDDI_TAG;
  // Public Methods
    public Vector getBusinessEntityVector( );
    public String getOperator( );
    public String getTruncated( );
    public boolean getTruncatedBoolean( );
    public void saveToXML(Element parent);
    public void setBusinessEntityVector(Vector s);
    public void setOperator(String s);
    public void setTruncated(boolean s);
    public void setTruncated(String s);
}
```

Hierarchy

```
java.lang.Object → com.ibm.uddi.UDDIElement → com.ibm.uddi.response.
BusinessDetail
```

com.ibm.uddi.response.BusinessDetailExt

This class encapsulates the UDDI operator response for a get_businessDetailExt( )
query. Use the getBusinessEntityExtVector( ) method to extract a Vector of
BusinessEntityExt objects.

Synopsis

```
public class BusinessDetailExt extends UDDIElement {
  // Constructors
    public BusinessDetailExt( );
    public BusinessDetailExt(String operator, Vector businessEntityExt);
    public BusinessDetailExt(Element base) throws UDDIException;
  // Field Summary
    protected Element base;
    public static final String UDDI_TAG;
  // Public Methods
    public Vector getBusinessEntityExtVector( );
    public String getOperator( );
    public String getTruncated( );
    public boolean getTruncatedBoolean( );
    public void saveToXML(Element parent);
    public void setBusinessEntityExtVector(Vector s);
    public void setOperator(String s);
    public void setTruncated(boolean s);
    public void setTruncated(String s);
}
```

Hierarchy

```
java.lang.Object → com.ibm.uddi.UDDIElement → com.ibm.uddi.response.
BusinessDetailExt
```

com.ibm.uddi.response.BusinessEntityExt

This class encapsulates information for a UDDI businessEntityExt record.

Synopsis

```
public class BusinessEntityExt extends UDDIElement {
  // Constructors
    public BusinessEntityExt( );
    public BusinessEntityExt(BusinessEntity businessEntity);
    public BusinessEntityExt(Element base) throws UDDIException;
```

```
    // Field Summary
      protected Element base;
      public static final String UDDI_TAG;
    // Public Methods
      public BusinessEntity getBusinessEntity( );
      public void saveToXML(Element parent);
      public void setBusinessEntity(BusinessEntity s);
  }
```

Hierarchy

```
java.lang.Object → com.ibm.uddi.UDDIElement → com.ibm.uddi.response.
BusinessEntityExt
```

com.ibm.uddi.response.BusinessInfo

This class encapsulates brief information for a UDDI businessEntity record. This
includes the businessKey, business name, and description. Use getServiceInfos( )
to retrieve a list of services offered by the business.

Synopsis

```
public class BusinessInfo extends UDDIElement {
  // Constructors
    public BusinessInfo( );
    public BusinessInfo(String businessKey, String name, ServiceInfos
        serviceInfos);
    public BusinessInfo(Element base) throws UDDIException;
  // Field Summary
    protected Element base;
    public static final String UDDI_TAG;
  // Public Methods
    public String getBusinessKey( );
    public String getDefaultDescriptionString( );
    public Vector getDescriptionVector( );
    public Name getName( );
    public String getNameString( );
    public ServiceInfos getServiceInfos( );
    public void saveToXML(Element parent);
    public void setBusinessKey(String s);
    public void setDefaultDescriptionString(String s);
    public void setDescriptionVector(Vector s);
    public void setName(Name s);
    public void setName(String s);
    public void setServiceInfos(ServiceInfos s);
}
```

Hierarchy

```
java.lang.Object → com.ibm.uddi.UDDIElement → com.ibm.uddi.response.
BusinessInfo
```

com.ibm.uddi.response.BusinessInfos

This class encapsulates multiple BusinessInfo objects. Use the getBusinessInfoVector( ) method to retrieve a Vector of BusinessInfo objects.

Synopsis

```
public class BusinessInfos extends UDDIElement {
  // Constructors
    public BusinessInfos( );
    public BusinessInfos(Element base) throws UDDIException;
  // Field Summary
    protected Element base;
    public static final String UDDI_TAG;
  // Public Methods
    public Vector getBusinessInfoVector( );
    public void saveToXML(Element parent);
    public void setBusinessInfoVector(Vector s);
}
```

Hierarchy

```
java.lang.Object → com.ibm.uddi.UDDIElement → com.ibm.uddi.response.
BusinessInfos
```

com.ibm.uddi.response.BusinessList

This class encapsulates the UDDI operator response for a find_business( ) query. Use the getBusinessInfos( ) method to retrieve a BusinessInfo object.

Synopsis

```
public class BusinessList extends UDDIElement {
  // Constructors
    public BusinessList( );
    public BusinessList(String operator, BusinessInfos businessInfos);
    public BusinessList(Element base) throws UDDIException;
  // Field Summary
    protected Element base;
    public static final String UDDI_TAG;
  // Public Methods
    public BusinessInfos getBusinessInfos( );
    public String getOperator( );
    public String getTruncated( );
    public boolean getTruncatedBoolean( );
    public void saveToXML(Element parent);
    public void setBusinessInfos(BusinessInfos s);
    public void setOperator(String s);
    public void setTruncated(boolean s);
    public void setTruncated(String s);
}
```

```
java.lang.Object → com.ibm.uddi.UDDIElement → com.ibm.uddi.response.
BusinessList
```

com.ibm.uddi.response.DispositionReport

This class encapsulates a UDDI disposition report. Depending on the API call, the
DispositionReport may contain error information or a success flag. For example,
a call to the get_businessDetail() query that fails will trigger a UDDIException
with an embedded DispositionReport object. A call to delete_business() will
return a DispositionReport object directly; if the deletion was successful, the
success flag will be set to true. Use getErrCode() to retrieve the UDDI error code
(e.g., E_invalidKeyPassed, E_fatalError); use getErrno() to retrieve the UDDI
error code number (e.g., 10210, 10500); or use getErroInfoText() to retrieve a
more complete description of the error. Use the success() method to retrieve the
success flag. Use getGeneric() to retrieve the UDDI version number of the UDDI
operator site.

Synopsis

```
public class DispositionReport extends UDDIElement {
    // Constructors
      public DispositionReport(Element el) throws UDDIException;
    // Field Summary
      public static final String E_accountLimitExceeded;
      public static final String E_authTokenExpired;
      public static final String E_authTokenRequired;
      public static final String E_categorizationNotAllowed;
      public static final String E_invalidCategory;
      public static final String E_invalidKeyPassed;
      public static final String E_invalidURLPassed;
      public static final String E_keyRetired;
      public static final String E_operatorMismatch;
      public static final String E_userMismatch;
      public static String UDDI_TAG;
    // Public Methods
      public String getErrCode();
      public String getErrInfoText();
      public int getErrno();
      public String getGeneric();
      public String getOperator();
      public boolean isValidElement(Element el);
      public void saveToXML(Element el);
      public boolean success();
}
```

Hierarchy

```
java.lang.Object → com.ibm.uddi.UDDIElement → com.ibm.uddi.response.
DispositionReport
```

com.ibm.uddi.response.ErrInfo

This class encapsulates information regarding a UDDI disposition report. The class is not typically used directly by UDDI client code.

Synopsis

```
public class ErrInfo extends UDDIElement {
  // Constructors
    public ErrInfo( );
    public ErrInfo(String value, String errCode);
    public ErrInfo(Element base) throws UDDIException;
  // Field Summary
    protected Element base;
    public static final String UDDI_TAG;
  // Public Methods
    public String getErrCode( );
    public String getText( );
    public void saveToXML(Element parent);
    public void setErrCode(String s);
    public void setText(String s);
}
```

Hierarchy

```
java.lang.Object → com.ibm.uddi.UDDIElement → com.ibm.uddi.response.
ErrInfo
```

com.ibm.uddi.response.RegisteredInfo

This class encapsulates the UDDI operator response for a get_registeredInfo( ) query. The object includes a list of all businessEntity keys and tModel keys that are controlled by the specified authentication token.

Synopsis

```
public class RegisteredInfo extends UDDIElement {
  // Constructors
    public RegisteredInfo( );
    public RegisteredInfo(String operator, BusinessInfos businessInfos,
        TModelInfos tModelInfos);
    public RegisteredInfo(Element base) throws UDDIException;
  // Field Summary
    protected Element base;
    public static final String UDDI_TAG;
  // Public Methods
    public BusinessInfos getBusinessInfos( );
    public String getOperator( );
    public TModelInfos getTModelInfos( );
    public String getTruncated( );
    public boolean getTruncatedBoolean( );
```

```
      public void saveToXML(Element parent);
      public void setBusinessInfos(BusinessInfos s);
      public void setOperator(String s);
      public void setTModelInfos(TModelInfos s);
      public void setTruncated(boolean s);
      public void setTruncated(String s);
    }
```

Hierarchy

```
java.lang.Object → com.ibm.uddi.UDDIElement → com.ibm.uddi.response.
RegisteredInfo
```

---

com.ibm.uddi.response.Result

This class encapsulates information regarding a UDDI disposition report. The class is not typically used directly by UDDI client code.

Synopsis

```
public class Result extends UDDIElement {
  // Constructors
    public Result( );
    public Result(String errno);
    public Result(Element base) throws UDDIException;
  // Field Summary
    protected Element base;
    public static final String UDDI_TAG;
  // Public Methods
    public ErrInfo getErrInfo( );
    public String getErrno( );
    public String getKeyType( );
    public void saveToXML(Element parent);
    public void setErrInfo(ErrInfo s);
    public void setErrno(String s);
    public void setKeyType(String s);
  }
```

Hierarchy

```
java.lang.Object → com.ibm.uddi.UDDIElement → com.ibm.uddi.response.Result
```

---

com.ibm.uddi.response.ServiceDetail

This class encapsulates the UDDI operator response for a get_serviceDetail( ) query or a save_service( ) publishing request. Use the getBusinessServiceVector( ) method to retrieve a Vector of BusinessService objects.

Synopsis

```
public class ServiceDetail extends UDDIElement {
  // Constructors
```

```
    public ServiceDetail( );
    public ServiceDetail(String operator);
    public ServiceDetail(Element base) throws UDDIException;
  // Field Summary
    protected Element base;
    public static final String UDDI_TAG;
  // Public Methods
    public Vector getBusinessServiceVector( );
    public String getOperator( );
    public String getTruncated( );
    public boolean getTruncatedBoolean( );
    public void saveToXML(Element parent);
    public void setBusinessServiceVector(Vector s);
    public void setOperator(String s);
    public void setTruncated(boolean s);
    public void setTruncated(String s);
}
```

Hierarchy

```
java.lang.Object → com.ibm.uddi.UDDIElement → com.ibm.uddi.response.
ServiceDetail
```

com.ibm.uddi.response.ServiceInfo

This class encapsulates brief information for a UDDI businessService record. This information includes service name, serviceKey, and associated businessKeys.

Synopsis

```
public class ServiceInfo extends UDDIElement {
  // Constructors
    public ServiceInfo( );
    public ServiceInfo(String serviceKey, String name);
    public ServiceInfo(Element base) throws UDDIException;
  // Field Summary
    protected Element base;
    public static final String UDDI_TAG;
  // Public Methods
    public String getBusinessKey( );
    public Name getName( );
    public String getNameString( );
    public String getServiceKey( );
    public void saveToXML(Element parent);
    public void setBusinessKey(String s);
    public void setName(Name s);
    public void setName(String s);
    public void setServiceKey(String s);
}
```

Hierarchy

```
java.lang.Object → com.ibm.uddi.UDDIElement → com.ibm.uddi.response.
ServiceInfo
```

com.ibm.uddi.response.ServiceInfos

This class encapsulates multiple ServiceInfo objects. Use the
getServiceInfoVector( ) method to retrieve a Vector of ServiceInfo objects.

Synopsis

```
public class ServiceInfos extends UDDIElement {
  // Constructors
    public ServiceInfos( );
    public ServiceInfos(Element base) throws UDDIException;
  // Field Summary
    protected Element base;
    public static final String UDDI_TAG;
  // Public Methods
    public Vector getServiceInfoVector( );
    public void saveToXML(Element parent);
    public void setServiceInfoVector(Vector s);
}
```

Hierarchy

```
java.lang.Object → com.ibm.uddi.UDDIElement → com.ibm.uddi.response.
ServiceInfos
```

com.ibm.uddi.response.ServiceList

This class encapsulates the UDDI operator response for a find_service( ) query.
Use the getServiceInfos( ) method to retrieve a ServiceInfos object.

Synopsis

```
public class ServiceList extends UDDIElement {
  // Constructors
    public ServiceList( );
    public ServiceList(String operator, ServiceInfos serviceInfos);
    public ServiceList(Element base) throws UDDIException;
  // Field Summary
    protected Element base;
    public static final String UDDI_TAG;
```

```
   // Public Methods
     public String getOperator( );
     public ServiceInfos getServiceInfos( );
     public String getTruncated( );
     public boolean getTruncatedBoolean( );
     public void saveToXML(Element parent);
     public void setOperator(String s);
     public void setServiceInfos(ServiceInfos s);
     public void setTruncated(boolean s);
     public void setTruncated(String s);
   }
```

Hierarchy

```
java.lang.Object → com.ibm.uddi.UDDIElement → com.ibm.uddi.response.
ServiceList
```

com.ibm.uddi.response.TModelDetail

This class encapsulates the UDDI operator response for a get_tModelDetail( ) query or a save_tModel( ) publishing request. Use the getTModelVector( ) method to retrieve a Vector of TModel objects.

Synopsis

```
public class TModelDetail extends UDDIElement {
   // Constructors
     public TModelDetail( );
     public TModelDetail(String operator, Vector tModel);
     public TModelDetail(Element base) throws UDDIException;
   // Field Summary
     protected Element base;
     public static final String UDDI_TAG;
   // Public Methods
     public String getOperator( );
     public Vector getTModelVector( );
     public String getTruncated( );
     public boolean getTruncatedBoolean( );
     public void saveToXML(Element parent);
     public void setOperator(String s);
     public void setTModelVector(Vector s);
     public void setTruncated(boolean s);
     public void setTruncated(String s);
   }
```

Hierarchy

```
java.lang.Object → com.ibm.uddi.UDDIElement → com.ibm.uddi.response.
TModelDetail
```

com.ibm.uddi.response.TModelInfo

This class encapsulates brief information for a UDDI tModel record. The information includes the tModel name and the tModelKey.

Synopsis

```
public class TModelInfo extends UDDIElement {
  // Constructors
    public TModelInfo( );
    public TModelInfo(String tModelKey, String name);
    public TModelInfo(Element base) throws UDDIException;
  // Field Summary
    protected Element base;
    public static final String UDDI_TAG;
  // Public Methods
    public Name getName( );
    public String getNameString( );
    public String getTModelKey( );
    public void saveToXML(Element parent);
    public void setName(Name s);
    public void setName(String s);
    public void setTModelKey(String s);
}
```

Hierarchy

```
java.lang.Object → com.ibm.uddi.UDDIElement → com.ibm.uddi.response.
TModelInfo
```

com.ibm.uddi.response.TModelInfos

This class encapsulates multiple TModelInfo objects. Use the getTModelInfoVector( ) method to retrieve a Vector of TModelInfo objects.

Synopsis

```
public class TModelInfos extends UDDIElement {
  // Constructors
    public TModelInfos( );
    public TModelInfos(Element base) throws UDDIException;
  // Field Summary
    protected Element base;
    public static final String UDDI_TAG;
  // Public Methods
    public Vector getTModelInfoVector( );
    public void saveToXML(Element parent);
    public void setTModelInfoVector(Vector s);
}
```

```
java.lang.Object → com.ibm.uddi.UDDIElement → com.ibm.uddi.response.
TModelInfos
```

com.ibm.uddi.response.TModelList

This class encapsulates the UDDI operator response for a find_tModel( ) query. Use the getTModelInfos( ) method to retrieve a TModelInfo object.

Synopsis

```
public class TModelList extends UDDIElement {
  // Constructors
    public TModelList( );
    public TModelList(String operator, TModelInfos tModelInfos);
    public TModelList(Element base) throws UDDIException;
  // Field Summary
    protected Element base;
    public static final String UDDI_TAG;
  // Public Methods
    public String getOperator( );
    public TModelInfos getTModelInfos( );
    public String getTruncated( );
    public boolean getTruncatedBoolean( );
    public void saveToXML(Element parent);
    public void setOperator(String s);
    public void setTModelInfos(TModelInfos s);
    public void setTruncated(boolean s);
    public void setTruncated(String s);
}
```

Hierarchy

```
java.lang.Object → com.ibm.uddi.UDDIElement → com.ibm.uddi.response.
TModelList
```

The com.ibm.uddi.util Package

com.ibm.uddi.util.AuthInfo

This class encapsulates the UDDI authentication token. Use the getText( ) method to retrieve the actual authentication token value.

Synopsis

```
public class AuthInfo extends UDDIElement {
  // Constructors
    public AuthInfo( );
    public AuthInfo(String value);
```

```
      public AuthInfo(Element base) throws UDDIException;
   // Field Summary
      protected Element base;
      public static final String UDDI_TAG;
   // Public Methods
      public String getText();
      public void saveToXML(Element parent);
      public void setText(String s);
}
```

Hierarchy

```
java.lang.Object → com.ibm.uddi.UDDIElement → com.ibm.uddi.util.AuthInfo
```

com.ibm.uddi.util.BindingKey

This class encapsulates information regarding a UDDI BindingKey, but is not typically used by client code directly.

Synopsis

```
public class BindingKey extends UDDIElement {
   // Constructors
      public BindingKey();
      public BindingKey(String value);
      public BindingKey(Element base) throws UDDIException;
   // Field Summary
      protected Element base;
      public static final String UDDI_TAG;
   // Public Methods
      public String getText();
      public void saveToXML(Element parent);
      public void setText(String s);
}
```

Hierarchy

```
java.lang.Object → com.ibm.uddi.UDDIElement → com.ibm.uddi.util.BindingKey
```

com.ibm.uddi.util.BusinessKey

This class encapsulates information regarding a UDDI BusinessKey, but is not typically used by client code directly.

Synopsis

```
public class BusinessKey extends UDDIElement {
   // Constructors
      public BusinessKey();
      public BusinessKey(String value);
      public BusinessKey(Element base) throws UDDIException;
```

```
// Field Summary
  protected Element base;
  public static final String UDDI_TAG;
// Public Methods
  public String getText( );
  public void saveToXML(Element parent);
  public void setText(String s);
}
```

Hierarchy

```
java.lang.Object → com.ibm.uddi.UDDIElement → com.ibm.uddi.util.
BusinessKey
```

com.ibm.uddi.util.CategoryBag

This class encapsulates multiple KeyedReference objects, each of which indicates a UDDI categorization. For example, a CategoryBag object may contain one or more NAICS codes. The class is usually passed as an argument to any of the find_xxx( ) functions.

Synopsis

```
public class CategoryBag extends UDDIElement {
  // Constructors
    public CategoryBag( );
    public CategoryBag(Element base) throws UDDIException;
  // Field Summary
    protected Element base;
    public static final String UDDI_TAG;
  // Public Methods
    public Vector getKeyedReferenceVector( );
    public void saveToXML(Element parent);
    public void setKeyedReferenceVector(Vector s);
}
```

Hierarchy

```
java.lang.Object → com.ibm.uddi.UDDIElement → com.ibm.uddi.util.
CategoryBag
```

com.ibm.uddi.util.DiscoveryURL

This class encapsulates the information for a UDDI DiscoveryURL.

Synopsis

```
public class DiscoveryURL extends UDDIElement {
  // Constructors
    public DiscoveryURL( );
    public DiscoveryURL(String value, String useType);
```

```
    public DiscoveryURL(Element base) throws UDDIException;
  // Field Summary
    protected Element base;
    public static final String UDDI_TAG;
  // Public Methods
    public String getText( );
    public String getUseType( );
    public void saveToXML(Element parent);
    public void setText(String s);
    public void setUseType(String s);
}
```

Hierarchy

```
java.lang.Object → com.ibm.uddi.UDDIElement → com.ibm.uddi.util.
DiscoveryURL
```

com.ibm.uddi.util.DiscoveryURLs

This class encapsulates multiple DiscoveryURL objects.

Synopsis

```
public class DiscoveryURLs extends UDDIElement {
  // Constructors
    public DiscoveryURLs( );
    public DiscoveryURLs(Vector discoveryURL);
    public DiscoveryURLs(Element base) throws UDDIException;
  // Field Summary
    protected Element base;
    public static final String UDDI_TAG;
  // Public Methods
    public Vector getDiscoveryURLVector( );
    public void saveToXML(Element parent);
    public void setDiscoveryURLVector(Vector s);
}
```

Hierarchy

```
java.lang.Object → com.ibm.uddi.UDDIElement → com.ibm.uddi.util.
DiscoveryURLs
```

com.ibm.uddi.util.FindQualifier

This class encapsulates a single UDDI FindQualifier, used to specify more precise search criteria. For example, a FindQualifier set to exactNameMatch mandates that only exact name matches be returned from a find_xxx( ) function call.

Synopsis

```
public class FindQualifier extends UDDIElement {
  // Constructors
    public FindQualifier( );
    public FindQualifier(String value);
    public FindQualifier(Element base) throws UDDIException;
  // Field Summary
    protected Element base;
    public static final String caseSensitiveMatch;
    public static final String exactNameMatch;
    public static final String sortByDateAsc;
    public static final String sortByDateDesc;
    public static final String sortByNameAsc;
    public static final String sortByNameDesc;
    public static final String UDDI_TAG;
  // Public Methods
    public String getText( );
    public void saveToXML(Element parent);
    public void setText(String s);
}
```

Hierarchy

```
java.lang.Object → com.ibm.uddi.UDDIElement → com.ibm.uddi.util.
FindQualifier
```

com.ibm.uddi.util.FindQualifiers

This class encapsulates multiple FindQualifier objects. The class is usually passed as an argument to any of the find_xxx( ) function calls.

Synopsis

```
public class FindQualifiers extends UDDIElement {
  // Constructors
    public FindQualifiers( );
    public FindQualifiers(Element base) throws UDDIException;
  // Field Summary
    protected Element base;
    public static final String UDDI_TAG;
  // Public Methods
    public Vector getFindQualifierVector( );
    public void saveToXML(Element parent);
    public void setFindQualifierVector(Vector s);
}
```

Hierarchy

```
java.lang.Object → com.ibm.uddi.UDDIElement → com.ibm.uddi.util.
FindQualifiers
```

com.ibm.uddi.util.IdentifierBag

This class encapsulates multiple KeyedReference objects, each of which indicates a UDDI identifier. For example, an IdentifierBag object may contain one or more Dun & Bradstreet D-U-N-S® Numbers. The class is usually passed as an argument to any of the find_xxx( ) function calls.

Synopsis

```
public class IdentifierBag extends UDDIElement {
  // Constructors
    public IdentifierBag( );
    public IdentifierBag(Element base) throws UDDIException;
  // Field Summary
    protected Element base;
    public static final String UDDI_TAG;
  // Public Methods
    public Vector getKeyedReferenceVector( );
    public void saveToXML(Element parent);
    public void setKeyedReferenceVector(Vector s);
}
```

Hierarchy

```
java.lang.Object → com.ibm.uddi.UDDIElement → com.ibm.uddi.util.
IdentifierBag
```

com.ibm.uddi.util.KeyedReference

This class encapsulates a single UDDI keyedReference record. See CategoryBag and IdentifierBag for additional details.

Synopsis

```
public class KeyedReference extends UDDIElement {
  // Constructors
    public KeyedReference( );
    public KeyedReference(String keyName, String keyValue);
    public KeyedReference(Element base) throws UDDIException;
  // Field Summary
    protected Element base;
    public static final String UDDI_TAG;
  // Public Methods
    public String getKeyName( );
    public String getKeyValue( );
    public String getTModelKey( );
    public void saveToXML(Element parent);
    public void setKeyName(String s);
    public void setKeyValue(String s);
    public void setTModelKey(String s);
}
```

Hierarchy

```
java.lang.Object → com.ibm.uddi.UDDIElement → com.ibm.uddi.util.
KeyedReference
```

com.ibm.uddi.util.KeyValue

This class encapsulates information regarding a UDDI KeyValue, but is not typically used by client code directly.

Synopsis

```
public class KeyValue extends UDDIElement {
  // Constructors
    public KeyValue( );
    public KeyValue(String value);
    public KeyValue(Element base) throws UDDIException;
  // Field Summary
    protected Element base;
    public static final String UDDI_TAG;
  // Public Methods
    public String getText( );
    public void saveToXML(Element parent);
    public void setText(String s);
}
```

Hierarchy

```
java.lang.Object → com.ibm.uddi.UDDIElement →
com.ibm.uddi.util.KeyValue
```

com.ibm.uddi.util.ServiceKey

This class encapsulates information regarding a UDDI ServiceKey, but is not typically used by client code directly.

Synopsis

```
public class ServiceKey extends UDDIElement {
  // Constructors
    public ServiceKey( );
    public ServiceKey(String value);
    public ServiceKey(Element base) throws UDDIException;
  // Field Summary
    protected Element base;
    public static final String UDDI_TAG;
  // Public Methods
    public String getText( );
    public void saveToXML(Element parent);
    public void setText(String s);
}
```

Hierarchy

```
java.lang.Object → com.ibm.uddi.UDDIElement → com.ibm.uddi.util.ServiceKey
```

com.ibm.uddi.util.TModelBag

This class encapsulates multiple TModelKey objects.

Synopsis

```
public class TModelBag extends UDDIElement {
  // Constructors
    public TModelBag();
    public TModelBag(Vector tModelKeyStrings);
    public TModelBag(Element base) throws UDDIException;
  // Field Summary
    protected Element base;
    public static final String UDDI_TAG;
  // Public Methods
    public Vector getTModelKeyStrings();
    public Vector getTModelKeyVector();
    public void saveToXML(Element parent);
    public void setTModelKeyStrings(Vector s);
    public void setTModelKeyVector(Vector s);
}
```

Hierarchy

```
java.lang.Object → com.ibm.uddi.UDDIElement → com.ibm.uddi.util.TModelBag
```

com.ibm.uddi.util.TModelKey

This class encapsulates a single UDDI tModelKey.

Synopsis

```
public class TModelKey extends UDDIElement {
  // Constructors
    public TModelKey();
    public TModelKey(String value);
    public TModelKey(Element base) throws UDDIException;
  // Field Summary
    protected Element base;
    public static final String UDDI_TAG;
  // Public Methods
    public String getText();
    public void saveToXML(Element parent);
    public void setText(String s);
}
```

java.lang.Object → com.ibm.uddi.UDDIElement → com.ibm.uddi.util.TModelKey

---

com.ibm.uddi.util.UploadRegister

This class encapsulates a single UDDI UploadRegister. UploadRegisters indicate the URL for a complete XML document and can be passed to several of the save_ xxx() functions. For example, an UploadRegister may indicate the URL for a UDDI businessEntity record; to publish the record, use the save_business(String authInfo, UploadRegister[] uploadRegisters) method. Note that not all UDDI operator sites support the UploadRegister facility.

Synopsis

```
public class UploadRegister extends UDDIElement {
  // Constructors
    public UploadRegister( );
    public UploadRegister(String value);
    public UploadRegister(Element base) throws UDDIException;
  // Field Summary
    protected Element base;
    public static final String UDDI_TAG;
  // Public Methods
    public String getText( );
    public void saveToXML(Element parent);
    public void setText(String s);
}
```

Hierarchy

java.lang.Object → com.ibm.uddi.UDDIElement → com.ibm.uddi.util. UploadRegister

Glossary

Apache SOAP

Open source Java implementation of the SOAP protocol. Hosted by the Apache Software Foundation.

BEEP

Blocks Extensible Exchange Protocol. Developed by Marshall Rose, and now an official IETF specification, BEEP is a framework of best practices for building new application protocols. BEEP is layered directly on TCP and includes a number of built-in features, such as an initial handshake protocol, authentication, security, and error handling. Currently, BEEP is not widely deployed, but it has the potential to replace HTTP as a viable protocol for remote procedure calls. See also *HTTP*.

binding element

The WSDL `binding` element specifies the implementation details for the XML messaging layer of a web service. WSDL includes built-in binding extensions for defining SOAP services.

bindingTemplate

A UDDI XML element that includes information about how and where to access a specific web service. See also *businessService* and *tModel*.

businessEntity

A UDDI XML element that includes information about a registered business, such as business name, description, address, and contact information.

businessService

A UDDI XML element that includes information about a registered web service or a group of related web services. This includes name, description, and an optional list of `bindingTemplates`. See also *bindingTemplate*.

deployment descriptor file

An XML file used by Apache SOAP to define and deploy a specific SOAP service. It contains the service URN, a list of service methods, application scope, Java provider, and Java-to-XML type mappings.

deserialize

A generic technique for receiving data over a network connection and reconstructing the specified variable or object. For example, a Java SOAP client might receive XML messages over a network connection and use the messages to reconstruct the correct Java objects. See also *serialize*, *XML data type*, and *type mapping registry*.

disposition report

A UDDI XML element that indicates
the success or failure of a UDDI operation. In the event of failure, the disposition report will include a
human-readable explanation of the
error.

DNS

Domain Name System. A distributed
system for translating domain names
to IP addresses. See also *IP address*.

GLUE

Web services platform created by The
Mind Electric, Inc. Includes support
for SOAP, WSDL, and UDDI.

green pages

A generic category of data used
within UDDI to specify technical
information about a web service.
Generally, this includes a pointer to
an external specification and an
address for invoking the web service.
See also *bindingTemplate* and *tModel*.

HTTP

Hypertext Transfer Protocol. HTTP
is the main protocol for exchanging
data between web browsers and web
servers. HTTP was originally
designed for remote document
retrieval, but is now used by SOAP
and XML-RPC for remote procedure
calls. See also *BEEP*.

IETF

Internet Engineering Task Force. The
IETF is the main standards body for
Internet protocols, including HTTP
and BEEP.

IP

Internet Protocol. This is the main
protocol used to route packets of
data throughout the Internet. See also
TCP.

IP address

A unique 32-bit address that identifies a machine on the Internet.

ISO 3166

A standard taxonomy of country
codes maintained by the Interna-
tional Organization for Standardization (ISO). For example, China has
the code CN, whereas the United
States has the code US. Using ISO
3166, companies registered with
UDDI can identify their geographic
headquarters or their main geographic areas of business. ISO 3166 is
also used for top-level Internet
domain country codes.

MIME

Multi-Purpose Internet Mail Extensions. MIME is a standard technique
for transmitting or attaching binary
data, such as images, audio, and
video.

mustUnderstand

A SOAP Header attribute, which indicates whether a specified header is
optional or mandatory. If set to true,
the recipient must understand and
process the Header attribute. Otherwise, it must discard the message and
return a Fault. See also *SOAP Header*.

NAICS

North American Industry Classification System. NAICS provides a six-
digit industry code for more than
19,000 industries. Beginning in 1997,
NAICS replaced the previous Standard Industry Classification (SIC).
NAICS is used within UDDI as a
standard taxonomy for classifying
businesses and business services.

port

A logical connection place where
TCP/IP servers listen for client
requests. HTTP uses port 80.

portType

The WSDL portType element com-
bines multiple message elements to
form a complete one-way or
roundtrip operation. For example, a

portType can combine a request message and a response message into a single request/response operation, such as are commonly used in SOAP services.

remote procedure calls

A generic technique whereby one application can connect over a network to a second application, invoke one of its functions, and receive the results of the call. Remote procedure calls (RPCs) are used in many distributed application frameworks, including CORBA, Distributed COM, Java RMI, SOAP, and XML-RPC.

rpcrouter

Apache SOAP servlet that receives SOAP requests and routes them to the appropriate service classes for processing.

SAML

Security Assertion Markup Language. Developed by the Organization for the Advancement of Structured Information Standards (OASIS), SAML facilitates the exchange of authentication and authorization information between business partners.

Semantic Web

A term coined by Tim Berners-Lee, the original inventor of the World Wide Web. Very broadly, the Semantic Web envisions a world in which applications can use and understand the Web as easily as humans now browse the Web. Berners-Lee has indicated that web services are an important actualization of his Semantic Web vision.

serialize

A generic technique for transforming a variable or object into a standard format for transmission across a network. For example, a Java SOAP client will serialize Java objects to a standard XML format and then transmit the XML over the network. See also *deserialize*, *XML data type*, and *type mapping registry*.

service description

Layer within the web service protocol stack that is responsible for describing the public interface to a specific web service. See also WSDL.

service provider

Within the web service architecture, the service provider is any host that implements a web service and makes it available on the Internet. Traditionally, this is the same as a server in a client/server architecture.

service registry

Within the web service architecture, the service registry is a logically centralized directory of services. Developers can connect to a service registry and publish new services or find existing ones. See also *UDDI*.

service requestor

Within the web service architecture, the service requestor is any consumer of a web service. The requestor utilizes an existing web service by opening a network connection and sending an XML request. Traditionally, this is the same as a client in a client/server architecture.

service type

See *tModel*.

SOAP

SOAP is an XML-based protocol for exchanging information between computers. Although SOAP can be used in a variety of messaging systems and can be delivered via a variety of transport protocols, the main focus of SOAP is remote procedure calls (RPCs) transported via HTTP. Like XML-RPC, SOAP is platform-independent. It therefore enables diverse applications to communicate with one another over a network connection.

SOAP Body

The SOAP Body element encapsulates the main "payload" of the SOAP message. The payload includes details regarding the remote procedure call, including the method name to invoke, method parameters, or return values. The Body element can also include an optional Fault element for specifying error conditions.

SOAP Envelope

The SOAP XML Envelope element encapsulates a single XML message being transferred via SOAP. The Envelope specifies the SOAP version, and consists of one optional SOAP Header and a required SOAP Body. See also *SOAP Header* and *SOAP Body*.

SOAP Header

The optional SOAP Header element provides a flexible framework for specifying additional application-level attributes for a specific SOAP message. The Header framework can be used in a diverse set of applications, including user authentication, transaction management, or payment authorization. See also *SOAP Envelope* and *mustUnderstand*.

SOAP::Lite for Perl

The SOAP library for Perl. Includes support for SOAP, XML-RPC, WSDL, and UDDI.

SOAPAction Header

The HTTP Header that can be used to indicate the intent of a SOAP message. Some SOAP servers require that clients specify a full SOAPAction value, such as the following: SOAPAction: "urn:xmethodsBabelFish#BabelFish". But other SOAP servers, including Apache SOAP, only require that clients specify a blank SOAPAction (e.g., SOAPAction: ""). The SOAPAction Header is required under SOAP 1.1, but is optional under SOAP 1.2.

SOAP-DSIG

SOAP Security Extensions: Digital Signature. SOAP-DSIG uses public key cryptography to enable digital signing of SOAP messages. This enables the client or server to validate the identity of the other party. SOAP-DSIG has been submitted to the W3C.

socket

A programming abstraction that facilitates network programming by insulating the programmer from the details of the underlying network protocol.

targetNamespace

A convention of XML Schema that enables an XML document to refer to itself. Any newly defined elements will belong to the specified targetNamespace. See also *XML Schema*.

TCP

Transmission Control Protocol. TCP is primarily responsible for breaking messages into individual IP packets and then reassembling those packets at the destination. See also *IP*.

TcpTunnelGui

A tool bundled with Apache SOAP that enables you to easily intercept and view SOAP requests and responses. A great tool for debugging SOAP applications.

tModel

Technical model. A UDDI XML element used to provide pointers to external technical specifications. Also referred to as a service type.

type mapping registry

Within Apache SOAP, the type mapping registry maps XML elements to Java classes and vice versa. By default, the registry is prepopulated with basic data types, including strings, vectors, dates, and arrays. If you are passing new data types, you need to explicitly register the new type and indicate which Java classes will be responsible for serializing and deserializing your new type. See also *serialize* and *deserialize*.

UDDI

Universal Description, Discovery, and Integration. UDDI currently represents the discovery layer within the web service protocol stack. UDDI was originally created by Microsoft, IBM, and Ariba, and represents a technical specification for publishing and finding businesses and web services. See also *UDDI cloud services*.

UDDI Business Registry

See *UDDI cloud services*.

UDDI cloud services

Also known as the UDDI Business Registry, UDDI cloud services represent a fully operational implementation of the UDDI specification. Launched in May 2001 by Microsoft and IBM, UDDI cloud services now enable anyone to search existing UDDI data or to publish new business and service data.

UDDI4J

An open source UDDI library developed by IBM.

UNSPSC

Universal Standard Products and Service Classification. UNSPSC provides standard codes for classifying products and services. The standard was developed in 1998 and is currently maintained by the nonprofit Electronic Commerce Code Management Association (ECCMA). UNSPSC provides coverage of 54 industries and includes over 12,000 codes for products and services. UNSPSC is used within UDDI as a standard taxonomy for classifying businesses and business services.

URN

Uniform Resource Name. A URN is a Uniform Resource Identifier (URI) that is both persistent and location-independent. For example, urn:isbn:0596000588 refers to the book *XML in Nutshell* (O'Reilly). URNs are frequently used to identify SOAP services.

W3C

World Wide Web Consortium. The W3C is the main standards body for web protocols and specifications, including HTML, XML, XML Schema, SOAP, and XML Encryption. See also *W3C XML Protocol Group*.

W3C XML Protocol Group

Created in September 2000, the W3C XML Protocol Group aims to standardize web service protocols. Its first goal is to create an official specification for SOAP.

W3C Web Services Activity

Created in January 2002, this Activity includes the W3C XML Protocol Working Group, as well as groups for Architecture and Description.

web service

A web service is any service that is available over the Internet, uses a standardized XML messaging system, and is not tied to any one operating system or programming language. Although not required, web services should also be self-describing via a common XML format and discoverable via a simple find mechanism.

web service protocol stack

An emerging stack of protocols used to create and describe web services. The current web service protocol stack consists of four layers: service transport (HTTP, FTP, BEEP, etc.), XML messaging (XML-RPC, SOAP), service description (WSDL), and service discovery (UDDI).

white pages

A generic category of data used within UDDI to specify business information, including business name, business description, and address. See also *businessEntity*.

WSDL

Web Services Description Language. WSDL currently represents the service description layer within the web service protocol stack. WSDL is an XML grammar for specifying a public interface for a web service. This public interface can include information on all publicly available functions, data type information for all XML messages, binding information about the specific transport protocol to be used, and address information for locating the specified service. WSDL is not necessarily tied to a specific XML messaging system, but it does include built-in extensions for describing SOAP services.

WSIF

Web Services Invocation Framework. WSIF is a framework created by IBM that enables a programmer to invoke a SOAP service without actually writing any SOAP-specific code. It also enables automatic invocation of SOAP services, based on WSDL files.

XKMS

XML Key Management Services is a proposed web service specification for distributing and managing public keys and certificates. XKMS has been submitted to the W3C.

XML

eXtensible Markup Language. An official recommendation of the W3C, XML represents a flexible framework for organizing and sharing data. XML is used heavily within the XML messaging, service description, and service discovery layers of the web service protocol stack.

XML data type

Indicates the type of data that may be placed inside a particular XML element. XML Schema includes built-in support for basic data types. including strings, integers, floats, and doubles. See also *XML Schema* and *type mapping registry*.

XML Encryption Standard

A proposed W3C framework for encrypting/decrypting entire XML documents or just portions of an XML document.

XML namespaces

Provides a standard mechanism for disambiguating XML elements and attributes that have the same name. The SOAP specification makes heavy use of XML namespaces.

XML Schema

A framework for defining rules for XML documents. XML Schema includes the ability to specify data types for individual elements, a key ingredient for remote procedure calls (RPCs).

XML-RPC

A protocol that uses XML messages to perform RPCs via HTTP. Like SOAP, XML-RPC is platform-independent, and it therefore enables diverse applications to communicate with each other over a network connection.

yellow pages

A generic category of data used within UDDI to classify companies or services offered. Data may include industry, product, or geographic codes based on standard taxonomies. See also *ISO 3166*, *NAICS*, *tModel*, and *UNSPSC*.

Index

We'd like to hear your suggestions for improving our indexes. Send email to *index@oreilly.com*.

About the Author

Ethan Cerami is a software engineer at the Institute for Computational Biomedicine at the Mount Sinai School of Medicine. He is also an adjunct faculty member at New York University's Department of Computer Science.

Colophon

Our look is the result of reader comments, our own experimentation, and feedback from distribution channels. Distinctive covers complement our distinctive approach to technical topics, breathing personality and life into potentially dry subjects.

The animal on the cover of *Web Services Essentials* is a spiny lobster (also known as a rock lobster). There are about 45 species of spiny lobster worldwide, ranging in size from 2 to 26 pounds. Spiny lobsters have spine-studded shells and long antennae. However, unlike American lobsters, they have no large front claws. Spiny lobsters also have larger tails than American lobsters. They are colorfully marked with bright green, blue, and yellow spots on an orange or brown shell. Spiny lobsters inhabit shallow-watered, rocky environments in tropical and subtropical waters worldwide, as well as in cold waters of the southern hemisphere. Spiny lobsters usually remain concealed in rock crevices during the day and come out to feed at night. They eat a wide variety of foods, including shellfish, crabs, small fish, sea urchins, and sometimes algae and seaweed. They reach sexual maturity at 7 to 10 years and can live for over 30 years.

Although they are reclusive, spiny lobsters seem to be more social than American lobsters and often share their dens in coral reefs. One of the stranger sights reported by fishermen and divers is the so-called "March of the Spinys," which is a mass migration of hundreds or even thousands of spiny lobsters that often takes place in October or November, usually after a period of prolonged storminess. During this time, spiny lobsters swim in single-file columns, moving from shallow to deeper waters. Although the lobsters are nocturnal creatures, these marches sometimes occur in broad daylight. To date, there is no scientific explanation for this phenomenon.

Claire Cloutier was the production editor and copyeditor for *Web Services Essentials*. Rachel Wheeler was the proofreader. Sarah Sherman and Jeffrey Holcomb provided quality control. Phil Dangler, Edie Shapiro, Sarah Sherman, and Derek Di Matteo provided composition assistance. Nancy Crumpton wrote the index.

Ellie Volckhausen designed the cover of this book, based on a series design by Edie Freedman. The cover image is a 19th-century engraving from the Dover Pictorial Archive. Emma Colby produced the cover layout with QuarkXPress 4.1, using Adobe's ITC Garamond font.

David Futato designed the interior layout. Mihaela Maier and Neil Walls converted the files from Microsoft Word to FrameMaker 5.5.6, using tools created by Mike Sierra. The text font is Linotype Birka; the heading font is Adobe Myriad Condensed; and the code font is LucasFont's TheSans Mono Condensed. The illustrations that appear in the book were produced by Robert Romano and Jessamyn Read using Macromedia FreeHand 9 and Adobe Photoshop 6. The tip and warning icons were drawn by Christopher Bing. This colophon was written by Rachel Wheeler.

Get even more for your money.

Join the O'Reilly Community, and register the O'Reilly books you own. It's free, and you'll get:

- $4.99 ebook upgrade offer
- 40% upgrade offer on O'Reilly print books
- Membership discounts on books and events
- Free lifetime updates to ebooks and videos
- Multiple ebook formats, DRM FREE
- Participation in the O'Reilly community
- Newsletters
- Account management
- 100% Satisfaction Guarantee

Signing up is easy:

1. **Go to: oreilly.com/go/register**
2. **Create an O'Reilly login.**
3. **Provide your address.**
4. **Register your books.**

Note: English-language books only

To order books online:
oreilly.com/store

For questions about products or an order:
orders@oreilly.com

To sign up to get topic-specific email announcements and/or news about upcoming books, conferences, special offers, and new technologies:
elists@oreilly.com

For technical questions about book content:
booktech@oreilly.com

To submit new book proposals to our editors:
proposals@oreilly.com

O'Reilly books are available in multiple DRM-free ebook formats. For more information:
oreilly.com/ebooks

O'REILLY®

Spreading the knowledge of innovators   oreilly.com

©2010 O'Reilly Media, Inc. O'Reilly logo is a registered trademark of O'Reilly Media, Inc. 00000

Have it your way.